MIGHTY
PREVAILING
PRAYER

MIGHTY PREVAILING PRAYER

Wesley L. Duewel

May God make you mighty in prayer

Wesley Duewel

FRANCIS ASBURY PRESS
of Zondervan Publishing House
Grand Rapids. Michigan

OHIO CHRISTIAN UNIVERSITY

MIGHTY PREVAILING PRAYER
Copyright © 1990 by Wesley L. Duewel

Francis Asbury Press is an imprint of Zondervan Publishing House,
1415 Lake Drive, S.E., Grand Rapids, Michigan 49506.

Library of Congress Cataloging in Publication Data

Duewel, Wesley L.
    Mighty prevailing prayer / Wesley L. Duewel.
        p.   cm.
    Includes bibliographical references.
    ISBN 0-310-36191-5
    1. Prayer–Christianity. I. Title.
    BV220.D84   1990
    248.3'2–dc20
                                                                89-28486
                                                                CIP

Edited by Craig Noll

Printed in the United States of America

90 91 92 93 94 95 / LP / 10 9 8 7 6 5 4 3 2 1

Contents

Foreword

IN KEEPING WITH his title *Mighty Prevailing Prayer*, the author at once bombards you with the strongest and best kind of praying. And he never lets up on it. This is no kindergarten book on prayer but a summons to the battlefield. And you know it! It challenges you to mature and militant praying. You are at once on the high road, not the low. As in the book of Acts, you are immediately taken into the Upper Room where followers of Jesus persist obstinately in prayer and supplication.

But isn't this the best way to learn prayer?

When I saw Babe Ruth hit home runs, it did something for me right away! It stepped up my hitting and my whole vision of baseball. I said to myself, "Can you hit a ball *like that?*" When you hit a home run, you touch all the bases. Great praying helps you through all the other forms of praying, and steps it all up!

The same thing happens when you see the praying of Jesus. You say to yourself, "Can a person pray *like that?*" Nor do you have to be old to become strong in prayer. Jesus was young and so were His disciples. In a few short years, His followers became mighty in prayer. How? By seeing and learning the best and greatest at once—through Jesus.

It's best to learn from the best—at once! Hitch your wagon to a star! You still have to cover all the ground, but you avoid a lot of unnecessary delay.

I learned prayer that way. What got me into it was revival. When I started to read the accounts of great revivals, I said, "I want that ... I'm going for it."

This book will help everybody—the mature and the immature in prayer. It is loaded with Scripture—almost a compendium. It will be a great help to leaders, churches, groups—to *anyone*.

Each chapter is complete in itself, and, taken together, they sparkle like the many facets of a diamond. Along with larger illustrations are a "thousand points of light" that dart along the way.

The style is the man—Wesley Duewel. He has his own style. Why not?

This book will wake you up for prayer and motivate you to be your best for God.

Armin R. Gesswein
Founder and Director
Revival Prayer Fellowship, Inc.

Preface

THIS LIFETIME COLLECTION of Dr. Duewel's jewels on prayer is priority reading. It is a superb manual. I see it as a desktop encyclopedia on the awesome subject of Mighty Prevailing Prayer. It should be a lifetime manual for the serious student of the prayer life. Immense profit in spirit will be developed when a family uses it as a daily devotional and practices its exhortations. I was stirred by its truths.

Leonard Ravenhill

CHAPTER 1

God Has Answers for You

ARE YOU LONGING for power in prayer, the ability to get urgent and needed answers? Do you feel deeply tested at times by the unexplained delay in answers to your prayers? Are you longing for the secret to answered prayer?

Prevailing prayer is prayer that obtains the answer sought. It overcomes delay, opposition, and unfavorable circumstances. It often involves the Spirit's guidance in how you pray and His deepening of your desire for the answer to prayer. It involves His specially empowering your prayer and strengthening your faith until you receive the answer from God.

Do you really know how to prevail in prayer, how to obtain difficult answers that you have long needed or desired? Is your prayer list effective in bringing blessing to others? Are you satisfied with the answers you are receiving?

God wants your prayer life to be filled with petitions and intercessions for others and for the advance of His kingdom. He wants answers to such prayer to become your thrilling and frequent experience. One of the great joys of prayer is securing wonderful answers that seem so long delayed and so humanly impossible.

God wants answers to your prayers to be frequent and blessed. He wants you to prove repeatedly the mighty power of prayer in your own experience. He wants you to become not only a prayer veteran but also a constant victor in situations where the answers bring great glory to God and great consternation and defeat to Satan.

He wants you to experience frequently His prayer-answering power, His intensely personal concern and love for you, and the tremendously varied means available to His wisdom. God is never perplexed or surprised, and never ultimately defeated. He desires you, through prayer, to share in bringing His will to pass on earth.

I invite you to join me in seeking God's answers to the tremendous needs you and I face. What are the keys that will unlock heaven's resources and release the prayer-answering power of God? What further steps can you and I take to bring God's sovereign and irresistible power to bear?

Let us sit at the feet of God. Let us listen for His word. Let us turn to the lives of some of the heroes of our faith to see how they were able to see God's power released and God's answers made known.

Prevailing prayer is at times so simple that even a child can get mighty answers—often in an amazingly short period of time. Even new believers sometimes pray with such faith and so much of the Spirit's help that mature saints of God are amazed and can only praise God for the answers.

On the other hand, Jesus Himself indicated that some situations or needs were far more difficult than others (Mark 9:29). There can be many reasons for such cases, as we shall discover in the coming chapters.

God does not deliberately hide His deepest truth from you. He does not reserve power in prayer for certain special occasions or prayer victories for some specially chosen favorites of His. Prayer is so vital to all of Christian life and to the advancement of Christ's kingdom that He desires all of us to be mighty in prayer, experienced in getting prayer answers, and undismayed by the most complex or longstanding needs.

We live in the glorious "now" of God. The whole of time is God's arena to work on behalf of and through His faithful ones. Anything God has ever done in the past, He is able to duplicate or exceed. He is forever the same in wisdom, power, and love.

His overarching eternal plans are unchangeable, but in working out the details, He has ordained to work in cooperation with His praying, obeying children. He adapts His working to your prayer and obedience. While He reserves the sovereign right to work independently, His normal plan is to work in cooperation with and through the prayer and obedience of His own.

God therefore delights to adjust the working out of His plans to your cooperating obedience, to your laying hold of His promise, to your preparing the way of the Lord. He has made it possible for you to prevail in prayer, and He is waiting now for you and me to prove the blessed possibilities and the glorious realities of prevailing prayer.

CHAPTER 2

The Importance of Prevailing Prayer

THE ROLE OF PREVAILING PRAYER

GOD INTENDS YOUR praying to secure divine answers. Prayer is not just God's diversion to keep from being lonely. He delights in your fellowship. He always draws nearer when you pray. Also, prevailing prayer is one of the most important ministries in God's kingdom plans.

Prevailing prayer is not simply a spiritual exercise to help you grow in grace. Certainly nothing is more beneficial to growth in grace than growth in the life of prayer. The more you prevail, the more you will learn the secrets of God's grace and the powers of His kingdom. The more you intercede, the more intimate will be your walk with Christ and the stronger you will become by the Spirit's power.

Prevailing prayer is God's ordained means for extending His kingdom, for defeating Satan and his empire of darkness and evil, and for fulfilling God's eternal plan and bringing into effect His good will on earth. It is God's means of covering the earth with His blessings. Prevailing prayer is God's priority strategy for our age and dispensation. The history of the church can never be fully written until Christ in eternity reveals the mighty hidden prayer involvement of all His praying people. What a joy that revelation will bring to Christ's prayer partners!

God the Son is seated at the right hand of the Father on His eternal throne and is today sovereignly ruling and extending His kingdom. Christ does not live primarily to judge, demonstrate divine power, speak sovereign fiats, or issue authoritative decrees. His special divine vocation and strategic role today is to intercede (Heb. 7:25).

The Holy Spirit is so integral to the divine plan for this age that He ceaselessly joins God the Son in His holy intercession. He also is responsible for involving you and enabling you to be a partner in God's strategy of intercession. He longs for you to rise above your weakness and become mighty in God for prayer. He is so concerned that you become effective as the intercessory partner of Christ that He intercedes for you with divine groanings too deep for human words (Rom. 8:26). You do not hear Him, but He is ceaselessly groaning for you and with you.

Prevailing prayer is the most divine ministry you will ever have. Nothing is more Christlike or involves more cooperation with Christ. No form of Christian service is both so universally open to all and so high in Christ's priority for all Christians as prevailing prayer. It is Christ's desire, Christ's call, and Christ's command. Lord, teach us to prevail!

THE OBJECTS OF PREVAILING PRAYER

Prevailing prayer can be intensely personal. You have every right to prevail for your personal desires and needs. Undoubtedly God plans that most of your prevailing be on behalf of others and for the extension of His kingdom. Yet He expects and welcomes your praying for personal and family needs and situations related to you personally. Scripture is very clear on this point.

Blind Bartimaeus prevailed in prayer for the restoration of his eyesight (Mark 10:46–52). The woman embarrassed and plagued by twelve years of hemorrhaging prevailed for her healing (Luke 8:43). The Greek woman from Syrian Phoenicia prevailed, and Jesus cast out the demon from her daughter (Mark 7:26). Jacob prevailed with God for the protection of his family (Gen. 32:9–13, 22–30).

More commonly, you prevail in prayer on behalf of others. Abraham prevailed for Lot (Gen. 18:22–33). Moses prevailed for Israel's victory over Amalek (Exod. 17:8–15). Elijah prevailed when he asked for fire to fall from heaven so that Israel would be saved from backsliding (1 Kings 18). Isaiah and Hezekiah prevailed for Israel's deliverance from Sennacherib (2 Chron. 32:20). Epaphras prevailed for the church at Colosse (Col. 4:12–13).

We must prevail in prayer for situations where God's will is being thwarted and where Satan is delaying and blocking Christ's cause. We must prevail for lives so ensnared and blinded by sin that they are unable or unwilling to pray for themselves. We must prevail for revival in the church, for spiritual and numerical growth of the church, and for the worldwide advance of the gospel.

There are physical, financial, and spiritual needs that call for prevailing prayer. Homes are being torn apart by Satan, lives are being destroyed, and churches need God's special answers. We must prevail for ministries of the church and Christian organizations. We must prevail for moral and spiritual needs of our nation.

The scope of prevailing prayer is as broad as Christ's church and as extensive as God's world. There is nothing within God's will that is outside the purview of prevailing prayer. Prevailing prayer is intercession intensified—intercession until the answer is received.

THE TIME SPAN IN PREVAILING PRAYER

In certain wonderful times prayer prevails in an instant. Moses' prayer for the healing of Miriam from leprosy was very brief. "O God, please heal her!" (Num. 12:13). But Moses had been walking close to God in a face-to-face relationship. He did not need to prepare his heart to obtain God's favor and ear. The situation was comparatively uncomplicated in that the wills and attitudes of other people were not involved, and Aaron and Miriam were already repentant. So Moses received an almost instant answer from God.

Elijah's prayer on Mount Carmel was exceedingly brief— scarcely half a minute in length. "Then the fire of the LORD fell" (1 Kings 18:38). Probably Elijah had not even reached the amen of his prayer. I am sure he would have prayed longer if God had not answered so instantly. But what a dramatic and nation-changing answer: "When all the people saw this, they fell prostrate and cried, 'The LORD—he is God! The LORD— he is God!'" (v. 39).

But remember, Elijah had been praying for three years as he hid from wicked Ahab and Jezebel. He had been carrying an intercessory prayer burden constantly and had had no other public form of ministry. He had announced to Ahab three years before that he himself stood in God's royal presence as one of His attending ministers of state (1 Kings 17:1). You can be sure Elijah was interceding day and night.

Sometimes what seems like a simple, instant answer to prayer is but the crowning climax of days, months, or even years of faithful intercession. When did Elijah prevail? On Mount Carmel, or at the Kerith ravine while the ravens fed him, or at Zarephath while hiding with the widow and her son? The answer is that it was all part of his prevailing in prayer. The answer proved that Elijah prevailed. But all the time while he was prevailing, God was with him supplying his needs and protecting him. Prevailing prayer always involves a price, and Elijah paid that price for at least three years.

Look again at Elijah. Immediately after the fire fell from heaven, Elijah went alone to the top of Mount Carmel and prevailed for rain. Again and again he prayed and expected the answer and then asked his servant to go and look out toward the sea. But only the seventh time did God's cloud appear—at first, only the size of a man's hand (1 Kings 18:44). Instant prevailing one hour does not guarantee instant prevailing in the next situation.

There is often great mystery concerning the time span required in prevailing prayer. The secret of prevailing prayer is simply to pray until the answer comes. The length of time is ultimately immaterial. It is God's answer that counts. The length of time required may often seem perplexing and may prove a test of your faith. We will consider this matter more carefully later.

Prevailing prayer may be repeatedly necessary in some situations before final achievement of God's will is secured. Thus, when Joshua was struggling against Amelek, as long as Moses interceded with uplifted hands "to the throne of the LORD," Joshua was winning. But when Moses lowered his hands, Joshua began to be defeated. By the help of Aaron and Hur, his hands were held up continuously till sundown and complete victory was won (Exod. 17:11–16).

Similarly, Epaphras prevailed in prayer day after day for the church in Colosse (Col. 4:12–13). Paul also prevailed continuously for the Jews, even though he was primarily an apostle to the Gentiles (Rom. 9:1–3).

THE LEVELS OF PREVAILING PRAYER

In order to prevail, the intercessor must often increase the intensity of his or her praying from one level to another. I suggest seven such levels. The first three are listed by Jesus in His Sermon on the Mount (Matt. 7:7). To these I add four more levels from Scripture.

Level 1: Ask	Matthew 7:7.
Level 2: Seek	The asking becomes longer and more intense.
Level 3: Knock	Interceding becomes even more urgent and insistent.

Level 4: Fast	To the previous crescendo of intensity and urgency of intercession, fasting is added.
Level 5: Prayer burden	The burden may be intense and brief or perhaps extend over a longer time.
Level 6: Wrestling in prayer	Very intense praying.
Level 7: Prayer warfare	Prayer battle, extending over a prolonged period.

Perhaps we should call these levels seven aspects or forms of prevailing prayer. Instead of giving up, we move into ever more determined intercession until we prevail. These levels of prayer intensity are not totally separate from each other. During prevailing in prayer, one level may merge into another almost without the intercessor's awareness of it.

A special prayer burden given by the Holy Spirit cannot be borne for a long period of time in its most intense form. It is too exhausting physically. Similarly, prayer burden in its very intense form may become almost synonymous with wrestling in prayer.

Prayer warfare may include all the preceding levels. In fact, prayer warfare is usually over a prolonged period of time and may involve alternating from one level to another as the Spirit guides.

The important thing is not to keep analyzing your prayer to see what level of intercession is yours at a particular time. Rather, be aware that the Spirit may guide you into one or all of these levels as He wills. Be available and ready to pray as He guides and empowers. In the holy partnership of intercession with Christ and the Holy Spirit, the prayer warrior is seeking to intercede constantly according to the mind of the Spirit. All this discussion will become increasingly clear and spiritually blessed as you advance in Christ's school of prayer.

Always remember that you never merit prayer's answers. You do not earn God's response by anything you do. You do not get answers because of physical exertion, praying in a loud voice, or working up some kind of emotional experience. In fact, the most intense prayer of all may at times be the most silent. On the other hand, when your heart cries out to God, you may well, like Jesus, have moments of "loud cries and tears" (Heb. 5:7). Many of God's prayer warriors over the centuries have at times experienced such prayer intensity.

Intensified prevailing prayer is God's ordained law and method for implementing His redemptive plan in this age till Jesus returns. It is the highest, holiest, and mightiest effort of which a child of God is capable. It is God's chosen way to bring heaven's power, heaven's resources, and heaven's angels into action on earth. Spurgeon says, "He who knows how to overcome with God in prayer has heaven and earth at his disposal."[1] Intensified prayer is clothed with the might of God Himself.

LEVELS OF UNITING IN PRAYER

Uniting in prayer is often essential in securing prayer answers. God always honors unity in prayer. When several are praying for the same need, God may choose one of the group to bear a special prayer burden or exercise special faith. This can strengthen and help all the group in their praying.

I point out five levels of uniting in prayer:

Level 1: Prayer partners
Level 2: Prayer groups
Level 3: Simultaneous prayer groups
Level 4: Calls to prayer issued by responsible and influential leaders to many people and groups
Level 5: Widespread movements of prayer

During widespread movements of prayer all five levels may be existing simultaneously as guided and motivated by the Holy Spirit. Uniting in prayer will be discussed more fully in later chapters.

CHAPTER 3

Prevailing Prayer—
The Need of the Church

THE GREAT NEED of our world, our nation, and our churches is people who know how to prevail in prayer. Moments of pious wishes blandly expressed to God once or twice a day will bring little change on earth or among the people. Kind thoughts expressed to Him in five or six sentences, after reading a paragraph or two of mildly religious sentiments once a day from some devotional writing, will not bring the kingdom of God to earth or shake the gates of hell and repel the attacks of evil on our culture and our civilization.

Results, not beautiful words, are the test of prevailing prayer. Results, not mere sanctimonious devotional moments, are the hallmark of the true intercessor.

We need great answers to prayer, changed lives and situations—answers that bear upon them the stamp of the divine. We need mighty demonstrations of the reality and concern of God and of His activity and power, which will force the world to recognize that God is truly God, that God is sovereign, and that God is involved in His world today. We need mighty answers to prayer that will bring new life to the church and new strength, faith, and courage to faint believers;

that will silence, dumbfound, and convict evil men; and that will thwart, defeat, and drive back the assaults of Satan.

The vast majority of Christians know very little about prevailing prayer, wrestling in prayer, or prayer warfare. We have seen too few demonstrations of prevailing prayer. We have known too few prayer warriors who had intercessory power with God and with people. We have met too few Elijah-type intercessors who were just like us, yet whose prayer lives were powerful and effective (James 5:16–18).

Intercession is more than an occasional heartwarming, emotional love to God, more than expressions of good will on our knees when we think of the sick and the suffering among our friends. Prayer is more than a cry of earnest desire when suddenly faced with a crisis need.

GOD'S PRIORITY WORK FOR YOU

Prevailing prayer is holy work, fervent labor. Epaphras, who was "always wrestling in prayer" for his congregation (Col. 4:12), prevailed in prayer. The apostles deliberately chose to give their attention to prayer (Acts 6:4). Then three verses later we are told, "So the word of God spread. The number of disciples in Jerusalem increased rapidly." Even a large number of the priests, perhaps the most difficult to win, "became obedient to the faith."

Murray wrote, "We have far too little conception of the place that intercession, as distinguished from prayer for ourselves, ought to have in the church and the Christian life. In intercession our king upon the throne finds His highest glory. In it we shall find our highest glory too. Through it He continues His saving work and can do nothing without it. Through it alone we can do our work, and nothing avails without it." He adds, "Where . . . we work more than we pray, the presence and the power of God are not seen in our work as we would wish."[1]

"Prayer was never meant to be incidental to the work of God. It is *the* work . . . in all work for God, prayer is the

21

working power of all that God would do through His people." Arthur Mathews says, "The spiritual history of a mission or a church is written in its prayer life."[2] What counts with God is not statistics but prayer depth and God's presence and power in lives, church service, and outreach. All our goal setting, effective management techniques, and computerized administration will accomplish little unless empowered by mighty prevailing prayer.

Whatever gets you too busy for prayer time, whatever distracts you from holy prevailing, whatever robs you of hunger for God, for souls, and for time for prayer warfare is a hindrance to God and His kingdom. You cannot afford it.

The great and godly people of the church have always been those who know how to prevail in prayer. There is nothing higher or holier in Christian living and service. In prevailing prayer you rise to your full potential as created in the image of God and as exalted to the heavenlies to share with Christ His intercessory throne (Eph. 1:20–21; 2:6).

Think of it: The very God who raised up Jesus to heaven after His death and resurrection, placing Jesus at His right hand on the throne of the universe, has also "raised us up with Christ and seated us with him in the heavenly realms" (Eph. 2:6). You sit potentially where Jesus sits—on the throne, to share His rule! When? Now! How? By intercession!

You have no greater ministry or no leadership more influential than intercession. There is no higher role, honor, or authority than this. You have been saved to reign through prayer. You have been Spirit-filled to qualify you to reign by prayer. You reign as you prevail in prayer.

GOD IS SEARCHING FOR PEOPLE TO PREVAIL

The greatest need of God today is for men and women who know how to prevail in prayer—mighty intercessors, tireless prevailers, people who will persevere in prayer battle and prayer conquest until heaven's powers are released and God's will is done in the practical situations on earth.

God's cause creeps forward timidly and slowly when there are more organizers than agonizers, more workers than prevailing prayer warriors. We need prayer warriors who have seen the heart of God, who have experienced the power and glory of the cross, who know the Bible meaning and significance of the day of judgment, heaven and hell. We need prayer warriors who feel the slavery, the absence of any eternal hope, and the doom of the unsaved; who feel the transforming power, joy, and glory from Christ of the saved. We need prayer warriors who pray as though God is God and as though Satan is Satan.

God seeks people to prevail in prayer. It is His ordained means to move the world toward righteousness and the people of the world toward salvation. God seeks people to prevail because He sees earth's millions in their sin and need, loves them infinitely, and longs to save them from sin, Satan, and hell. The price for their atonement is already paid. Calvary's work is finished triumphantly, forever. All things are ready, but man is blinded, fettered, and hardened by sin.

God's only hope for earth's millions is prevailing prayer. For this reason Jesus is prevailing day and night and needs our prevailing cooperation. God has ordained to save the nations through prayer (Ps. 2:8). It is part of His eternal decree. Therefore Jesus prays, and therefore we must pray.

WE ARE FAILING GOD

Millions of feeble, careless Christians are failing God's great heart of love; failing their crucified, resurrected, and enthroned Savior; failing their tender, groaning Intercessor-Spirit. God longs to be gracious (Isa. 30:18), but He is hindered by our failing to fulfill the role for which He created us, saved us, and preserves us alive today.

Churches, missionary organizations, and Christian institutions are highly organized, well staffed, and, on the whole, busy in significant labor. But where are the results? We have not prayed them to pass yet. We have failed to teach our people the role of prevailing prayer. We have failed to model for them powerful lives of prevailing prayer and to lead them in it.

Only a fool fails to pray, but millions of Christians seem almost greater fools. They believe in prayer. They pray rather casually and often ineffectively, but they have never given themselves to the work of spiritual conquest through prevailing prayer. Knowing God's mighty power is always released through prayer, they nevertheless fail to pray until they prevail.

"Where are the Christian leaders who can teach the modern saints to pray and put them at it? . . . Where are the apostle leaders who can put God's people to praying?"[3] Only those who prevail in prayer produce a host of followers who know how to prevail. Prevailing apostles produce prayer warriors. Comparatively prayerless pulpits will produce prayerless and powerless congregations. Who will call today's generation to prayer and teach them to pray? Where are our prayer giants?

WANTED: GIANTS IN PRAYER

Many years ago, E. M. Bounds wrote:

We need this prayerful leadership; we must have it, that by the perfection and beauty of its holiness, by the strength and elevation of its faith, by the potency and pressure of its prayers, by the authority and spotlessness of its example, by the fire and contagion of its zeal, by the singularity, sublimity, and unworthiness of its piety, it may influence God and hold and mold the church to its heavenly pattern.

Such leaders, how mighty they are felt! How their flame arouses the church! How they embattle and give victory by the conflicts and triumphs of their own faith! How they fashion it by the impress and importunity of their prayers! How they inoculate by the contagion and fire of their holiness! How they lead the march in great spiritual revolutions! How the church is raised from the dead by the resurrection call of their sermons! Holiness springs up in their wake as flowers at the voice of spring, and where they tread the desert blooms as a garden of the Lord. God's cause demands such leaders.[4]

God longs to reveal His mighty power and redemptive love more outstandingly and more constantly. What hinders Him? The lack of adequate prevailing prayer. Just as the orchard owner Jesus described came seeking fruit (Luke 13:6–7), so God seeks for prevailing prayer veterans among His people. Listen to Andrew Murray again:

> He looks if the church is training the great army of aged men and women, whose time of outward work is past, but who can strengthen the army of the "elect, who cry to him day and night." . . . He looks to the thousands of young men and young women in training for the work of ministry and mission, and gazes longingly to see if the church is teaching them that intercession, power with God must be their first care, and in seeking to train and help them to it. He looks to see whether ministers and missionaries are understanding their opportunity, and laboring to train the believers of their congregations into those who can "help together" by their prayer, and can "strive with them in their prayers." As Christ seeks the lost sheep until He finds it, God seeks intercessors.[5]

We need a new intense and radical commitment to prayer, leaders who know and prove the power of prayer, congregations growing ever more mighty in prayer. We need prevailing leadership to mold a new generation of prayer warriors.

GOD HAS ORDAINED OUR PREVAILING

God has ordained a glorious role for His Son and for us in holy, though unworthy, partnership with His Son. Oh, that God would help us sense the wonder of these realities!

God Has Ordained Christ to Be the Great Intercessor

1. *The Son is the revelation of God the Father.* All that you learn of God you learn through the Son. No one has ever seen God the Father (John 1:18), but whoever sees the Son, sees the Father (14:9). Therefore, whenever God has appeared as a visible being, it is God the Son who appeared. God the Son is

the Word of God. Therefore, whenever God has spoken it was through God the Son.

2. *The Son is God's ordained representative.* God created us through the Son (John 1:3, 10). All life that we have came from God through the Son (1:4; 6:33; 11:25). The Son was God's Mediator with us, even when He came as the preincarnate Jehovah. It was undoubtedly He who walked with Adam and Eve in the garden, with Enoch over the years, and with His friend Abraham; He spoke face-to-face with Moses and made Himself visible to Isaiah (John 12:41), Daniel, and the apostle John on Patmos. Over the centuries since Creation, Christ has been coming to us again and again (Mic. 5:2, margin). He came to us in His incarnation; now He comes to us constantly as Immanuel, God with us.

3. *The Son is ordained to be responsible for humankind.* He has always taken upon Himself our needs (Isa. 53:4; 63:9). He was responsible for providing atonement for humankind (53:6). From Creation on, He is the Intercessor for humankind, and now having entered the sanctuary of heaven on our behalf, He is and will be our High Priest forever (Heb. 6:19–20). His high-priestly sacrifice of Himself was once for all, but His intercessory role continues forever (7:25). Thus God the Son, our Lord and Savior, is the great, continuing, and perfect prevailing Intercessor.

God Has Ordained Us to Intercede with Christ

God has created us in His image to be godlike in personality and in character. God has created us to have fellowship with the triune Jehovah. God has ordained us from all creation to have a special relationship to God the Son. We are created spiritually to fellowship with the Son (1 Cor. 1:9) and to be the bride of the Son (Isa. 62:5; John 3:29; Eph. 5:25–26; Rev. 21:9).

We are also created, saved, and called to intercede and thus to prevail until God's answer appears. Since prevailing intercession is Christ's great priority today, it must become ours as His representatives here. He has given us the Holy Spirit to enable us to see people and needs from His perspective. He has ordained that the Holy Spirit enable us in our prayer weakness (Rom. 8:26). He has authorized us to use the authority of His name in prayer (John 14:13–14; 15:16; 16:23–24).

He has made us to be priests to God, which certainly includes the intercessory role of all priests (Rev. 1:6). We are to be not only holy priests (1 Peter 2:5), however, but royal priests (v. 9), appointed to serve our King. In the light of other Scriptures, this responsibility obviously includes our being given a kingly role in our intercession. We become interceding royalty. We, like Jesus, rule and extend Christ's rule by our prevailing intercession. We are to share Christ's sovereignty by our prevailing prayer.[6] He delegates royal authority to us.

"God has voluntarily made himself dependent also upon our prayer. . . . In prayer the church has received power to rule the world." Through our prayers God acts and speaks. While God is ever free and acts in sovereign freedom, yet He seems to have bound Himself, at least to a large degree, to our intercession.[7] Hallesby calls prayer "the conduit through which the power of heaven is brought to earth." He adds that our believing prayer "is unquestionably the means by which God, in the quickest way," will be able to give to our world His saving power through Christ. Calvin also taught that prayer was a means by which the power of Satan can be overthrown and the kingdom of God advanced.[8]

THE GLORY OF PREVAILING PRAYER

The highest glory of Christ upon His sovereign throne today is the glory of His prevailing intercession.[9] It becomes our most glorious ministry also. There is no more Christlike role than to be a co-intercessor with Christ for the priorities upon His heart. In no other way can a Christian be a greater strength and blessing to Christ's church. In no other way can you do more to advance Christ's kingdom and bring glory to the name of Jesus. Prevailing intercession is your supreme service while on earth.

Prevailing prayer is glorious because it unites you with the heartbeat of Christ. It is glorious because in prevailing prayer you share the vision of Christ, the purpose and holy determination of Christ, and often the costly soul agony and burden of Christ. Prevailing intercession is the most Christly of all labor, as well as the most Spirit-controlled. The Spirit shares with you Christ's passion until you are convulsed by the same heart-cry as the Son and the same groanings as the Spirit (Rom. 8:26).

It is glory to weep with Christ, love with Christ, and burn with the passionate longing of Christ. It is glory to share with Christ the intercessory battle and triumph. Sometimes you begin to sense the power and joy of the coming age (Heb. 6:5) as your prevailing breaks through to victory. Glory begins as you feel the Spirit's assurance that your prayer has been heard and answered. The visible results are not always immediately evident, but you know you have prevailed according to the will of God, and you know God's answer is sure.

All prevailing prayer will receive its final and supreme glory when you reach the glory world, with its unveilings of the rewards of answered prayer. What honor awaits God's prevailing prayer warriors at the judgment seat of Christ when the honors and rewards of eternity are announced and conferred (1 Cor. 3:11–15; 4:5; 9:25)!

Then you will be amazed to see how your prevailing was united with the prevailing of others of God's prayer warriors and with the very intercession of Christ, the Son of God. Then you will discover the hidden prevailing saints who over the ages were the secret of God's mighty working. Then you will see that all holy intercession begins in the heart of God, is shared with you by the Holy Spirit, is "amened" and presented to the Father by the Son, and is aided by God's holy angels. Then you will see that no prevailing prayer was ever in vain. You will bow before God in wonder, love, and adoring amazement to think that you, unworthy you, have had such strategic partnership with Christ in His throne ministry and eternal victories!

Lord, teach us the privilege, the responsibility, and the glory of prevailing prayer!

CHAPTER 4

Prayerlessness Is Sin

THERE IS NO easier sin to commit than the sin of prayerlessness. It is a sin against man and a sin against God. Are you guilty of that sin today? On some occasions the Bible specifically addresses the sin of failing to pray for others. Samuel said to Israel, "As for me, far be it from me that I should sin against the LORD by failing to pray for you" (1 Sam. 12:23). It would have been a sin against them and against God, who loved them so much.

You can sin not only by doing what is wrong but by not doing what is right, by not doing your duty. "Anyone, then, who knows the good he ought to do and doesn't do it, sins" (James 4:17). Jesus said, "That servant who knows his master's will and . . . does not do what his master wants" commits such a sin (Luke 12:47).

Such sins of omission do not separate you from God, but they certainly grieve His heart. They show disrespect to the Word of God, to the love of Christ, and to the tender Holy Spirit, who seeks to remind you of what you should do. Sins of omission weaken your spiritual life, make you comparatively useless to God, and rob you of the rewards God longs to give you.

A SIN OF NEGLECT

O. Hallesby has written, "A child of God can grieve Jesus in no worse way than to neglect prayer. . . . Many neglect prayer to such an extent that their spiritual life gradually dies out."[1] Those who are careless about prayer show that they are careless about other spiritual things. They are rarely ready to be used by God. Prayerlessness means unavailability to God—a sin against God's love.

Prayerlessness proves that the person has very little real love for God. It is not difficult to make time to speak to those we love. "Brethren, the crying need of the church is her laziness after God," says Samuel Chadwick. Andrew Murray adds, "The sin of prayerlessness is a proof . . . that the life of God in the soul is in deadly sickness and weakness."[2]

The prayerless person is more carnal than spiritual. The Holy Spirit is the Spirit of prayer (Zech. 12:10, margin). He prompts us to pray, guides us in prayer, and helps our weakness in prayer (Rom. 8:26). Prayerless Christians are not filled and controlled by the Spirit, no matter what they may profess. One's neglect to pray can be a sin against God.

A SIN OF DISOBEDIENCE

Not only is prayerlessness neglect, it is disobedience. This disobedience can take many forms.

We are responsible to pray for all leaders, specially the leaders of our government and of other nations. Do you? "I urge, then, first of all, that requests, prayers, intercession and thanksgiving be made for everyone—for kings and all those in authority" (1 Tim. 2:1–2). Not to include these topics in your private or public praying is a sin of disobedience.

On two separate occasions Jesus commanded, "Ask the Lord of the harvest, therefore, to send out workers into his harvest field" (Matt. 9:38; Luke 10:2). If you do not pray for evangelism and missions, you are directly disobeying Jesus' command. This is a sin of disobedience.

Jesus taught us in the Sermon on the Mount that we should pray, "Your kingdom come" (Matt. 6:10). The Christian has no option. He or she must pray regularly for the advance of Christ's cause, for the hallowing and glorifying of Christ's name, for God's blessing on the church. Not to do so is a direct sin of disobedience to Christ. Examine your prayer life and see if you have been grieving God frequently by such disobedience.

Jesus gave us a model prayer to teach us: "This, then, is how you should pray" (Matt. 6:9). In fact, we should often use these exact words, because Jesus commanded us, "When you pray, say . . ." (Luke 11:2). In this model prayer, Jesus taught that normally we should first pray for God's name, kingdom, and will to be done before we begin to pray for our personal needs (Matt. 6:9–13; Luke 11:2–4).

Therefore, regularly to center most of your praying on yourself, your family, and your immediate circle of friends, rather than on Christ's kingdom, His church, world needs, and world evangelization is contrary to Christ's example when He said, "This, then, is how you should pray" (Matt. 6:9). To pray for oneself is petition, not intercession. Intercession is prayer for others. Prevailing prayer is usually prayer for others.

For Christians day after day to pray primarily for themselves, their own family, and their immediate circle of friends and not to pray primarily first for others, as Jesus taught, is a form of sin. For Christians to be so self-centered that they never weep like David as they pray for their enemies' welfare or salvation; for Christians never to weep over their own city or area, as Jesus wept over Jerusalem; for Christians never to pray with a broken heart for the poor and the homeless, ones who are starving, those in prison, orphans, widows, the bereaved, those enslaved by drink, drug addicts, and abused children and wives is to sin against Paul's injunction to "mourn with those who mourn" (Rom. 12:15).

Job asked, "Have I not wept for those in trouble? Has not my soul grieved for the poor?" (Job 30:25).

For Christians to know that Christ has taught—and commanded—them to pray and is waiting for their prayer partnership and still fail to pray is direct disobedience.

For a Christian to know that Christ desires that the world be given a chance to be saved, that Christ has commanded us to pray for workers in His harvest, and that lasting spiritual results from evangelism come only when the evangelism is covered with prevailing prayer—for a Christian to know all this and still fail to pray is direct disobedience of a most serious kind. It raises a doubt as to how much we love people and how much we really love Jesus.

Not to pray regularly and faithfully for others is to prove that our love is very selfish, that our vision is very limited, and that we have not yet learned the heartbeat of Jesus, who loves and longs for the welfare and salvation of the whole world.

A SIN AGAINST YOUR OWN SPIRITUAL LIFE

Prayerlessness is also a sin against your own spiritual life. You cannot grow in grace when you neglect prayer. You cannot develop a close walk with Jesus if you do not frequently commune with Him. You cannot share His heartbeat if you seldom intercede with Him.

Prayerlessness robs you of the consciousness of the near presence of Jesus. It robs you of the awareness of the smile on His face, of the blessedness of listening to His voice. It robs you of the touch of His hand upon you and of much of His guidance. It robs you of His power.

Prayerlessness is all the more serious sin against yourself, since prayer is so blessedly simple. All you need to do to learn to pray is to pray. It is so spiritually natural that new Christians almost begin to pray without being taught. Even little children can easily learn a very real, personal and satisfying prayer life as they talk to Jesus.

A SIN AGAINST GOD

We may call prayerlessness a weakness, being so busy and preoccupied that we neglect what we know we should do. We may make many excuses, but God calls it disobedience. That is sin against God.

Prayerlessness is not only a direct sin against others, it is a direct sin against God Himself (1 Sam. 12:23). Jesus told us that we "should always pray and not give up" (Luke 18:1). Forsyth has said that for the Christian, "the worst sin is prayerlessness."[3] Why? Because it shows our indifference and disobedience to God.

Prayerlessness is an evidence of what our attitude is to God. It is a kind of unfaithfulness and lovelessness.[4] Our relation with God is not what it should be if we do not love Him enough to find time to get alone and listen and talk to Him. Prayerlessness proclaims to God and to Satan that our relation to Jesus is not very loving and close. An adequate relation to Jesus always includes prayer—both the desire and the actual practice.

YOU WILL REGRET PRAYERLESSNESS

The regret of prayerlessness begins in this life when we suddenly need to prevail in prayer and then realize how far we have drifted, how casual our relation to Him is, and how weak our prayerlessness has left us. When we suddenly need strong faith, our faith proves feeble and wavering because we have exercised it so little. God in His mercy may still hear us, but our hearts feel guilty for so neglecting Him and disobeying Him in our prayer life.

We need to ask His forgiveness instantly. Remember, forgiveness can be received in a moment if we truly repent and take steps now to do God's will. But power in prayer is not restored in a moment. Normally, it is the result of faithfulness in a life of prayer.

God keeps a record not only of our thoughts and words but also of our prayers. Ravenhill writes, "I believe most of us will need the tears wiped from our eyes when the books are opened at the judgment bar of God, and our personal record is read."[5]

When you and I stand with Christ in eternity, perhaps the

most amazing feature of our lives as we look back will be our prayerlessness. "If there are any regrets in heaven, the greatest will be that we spent so little time in real intercession."[6]

If, as Andrew Murray taught, Christ intended prayer to be the great power by which His church would do its work, then certainly the neglect of prayer by the church is the greatest reason for its powerlessness. He added, "Satan will bring forth all his power to prevent us from becoming men of prayer."[7] How disappointed God is with the spiritual life of pastor and people when they are weak in prevailing prayer and the prayer of faith. God has given us no greater means of bringing down His blessing and power upon our lives and work.

There is probably no single sin that you and I ought to acknowledge with deeper shame than the sin of prayerlessness. Perhaps never in the history of the church have we church leaders and our congregations been busier and more organized in church activity. But where is the power that attracts the unsaved, that causes them to tremble in the presence of God, that brings them to real repentance and transformed lives, and that then makes them a part of an actively witnessing community? Being busy is not enough. We must be blessed and empowered, used mightily by God.

Never has the cause of God needed more visible illustration of the possibilities and power of prayer than does the church in our age. It is prayer power that makes saints and that produces holy character, ethical living, and fruitful witnessing. God forgive our prayerlessness and call us all again to a life of prevailing prayer.

WE CAN BE SAVED FROM PRAYERLESSNESS

Chadwick has written, "It would seem as if the biggest thing in God's universe is a man who prays. There is only one thing more amazing, that is, that man, knowing this, should not pray."[8] Lord, make us giants in prayer! Prayerlessness is the sin of the casual Christian. The absence of truly prevailing prayer is the sin of many praying Christians. Thank God, there is a way to a life of prayer and empowerment through prayer.

We must have an entirely new relationship to Jesus. Says Andrew Murray, "It is vain for us, with our defective spiritual life, to endeavor to pray more or better. It is an impossibility."[9] We must see Jesus as the Lord who waits to save us from prayerlessness. We must believe Him for a new life of closer fellowship with Him, a life in His love and communion beyond anything that we have known thus far.

Jesus longs to save you from a defective spiritual life and a defective prayer life. He must become more personally real to you. You must value His infinite love more than ever before. You must reciprocate His longing for communion with you. Be willing to take time to share His prayer burden with Him as He intercedes at the right hand of the Father.

The resurrected, enthroned Lord Jesus, your great Intercessor, through His Holy Spirit, will teach you the life and power of prayer. May the Spirit fill you with the spirit of intercession.

Learning to prevail in prayer demands willpower. It demands recognizing your spiritual priorities. Ravenhill has said, "Prayer is a battle for full-grown men, fully armed and fully awake to the possibilities of grace."[10]

God teach us the role and priority of prayer! God give us a thirst and relish for prayer, for meeting face-to-face with the Lord Jesus! God give us the determination to prepare ourselves to pray, to set apart time and follow the example of Christ in prayer! God teach us to meet the conditions of prayer, to cultivate the hunger for prayer, to experience the joy of prevailing intercession and the power of God that comes upon our life and others as we pray!

CHAPTER 5

The Prevailing Christ

HE PREVAILED AS THE PREINCARNATE CHRIST

THERE ARE INDICATIONS in Scripture that our ascended Lord, the enthroned Christ, has had an intercessory role from the time of Adam and Eve till today. It will continue at least until all of the church has been united with the Lord in heaven. Was there instant intercession by the preincarnate Jesus when Adam and Eve sinned? Is not that why they did not instantly die physically when they did spiritually?

We know that Jesus accompanied Israel throughout their desert wanderings (Exod. 14:19; 33:14; Isa. 63:9; 1 Cor. 10:4). The statement, "My Presence will go with you," in Exodus 33:14 is literally "My face will go with you." Christ is the only visible face of Jehovah. If Jehovah-Jesus in His preincarnate form constantly accompanied Israel, sharing their sorrows, undoubtedly He interceded for them constantly, adding His intercession and amen, for example, to the intercession of Moses (Exod. 32) and the prophets (Isa. 62). Hints of Christ's existence, presence, and ministry are given in the Old Testament, but all becomes clear and explicit in the New Testament.

One of the most startling passages that both veils and yet reveals Christ's prevailing intercession is found in Isaiah 62:1. Many commentators see this verse as the voice of God or the voice of the Servant of Jehovah—in other words, the preincarnate Christ. "For Zion's sake I will not keep silent, for Jerusalem's sake I will not remain quiet, till her righteousness shines out like the dawn, her salvation like a blazing torch." In what way will He not keep silent? The answer is found in verses 6 and 7: "I have posted watchmen on your walls, O Jerusalem; they will never be silent day or night. You who call on the LORD, give yourselves no rest, and give him no rest till he establishes Jerusalem and makes her the praise of the earth."

Because the preincarnate Christ is determined not to be silent (Isa. 62:1), He calls on those who call on the Lord—in other words, who intercede—never to be silent. God's purpose for Jerusalem (the literal Jerusalem then, but more fully now the spiritual Jerusalem, the church) is so great and urgent that He and we must unite together in ceaseless prevailing prayer. Oh, the billions of times Christ has interceded for His people over the centuries!

CHRIST PREVAILED ON EARTH

Christ prevailed when He was here on earth far more than His disciples realized at the time. He made no ostentatious display of His communion with the Father or of His intercession but usually slipped away quietly to get alone in prayer. He arose early to be able to intercede uninterruptedly.

We know the agony of His prayer wrestling in Gethsemane—a prayer of such prevailing and at such a cost of soul energy that we stand aghast at the record. Isaiah tells us, "He poured out his life unto death, and was numbered with the transgressors. For he bore the sin of many, and made intercession for the transgressors" (53:12). So the cross and the agony of Gethsemane go side by side. What He had been doing in secret with the Father and what He agonized for in the garden became vocal and open on the cross, when He said, "Father, forgive them."

Jesus Christ is the Intercessor-Savior. Hebrews tells us, "During the days of Jesus' life on earth, he offered up prayers and petitions with loud cries and tears" (5:7). F. F. Bruce speculates on the writer of this verse, "He probably knew of a number of incidents in the life of Jesus when He 'offered up prayers and supplications with strong crying and tears.'"[1] Obviously, Gethsemane was one of these times.

How gladly we would all welcome more details of how Jesus prevailed in prayer. Moses, Elijah, Isaiah, and Daniel were all mighty in prevailing prayer, but never such prevailing as that of Christ, the Son of Man, as He interceded on earth as our great High Priest.

Never was any human being busier than our Lord during His earthly ministry. Mark tells us of occasions when He did not even have time to eat. On other occasions He did not take time to sleep. He was ministering by day, and people came for interviews at night. He was teaching, healing, journeying, and blessing, but He withdrew alone to pray. It was probably during those early morning hours and all-night hours, when He could be more alone with the Father, that He again and again prevailed with strong crying and tears. Christ Himself tells us how deeply and how often He longed to save Jerusalem (Matt. 23:37; Luke 13:34; 19:41). The revival at Pentecost and afterward undoubtedly was chiefly the result of the prevailing intercession of Jesus.

E. M. Bounds wrote, "His life crises were distinctly marked, His life victories all won, in hours of importunate prayer." According to Thomas Payne, "His prayers were stronger than all the forces of earth and hell together. . . . It was to Him the real battlefield."[2]

His prayers brought all-essential victories. He prayed, and the disciples did not lose their faith and did not disband at the Crucifixion (Luke 22:32). He prayed, and through Gethsemane's agony He was able to bear the weight of the sins of the world.

It was not customary in Jesus' day to kneel for prayer. But Jesus was in such agony of prevailing prayer that He kneeled down as He prayed (Luke 22:41). Matthew and Mark add that He fell to the ground on His face in His prayer wrestling (Matt. 26:39; Mark 14:35). Jesus prevailed till He had assurance of victory, and rising from His agony, He demonstrated the quiet poise of total victory. He had prayed as no one ever prayed and had prevailed as no one had ever prevailed, and it was all for our sakes. Prevailing prayer is almost always for the sake of others.

Prevailing prayer was His lifelong vocation. All that Christ accomplished during His earthly ministry was born in intercession, covered and saturated with intercession, and empowered and anointed as a result of intercession. Says Andrew Murray, "Every act of grace in Christ has been preceded by, and owes its power to intercession."[3]

Christ chose to minister, not primarily through the power and attributes of His essential deity as Son of God, but, rather, as Son of Man. His favorite term for Himself was Son of Man. He chose to face life and Satan on the same level that we do. His baptism occurred as He prevailed in prayer, and the Holy Spirit came upon Him as he prayed. Why was He praying? No doubt during His years in Nazareth He had already been praying day after day as He worked in the carpenter's shop. Prayer was a part of all He did. It was His very life breath.

Jesus won His forty-day battle in the desert with Satan through prayer. He selected His apostles through prayer. He depended totally upon the Holy Spirit, just as you and I must do, and He received the Holy Spirit, just as you and I do— through prayer. Jesus prevailed daily. He could not live and minister without prevailing prayer, as Hebrews 5:7 indicates.

JESUS STILL PREVAILS IN PRAYER

Jesus, on heaven's throne today, is still our High Priest as well as our King. His priesthood is permanent (Heb. 7:24). He is still the Son of Man. He reigns today and intercedes today as

39

the Son of Man. When He comes again, He will come as the Son of Man.

As Son of Man, where does His priority lie? As enthroned Son of Man, what does Jesus live to do? Does He live to welcome the saints to heaven at their death? I am sure He welcomes them, but the Bible does not say so. Does He live to grant interviews to saints and angels? He most probably often does this, but the Bible does not say so. Does He live to enjoy heaven's music? I am sure He thrills to it. He created us to be able to enjoy music along with Him, but there is something more important than listening to music. Does He live to reign? Most certainly He does—and He will reign for ever and ever.

But the Bible emphasizes one role of Jesus today above all others—He is *Priest* forever (Heb. 5:6; 6:20; 7:17, 21). His priesthood is permanent (7:24) because He always lives to intercede (v. 25). His sovereign throne is a throne of grace, both because of His atonement and because He ever lives to intercede for us. His is a priestly throne (8:1).

Romans 8:34 associates two facts: Christ at the right hand of God, and Christ interceding for us. What does this intercession for us imply? Many commentators feel that His very presence seated on the throne of heaven is sufficient in itself as a glorious intercession. They doubt that He is actually praying. They feel that He does not need to make any requests of the Father; His just sitting on the throne is all the request necessary.

But Jesus is the same yesterday, today, and forever (Heb. 13:8). While on earth, He loved us, yearned for us, and prayed for us (John 17). He prayed for Peter personally (Luke 22:32). As Son of Man, He is as intensely concerned about and interested in each one of us as He ever was. He is still as sympathetic as He ever was (Heb. 4:15). The Greek word used here, *sympatheō,* means to suffer with. The whole argument of Hebrews 4:15–16 is that we are to come to the throne of grace (where Jesus is interceding) with confidence because He does sympathize and suffer with our pain. He is touched and moved by our need and feels its pain. He feels for us as infinitely as He ever did.

40

His throne of intercession for us is a throne of feeling intercession, a pained intercession. We sing the hymn, "Does Jesus care when my heart is pained?" And then we sing the chorus, which resounds our profound conviction, "Oh yes, He cares, I know He cares. His heart is touched with my grief."

I agree with Andrew Murray that every blessing we receive from God, every answer to prayer, bears this divine stamp upon it: "Through Christ's intercession."[4] Christ is not sitting passively in blissful royal dignity, unmoved, while you intercede. No! Never! You intercede because He intercedes. The Holy Spirit conveys to you the heartbeat of Jesus. You feel but the faintest burden of concern as compared with the infinite concern that Jesus feels for you and with you.

Jesus enters into all the struggles and spiritual warfare of the church. The Jesus who felt all the sorrows and pain of Israel in her sin (Isa. 63:9) feels all the heartbreak of the world yet today. He is our eternal High Priest. He is prevailing today on heaven's throne—not only by His presence and because of His wounds at Calvary, but through His continuing holy pleading, His intercession. Not till Satan is cast into the lake of fire, the warfare with sin is forever over, and the last lost sheep is in the fold will Jesus cease to prevail in intercessory burden for our world.

The death of our Lord Jesus Christ upon the cross marked the end of His humiliation and suffering, the completion of God's provision of atonement, and the crushing defeat of Satan. Jesus' exaltation then began in four glorious steps. First, Jesus went to the unseen world of spirits and announced His complete triumph over Satan (1 Peter 3:19).

Second came His triumphant resurrection, which announced to the universe that His atoning sacrifice was accepted by God the Father, that all His claims to be the Son of God were validated (Rom. 14:9), and that all His own would themselves one day be resurrected just as He was resurrected (1 Cor. 15:20; 2 Cor. 4:14).

Third, Jesus visibly and victoriously ascended to the Father in heaven. He went through the heavens (Heb. 4:14) and was escorted and received up into glory (1 Tim. 3:16). This triumphal procession into the gates of heaven is probably described in Psalm 24:7–10. As the glorified Son of Man, He is now officially resident with God the Father and is preparing a place for us (John 14:2). This is a blessed mystery, the full significance and result of which we shall one day realize.

Fourth, Jesus is now enthroned at the right hand of the Father (Mark 16:19). He Himself foretold this event when He quoted the prophecy of David, "The Lord [God the Father] said to my Lord [God the Son]: 'Sit at my right hand until I put your enemies under your feet'" (Matt. 22:44; Ps. 110:1). In His trial before the Sanhedrin Jesus announced, "I say to all of you [the entire world of saved and unsaved]: In the future you will see the Son of Man sitting at the right hand of the Mighty One" (Matt. 26:64).

This enthronement of Jesus is already an accomplished fact:

1. *He is already exalted to the place of highest honor and majesty* and is given the name above every name in heaven, on earth, and under the earth (i.e., over every satanic and demonic power; Phil. 2:9).

2. *He is already actively involved in the government of the universe* (Heb. 1:4). He is seated, which shows His sovereignty is an accomplished fact. He is at the right hand of God the Father—the place of supreme authority and highest honor. His reign is cosmic, over the whole universe. The glorious Father, says Paul, has "seated him at his right hand in the heavenly realms, far above all rule and authority, power and dominion, and every title that can be given, not only in the present age but also in the one to come. And God placed all things under his feet and appointed him to be head over everything" (Eph. 1:20–22).

3. *His reign is priestly.* He is our High Priest-Sovereign. His throne involves both kingship and priesthood. He is still the Messiah—the Anointed One—our Prophet, Priest, and King (the three classes of people who were anointed in the Old Testament times). He is the "high priest, who sat down at the right hand of the throne of the Majesty in heaven" (Heb. 8:1).

As High Priest, He offered Himself as the supreme and final sacrifice on the cross. When He "had offered for all time one sacrifice for sins, he sat down at the right hand of God" (10:12).

If His sacrificing activity is already completed forever, then in what way does He now serve as our High Priest? In the other major activity of the priesthood—intercession for others. "Because Jesus lives forever, he has a permanent priesthood. . . . He always lives to intercede for them. Such a high priest meets our need" (Heb. 7:24–26).

Christ is today the interceding Sovereign of the universe. His throne is one of intercession. One day He will rule by the rod—by His almighty power. Today He rules by His uplifted and extended hand—by prayer. His intercession is not symbolic but real, as real as it was when He interceded on earth. He is on the throne interceding for us and waiting for us to join Him as intercessors.

CHAPTER 6

Your Welcome to the Throne

HOW WE APPROACH CHRIST'S THRONE

ALL PRAYER IS an approach to the throne of God. Prayer is not a casual or trivial act but instead is an amazing privilege, a glory of God. He condescends to permit your approaching His throne. But God has given you the gracious birthright of coming at any time and as often as you desire. The whole foundation of prevailing prayer is that God has given you constant, instant access to His throne and that He desires you to take a responsible and active role in His throne concerns.

On the one hand, you should always remember that you are approaching the actual Sovereign of the universe, seated in majesty on His throne. This picture is real, not merely symbolic. The hymn writer sang:

> Thou art coming to a king;
> Large petitions with thee bring.

You are a kingdom official on kingdom business. Prevailing prayer is urgent kingdom business.

On the other hand, you should always remember how loved you are, how awaited and constantly welcome. You disappoint your heavenly Father if you do not come often and with freedom. You disappoint the Savior if you do not come interceding in His name. He longs to "amen" your prayer (Rev. 3:14) and join you in intercession.

1. *Approach, remembering it is a throne of grace.* It is indeed the throne of the universe—but it is equally the throne of grace (Heb. 4:16). Justice is its foundation (Ps. 89:14), but it is a throne of grace. The book of Revelation pictures the Lamb of God upon the throne, and twenty-six times Christ is called the Lamb.

The throne of God is a throne of grace because God is the God of all grace (1 Peter 5:10). His Spirit is the Spirit of grace (Heb. 10:29). Twelve times the Bible speaks of "the grace of our Lord Jesus." It is because of God's grace that His throne is open to you. This is His day of grace, when He longs to be gracious. Prevailing prayer enables God to be gracious.

2. *Approach the throne with confident boldness.* The word *parrēsia* in Hebrews 4:16 means freedom; unreservedness of speech; the absence of fear in speaking boldly, hence, confidence; and cheerful courage.[1] That is exactly the glorious freedom God gives you in entering His presence.

When your King urges you to come and make your requests known, why should you doubt Him? With the Lord, who loved you enough to die for you, asking you to join Him in His intercession, why should you hesitate or fail to be eager to intercede and prevail in prayer?

3. *Approach the throne with openness and sincerity.* The all-seeing eye of God has observed every aspect of the need you bring before Him. He knows how it will influence His royal purpose and how urgently it is needed. He knows all the reasons why the need is there. He desires you to share openly and fully, hiding nothing. Just as Hezekiah spread the threatening letter of Sennacherib before the Lord (Isa. 37:14), so you should present all the facts and reasons (1:18; 43:26). The more fully you share the situation with the Lord, the more easily you will be able to prevail in prayer.

4. *Approach the throne with faith.* A throne is a place where

royal answers are given, where needs are presented and discussed. It is the place where the king makes decisions. Remember, when you are a child of God, you do not come as a roving beggar, hoping to get crumbs and leftovers. You come as a prince and member of the royal family. You come as an official of the King's court. You come as the kingdom partner and prayer partner of the Son of the King.

During the days of the Persian empire, only the most privileged of the nobility were permitted to stand in the presence of the king, and then only a few at a time. It was thought to be the highest privilege of a human being. But you are given permanent and instant access to the throne room of the King of the universe at any time. You are commanded to come and ask. Remember, prevailing prayer is primarily for things related directly or indirectly to the King's own interests and desires.

If you can ask help or a favor from another, how much more can you petition the Almighty God for that which causes Him no embarrassment or loss but, on the contrary, advances His kingdom. Charles Spurgeon urged, "When we pray, we are standing in the palace, on the glittering floor of the great King's own reception room, and thus we are placed upon a vantage ground. In prayer we stand where angels bow with veiled faces; there, even there, the cherubim and seraphim adore, before that selfsame throne to which our prayers ascend."[2]

5. *Approach the throne with love and joy.* Approach eagerly and lovingly, for God is your Father. Approach with loving gratitude for all God's goodness to you. Remember how faithful He has been to you. Approach with love burning and glowing in your heart for Jesus, for His kingdom, and for those you pray for. Love because God loves.

Approach the throne with eager joy. You are asking for things God longs to do. He has ordained that, even though He desires to do what you ask for, normally He does not act until you pray. God is thus even more glad for you to come in prevailing prayer than you are glad for the opportunity. Your prayer time is always a joy time to the Lord.

Approach with joy because you have the privilege, instant access, and eager welcome at the throne. Approach with joy because God's throne is a throne of grace. Approach with joy because of all God's "very great and precious promises" (2 Peter 1:4). Approach rejoicing not only for what God is able to do but also for what you are expecting Him to do.

But there is something even greater and more amazing than access to the throne. The Bible also assures you that you actually sit down with Christ on His throne.

THE REALITY OF THRONE LIFE

Jesus promises, "To him who overcomes, I will give the right to sit with me on my throne, just as I overcame and sat down with my Father on his throne" (Rev. 3:21). But that sitting is future, after we join Him in heaven, after the judgment seat of Christ, when He gives to us His rewards and honors.

Even now Jesus wants you to exercise an active throne life. Christ has identified with us so fully that He provides for each true follower a gracious provision beyond our asking or thinking. It would be audacious and even blasphemous for you to suggest or claim the life that I now present if God's inspired Word did not clearly teach it.

Christ's provision for you is that by God's grace and your faith you can appropriate and experience to a sacred degree Christ's death, resurrection, and exaltation. You can know the reality of being crucified with Christ (Gal. 2:20), raised with Christ (Eph. 2:6), and now seated with Christ already on His throne.

God has already "blessed us in the heavenly realms with every spiritual blessing in Christ" (Eph. 1:3). We are members of the body, of which He is head, so what happened to Him happens spiritually to us. He is the Vine and we are the branches. We are in Him and He in us. The language is figurative, but the words are to be taken as true spiritual reality.

Potentially, you are already exalted to the throne where He reigns actually. Although you are still here on earth, your spirit

47

is in the heavenlies with Christ. You are in the world but not of it (John 17:11, 14). In spirit, you are lifted above the worldly, the earthly, and the temporal. Bishop Moule in his commentary on Ephesians 6:2 points out that because you are embodied "in Christ," you are beside Him on His throne of intercessory dominion. "Believers are bodily in heaven in point of right, and virtually so in spirit, and have their own place assigned there, which in due time they shall take possession of."[3]

You are spiritually to share Christ's exaltation now. You are to participate in a throne life and role now. You will possess in heaven visibly only what you possess now spiritually. Since all things are under Christ's feet (Eph. 1:22) and you are "in Christ," then all things are potentially under your feet also.

Paul assured the believers in Rome, "The God of peace will soon crush Satan under your feet" (Rom. 16:20). Is not this what Jesus referred to when He said, "I have given you authority to trample on snakes and scorpions and to overcome all the power of the enemy" (Luke 10:19)? This conquest must be accomplished through prevailing intercession. Then you realize the power to crush Satan. By faith, in virtue of Christ's cross and in His name, you can even issue commands to Satan. From your position where you are seated with Christ on the throne, you look down in spiritual vision upon Satan. In the words of Luther,

> And though this world, with devils filled,
> Should threaten to undo us,
>   We will not fear, for God hath willed
> His truth to triumph through us.
>   The Prince of Darkness grim,
> We tremble not for him;
>   His rage we can endure,
> For lo, his doom is sure;
>   One little word shall fell him.

You sit beside Christ on His throne, triumphant in Him, triumphant through Him.

This truth is so amazing that Paul was afraid we would not comprehend it in all its beauty. So before he explains it to the Ephesians, he tells them that he continually asks that God the Father would give them "the Spirit of wisdom and revelation" and that the eyes of their heart might be enlightened so that they could realize and truly know their hope and riches in Christ, and Christ's "incomparably great power for us who believe." He then describes how that power raised Christ to heaven's throne and put all things under His feet. Then Paul overwhelms us by saying that we are there seated with Christ (Eph. 1:17–2:6). May God help us to grasp the power and authority given us through prayer by virtue of this amazing truth. This teaching is the foundation of all prevailing prayer and explains why, by prayer, you can attack and rout Satan.

In yourself you are a weak human being. But in Christ you are seated beside Him on His sovereign throne, and He delegates to you the privilege of praying in His name, resisting Satan, your already-defeated foe, and crushing Satan under your feet because Satan is under Jesus' feet.

Huegel reminds us that you do not work up to this throne life little by little. It is not by your struggling, praying, and fasting that you finally attain throne life. Throne life is God's gift of grace to you in Christ.[4] Having realized God's gift of throne life, you may at times wrestle and fast as you prevail in prayer. But it is the expression of throne life, not a means to enter into it.

The full realization of the throne life "naturally presupposes many steps: surrender, consecration, the Spirit's infilling, victorious living—all are involved and presupposed."[5] The cross is the door to the Christian life, to the Spirit-filled life, and to the enthroned life. You have no power, victory, or authority of your own. All is by grace; all is because of the cross.

Andrew Murray calls the royal power of prayer, wherein our will is united with Christ's will, the highest proof that we are created in the likeness of Christ. "He is found worthy of entering into fellowship with Him, not only in adoration and worship, but in having his will actually taken up into the rule of the world, and becoming the intelligent channel through which God can fulfill His infinite purpose."[6] To Moses it was given by intercession to place his hand upon God's throne (Exod. 17:16, margin). To you, by grace, it is given to sit with Christ on His throne and there to intercede and prevail for His kingdom.

We are so identified with Christ that if we are one with Him in His death on the cross, we cannot be other than one with Him in His resurrection and one with Him on His throne. Throne life is as real as your crucifixion with Christ is real (Gal. 2:20). Throne life is to produce as definite results as crucifixion with Christ does.

In the same way that you are to count yourself "dead to sin but alive to God in Christ Jesus" (Rom. 6:11), you are to count yourself now enthroned with Christ, your reigning Lord. Just as surely as because of Romans 6:11 you are exhorted in verse 12, "Therefore do not let sin reign in your mortal body," just so certainly you, because you are enthroned with Christ, the interceding High Priest-King, are to be a king and priest with Christ (Rev. 1:6). You are to reign by your prayer just as Jesus reigns by prayer. Reigning means prevailing. May God write this powerful truth deeper and deeper on our hearts and use it ever more significantly in our prevailing prayer.

THE NORMALITY OF THRONE LIFE

Jesus wants it to be normal for you to exercise throne authority in your prevailing prayer. It is not presumption to act on God's Word. You are not to tremble before Satan but are to confront him from the throne. You are not to cower in the dust before him. You are to initiate prayer attacks on Satan's strongholds, force his retreat, and release his captives. Nothing but throne life and your exercising your delegated throne authority befits you as a priest and king of God through Christ (1 Peter 2:9). Prevailing prayer alone is adequate and befitting for you as one enthroned with Christ.

Enthroned intercessors manifest no proud, superior authority. It is only because of their Spirit-imparted pervasive humility that God is able to use them so mightily. It is those who humble themselves under God's mighty hand that the Spirit empowers to pray flaming lightning bolts from the throne. Enthroned prayer warriors do not go on tours demonstrating their prayer power. They are often hidden saints mighty only in God.

In all other respects, theirs is a normal life—Spirit-filled, sanctified to God's will, and radiant with His presence and joy. They are not unbalanced, abnormal, or fanatical. They are not boasting of a superior spirituality. They are wholesomely normal in their home life, work life, and church life. But in the hidden place of prayer they have power with God and exercise the prayer authority of Christ's throne.

You will note perhaps their quiet sense of spiritual responsibility, their sensitivity and deep concern for the needs of the kingdom and of our hurting world. Rivers of love, joy, peace, patience, and goodness flow out from their innermost being (John 7:38; Gal. 5:22–23). They carry with them a special portion of God's presence. Blessings seem to attend their word and their work. In them reside quiet power, intensity of commitment, active faith, and a disciplined and devoted life of prayer.

Throne life honors God; it takes Him at His word. It knows His holy heartbeat and loves with the love of Christ. It rejoices in the triumph of Christ. It often recognizes the hidden workings of God that others do not see. It does not judge from the external but is granted deeper understanding of God's purpose and goal. It "amens" the promises of God, echoing the amens of Jesus Himself (Rev. 3:14). Throne life sees God as God, permits God to be God, and gives God the opportunity He desires to get great glory through great answers to prayer.

REIGNING IN LIFE

Throne life, by prevailing intercession, is but one aspect of your reigning in life. "How much more will those who receive

51

God's abundant provision of grace and of the gift of righteousness reign in life through the one man, Jesus Christ" (Rom. 5:17). When does this reign in life occur? Obviously, by the grace of Jesus Christ we are to reign now. Its ultimate fullness will be in eternity. Christ's abundance not only provides abundant life now, but our reigning in life.

Vine comments, "That we are to reign in life involves much more than participation in eternal life; it indicates the activity of life in fellowship with Christ in His kingdom. There is stress on the word 'reign.'" This throne life, comments another, is "a life divinely owned and legally secured, 'reigning' in exalted freedom and unbiased might through that other matchless 'One,' Jesus Christ."[7]

Reigning in life certainly includes our being free from the dominion of sin and being more than conquerors through Christ (Rom. 8:37). It includes being equipped "with everything good for doing his will" (Heb. 13:21). It includes overcoming evil with good (Rom. 12:21) and having a faith that overcomes the world (1 John 5:4). It certainly includes sharing Christ's throne as a royal priest unto God (1 Peter 2:9).

All authority in heaven and earth has been given to Jesus (Matt. 28:18). Because of His universal authority you ask whatever you will in His name and are assured of God's answer. Only because of His authority can you prevail in prayer or dare to face Satan in prayer warfare.

ACTING FAITH

Throne life includes the privilege under the guidance of the Spirit to use the delegated authority of the name of Jesus and to give the command of faith. Huegel has called this a kind of "executive authority," which he considers the highest privilege of throne life.[8]

This is the most amazing privilege of all. It is a special form of acting faith. When Moses at the Red Sea cried unto the Lord, God answered, "Why are you crying out to me? Tell the Israelites to move on" (Exod. 14:15). Moses had faith. In the previous two verses he told Israel how God was going to deliver them. "Do not be afraid. Stand firm and you will see the deliverance the LORD will bring you today. . . . The LORD will fight for you; you need only to be still." He believed God would answer immediately, and yet he "cried out" to the Lord. God's answer was, "You don't need to keep asking. Act your faith."

Israel had been guided by God. Moses had been interceding. Now what he needed was not more prayer but the acting out of the faith of his heart.

When Elijah, by God's guidance (2 Kings 2:6), led Elisha to Jordan, he did not pray for the water to divide. He took his cloak and rolled it up and struck the water, which immediately parted (v. 8). When Elisha returned to carry on the Lord's commission, he called out, "Where now is the LORD, the God of Elijah?" (v. 14), and struck the water again. He found the Lord was right there, and the water divided before him.

This enacted faith is a privilege of the throne life. People who are accustomed to prevailing prayer will often meet crises when they must express their faith by action. Because they are enthroned, they will be able to obey God, and He will validate their faith.

THE COMMAND OF FAITH

The command of faith is probably the most dramatic form of throne authority. Both the Old and New Testaments contain many examples of using such a command, which is possible to us because of our throne life. It will be discussed in detail later.

CHAPTER 7

Why Is Prevailing Necessary?

WE ALL EXPERIENCE situations in which prayer answers are much more difficult than in others. Over whom or what must we prevail in prayer? Let me point out that you must prevail over yourself, over situations, sometimes over people, and perhaps almost always over Satan. There is also a sense in which you must prevail before God.

YOU MUST PREVAIL OVER YOURSELF

You must prevail over your schedule of activities. Life is so full that it is often difficult to find the necessary time for the prolonged prayer that may be required in prevailing. Prevailing may necessitate adjusting your priorities. In addition, Satan always seems to be able to manipulate circumstances or people to interrupt you or call you on the phone just when you want to concentrate on prayer. When you need to prevail, you find time alone with God more difficult than usual. You may have to sacrifice good and urgent activities in order to give adequate time to intercession.

You must at times prevail over weariness. After you have been active and working diligently and then stop to get alone with God, you may find that your natural physical weariness catches up with you. Sometimes when you are tired, the spiritual thing to do may be to take a brief nap before you begin your more intense prayer. After several hours of prayer, you may need to refresh yourself with a drink of water or snack on a piece of fruit or small quantity of simple food to help you wake up. You may need to vary your posture or to walk about your room if the location of your praying permits it. When you are not well, you may need to prevail over pain.

Some people have to prevail over personal laziness or restlessness. They are too undisciplined to find prolonged prevailing prayer easy. They need to determine by the grace of God to learn to discipline themselves. They can make this need a special object of prayer and receive God's real help at the point of weakness.

Some people are so spiritually weak that they have never learned how to pray with real soul hunger for any needs except for their own personal crises. They need to develop a loving concern for others, learn to make and use prayer lists, and make time for intercession a part of their daily schedule. They can learn to prevail over their weak spiritual life and their comparative prayerlessness.

You may need to prevail over a tendency to doubt. Perhaps you have a questioning nature that predisposes you to doubt. Perhaps you have not taught yourself to concentrate, and you have developed a pattern of thinking that lets your mind jump from one thought to another. These human tendencies are not sinful, but they need to be brought to the cross and the Spirit's help received.

Some people are so unspiritual that not only does their physical nature shrink from prayer but their carnal nature fears prayer involvement, holds them back from earnest, prolonged praying, and finds a multitude of excuses why not to prevail. Satan takes advantage of any natural tendency to procrastinate and specially attacks prayer time. A spiritually healthy, mature Spirit-filled person rejoices in the opportunity to pray, finds extra time for prayer, and often hungers for more time alone with Christ in prayer. Such a person is eager to sacrifice other things in order to be able to intercede with Christ.

In some aspects of prevailing prayer, such as wrestling in prayer or prayer warfare, God may lead you to add fasting to your intercession for a time. Then you may need to prevail over a desire for food.

Perhaps before you really begin to experience prevailing prayer, you will need to confess before God your past prayerlessness, your lack of hunger for God's presence or for God's will to be done, your lack of desire and determination to persevere until you obtain prayer answers to major needs. You may need to ask God to deliver you from inner hesitations, fears, and unwillingness to pay the price of victory. We cannot earn prayer's answers, but there is a price of self-effort, priority setting, and willingness to sacrifice self-interest so that God's will may prevail. Ask God to give you new boldness, determination, and faith.

YOU MUST PREVAIL OVER SITUATIONS

The situations about which you pray are often very complex. There may be so many interrelated aspects that it is almost impossible to discover what is hindering or blocking the way. Organizational structures, government laws, traditions, or habits of thinking and long-established methods may be so involved and intricately intertwined that prayer answers seem impossible.

To bring about changes in some aspects of situations, the actions of a number of people must be coordinated and timed in such detail that there always seems to be something hindering. Once you get prayer answers for one aspect of a situation, you may discern other hindering factors.

It may take a whole series of prayer answers before an exceedingly complex situation yields to the will of God. This process may require extended periods of prayer. Repeated roadblocks and unyielding complex situations can leave you frustrated and almost hopeless.

Never say "impossible" when you are praying for something in the will of God. God is sovereign over nature and over people. God can act in wisdom, grace, and power until one aspect of a situation after another yields with a divine domino effect until God's complete answer is given and His full will done. Never rule out an intervening act of God. Never doubt the possibility of miracle.

YOU MUST PREVAIL OVER PEOPLE

God has created each of us with the power of choice and a will of our own. Human will in one or more people may seem almost to eliminate the prayer answer you seek. It is almost impossible to predict the psychological working of minds and even more impossible to influence or control them. People can be obstinate, stubborn, and resistant to all suggestions and change. Over and over God called Israel stiff-necked. Moses agreed that Israel was stiff-necked. (Perhaps today we would term this attitude one of being bullheaded or pigheaded.)

Ambition, pride, jealousy, envy, and even hatred can poison minds and hearts. People not only become inflexible by habit and deaf to all entreaty, but they can become hardened by sin. What will it take, you ask, to change some person's attitude or decision?

The only hope is for God to change what you cannot change without His help. Therefore you pray. God has a way to speak to a person's conscience, to his or her common sense and better judgment. God has a way to bring new suggestions to a person's mind, until that one sees reasons for and advantages of a changed course of action. It may take a series of circumstances to bring new light on the situation or pressure on the person. But all such changes are possible for our sovereign God.

God will never treat people as robots or manipulate them. God will never violate an individual's free will. But God has ways of coordinating events, effects, and actions of other people until the most obdurate do change. It may take continuing intercession over a long period of time or amassed prayer from a number of prevailing prayer warriors, but prayer can prevail, until the person changes, no matter how reluctantly.

When Israel faced the overwhelming odds of the many diverse and entrenched armed nations occupying Canaan, God said to them symbolically, "I will send my terror ahead of you and throw into confusion every nation you encounter. I will make all your enemies turn their backs and run. I will send the hornet ahead of you to drive the Hivites, Canaanites and Hittites out of your way" (Exod. 23:27–28).

Just as the conquest of Canaan was a process of conquest, a series of divinely enabled victories over an extended period of time, so prevailing in many situations where willful and obstinate people are involved may require repeated prevailing and militant prayer warfare. But when your intercession prevails with Christ, there is no person that cannot be brought to submission to Christ's will or else be moved out of the way.

YOU MUST PREVAIL OVER SATAN

The instigating, manipulating, coordinating mastermind behind much over which you must prevail is Satan. He works through his many demons to do all in his power to keep you from prayer, to shorten your prayer time, to distract you while you pray, and if at all possible, to get you to give up before you prevail in prayer.

Satan would rather have you do anything but pray. He would rather have you busy working for God than praying to God. More than anything else you can ever do, prevailing prayer has the potential to hinder Satan, to damage his kingdom, and to rob him of his human followers and slaves.

Prevailing prayer, more than anything else, links you with God and His almighty kingdom power. It uniquely brings into action the divine and worldwide ministry of God's holy angels. The Bible pictures the almost indescribable power of some of God's angels (1 Chron. 21:15; Isa. 37:36; Dan. 6:22). Prevailing prayer unites you with all the forces of heaven.

Satan has intense and constant hostility to human beings

because he is so anti-God. There is only one way Satan can try to hinder God and frustrate God's plan: by focusing on us human beings—we who are so loved by God, so godlike in power and potential, and so integrated into God's plan. Satan dreads and fears prevailing prayer more than all your other activities for God and with God.

Satan usually knows his priorities, and since prevailing prayer can restrain, bind, and defeat him more than all else, Satan makes his priority to hinder, divert, or stop prevailing prayer. All prayer is a threat and an extreme danger to him. Prevailing prayer terrifies him more than all else and makes him desperately opposed. It seems that his priority assignment for his demon followers is to oppose and hinder prayer.

Prevailing prayer, thus, must again and again be focused on Satan and our unceasing battle with his forces, intrigues, and machinations. Our prevailing prayer often must become mighty prayer warfare. Prayer warfare will be treated in much more detail later.

We have not prevailed until Satan is defeated. The defeat begins in the unseen world of spirit but becomes visible as prayer is answered for us.

CHAPTER 8

You Must Prevail Before God

TO PREVAIL INVOLVES being spiritually strong, committed to the prayer goal, and persevering until God's answer of victory is received. Not only may prevailing prayer involve prevailing over ourselves, situations, other people, and Satan, but there may be an element of prevailing before God.

Prevailing may involve God's most perfect time. Only God knows at which point of time there would be the greatest spiritual returns and the most strategic advantage to His kingdom from your receiving the answer to your prayer. God's clocks keep perfect time. God's time is the best of all times. To obtain the highest kingdom results God may need to delay your answer. Included in this timing may be special blessing for you. God may see that it is best for your spiritual growth and eternal reward for you to prevail at some length before the answer reaches you.

1. *God may be testing your depth of desire.* We are assured that we find Him when we seek Him with all our heart (Jer. 29:13). If we are willing to do without God's answer, our desire is not yet deep enough. The longer we pray with real soul travail, the deeper our desire becomes.

2. *God may be testing your humility.* If there is desire for personal prestige or self-glory, your prayer will probably not be granted. It is very easy to want something sincerely for God's glory but yet to be glad if it becomes known that you helped pray it to pass! God may test, deepen, and purify your humility by delaying the answer.

In the case of the Greek woman from Syrophoenicia (Matt. 15:21–28), Jesus tested her in this way. At first He kept silent, until His disciples said, "Send her away, for she keeps crying out after us." But she kept pleading until she prevailed. Probably Jesus was deepening both her desire and her humility.

3. *God may use your time of prevailing to search and purify your motive.* Wrong motives can block any prayer, even if the desire sought is in the will of God. "When you ask, you do not receive, because you ask with wrong motives" (James 4:3). Motives can be very complex. You may seek an answer from God for several reasons, one of which may be unacceptable to God. It is for your good that God purifies your motives, even if He must delay His answer in order to do so.

While you plead for His answer, He may remind you of a spiritual need you have overlooked or forgotten in your own life. Has any disunity in your attitude or relation to others, whether in thought or action, blocked God's answer to your prayer (Matt. 5:23–24)? Jacob's relations with his brother Esau were probably probed by God during his night of prevailing prayer.

Have you grieved God with any sin of omission or any sin of thought, word, or deed? The psalmist said, "If I had cherished sin in my heart, the Lord would not have listened" (Ps. 66:18).

What kind of prevailing was involved when Jesus prevailed in the Garden of Gethsemane? Most probably His intense intercession occupied three hours. He was prevailing on our behalf. Probably several aspects of prevailing were included. His prayer, "If it is possible, may this cup be taken from me" (Matt. 26:39), indicates that he was prevailing over Himself, over His natural humanity. He was certainly prevailing over Satan also, and Satan was totally defeated. There may have been other hidden aspects of prevailing of which we are not aware.

Over what did Elijah prevail on Mount Carmel? Elijah knew he was in the will of God. He had announced three years before that there would be no rain or dew except at his word (1 Kings 17:1). God had given him step-by-step guidance—to the Kerith ravine, to Zarephath, back to King Ahab, and each step in the challenge to Baal on Mount Carmel. God had supernaturally fed him by ravens, multiplied the widow's flour and oil, raised the widow's son to life, and sent fire from heaven to consume the sacrifice and altar on Mount Carmel.

Elijah had been praying for the nation to be turned back to God and for idolatry to be destroyed from among them. Now the people had endorsed the form of the contest that Elijah had with the prophets of Baal. They had seen these prophets put to shame, had seen God's fire descend from heaven as Elijah prayed, and had leaped to their feet shouting, "The LORD—he is God! The LORD—he is God!" (1 Kings 18:39) They had seized the false prophets of Baal, who were then destroyed.

Elijah announced to King Ahab that now God would send rain. Elijah then went to his knees on the top of Mount Carmel and prayed for rain, but no rain came—not even a cloud appeared in the sky. Seven times Elijah sent his servant to search the sky for rain. But Elijah persevered in prevailing prayer, bowing down to the ground with his face between his knees in intense intercession. Then the servant spotted a small cloud the size of a man's hand. Elijah had prevailed before God, and soon the rain was pouring down in torrents.

Note the various aspects of prevailing in Jacob's night of prayer (Gen. 32:9–31). His life had not been flawless, yet God had an eternal purpose for him, for which Jacob needed spiritual preparation. The immediate need was to prevail for the safety of his family. Above all, he needed to be a new, more spiritual Jacob. Jacob became Israel by prevailing with God. Both symbolically and literally he prayed till he prevailed. It is a model of what it means to prevail before God.

1. *He was returning at God's command* (Gen. 31:3). Prevailing is often required, even when you are asking in God's will.

2. *He was returning at God's promise.*

3. *He pleaded the promise of God.* Your prayer takes on a new dimension of faith and power when you claim God's promise.

4. *He had proofs of God's presence and approval.* Laban testified that God spoke (Gen. 31:24–29). God's angels accompanied Jacob (32:1).

5. *Difficulties, obstacles, and delays are no proof of being out of the will of God.* Esau came with his private army. Satan's attacks most likely prove you are in God's will.

6. *He went instantly to prayer* (Gen. 32:9–12). No spiritual victories are won without instant, frequent recourse to God. Jacob reminded God of His command, promises, and previous blessings and presented a specific request.

7. *He humbled himself* (Gen. 32:10). He called God Elohim (mighty) and Jehovah (Lord), confessing his own unworthiness and his poverty apart from God.

8. *He did what he could to help answer his own prayer.*

9. *He was unable to sleep.* When God keeps you awake, He has something to say to you.

10. *He committed all into God's merciful hand*—wives, servants, children, and possessions.

11. *He prayed on alone* (cf. Hos. 12:4). He wrestled literally and symbolically. It was a spiritual struggle. He wept. Note these translations of the verb in Hosea: he pleaded (LB, JB), begged God's favor (NEB), and entreated God for mercy (BV).

12. *He refused to let go until God blessed him.* He persisted in holy boldness. The more he realized who the Wrestler was, the more determined he was to be blessed by Him. Whatever the cost, he held on, even when he suffered.

13. *He quit fighting and began clinging.* He insisted only on God's blessing.

14. *He got a new name.* This change indicated a new nature. He received a new face-to-face understanding of God. His name indicated a new royalty—he became a prince.

15. *His power with God preceded his power with men.* When he

had prevailed before God, he had no problem prevailing before his brother.

THE DYNAMICS OF PREVAILING PRAYER

All prevailing in prayer depends on the full enabling, guidance, and empowering of the Holy Spirit. From one viewpoint, there is only one source and dynamic of prevailing prayer—God the Spirit. Only as He fills us, possesses us, yearns through us, permeates and empowers every aspect of our praying, and discloses to us the priorities for our praying—that is, only as He is Lord of our praying—can we prevail.

From another viewpoint, there are eight all-important dynamics of prevailing prayer:

1. Desire
2. Fervency
3. Importunity
4. Faith

5. The Holy Spirit
6. Uniting in prayer
7. Perseverance
8. Praise

As you study the scriptural accounts, the biographies of God's holiest prayer warriors, and the thrilling narratives of answered prayer, you see repeated mention of how these eight dynamics have been used by the Spirit to lead God's prayer veterans to outstanding victories for Christ.

In some prayer battles, one or more of these dynamics seem to predominate, but in most cases most of them have been used by the Holy Spirit as He has prevailed and triumphed through the prayers of God's children. No two situations are identical in their need or in the activities Satan employs to try to prevent or limit Christ's victory. The people involved in the situations prayed for differ in their attitudes, personalities, and prejudices.

Sin has darkened the understanding, perverted the desires, and enslaved the wills until many of the problems that need to be solved are very complex. Some needs have existed for so long that they seem impossible to change. Some people are so resistant to God's will, so hardened in their sins, and so bound by Satan that there is a tremendous prayer struggle in envisioning and believing for God's answers.

Satan will not give up his strongholds without strong resistance and spiritual battle. He is not only insolent and inveterate in his hatred of God and man, but he is full of wrath at his repeated defeats by the prayer offensives of God's children.

Your prayer, however, can prevail over all circumstances and over all the cunning deception and the demonic power that Satan can marshal. God has ordained that Satan be routed and defeated by your prayer.

But who feels sufficient to take on in spiritual conflict the embattled forces and strongholds of Satan? Who dares to invade territory Satan claims for his own? Who dares to rouse the wrath of Satan by attacking his powerful forces and breaking the chains by which he has fettered his captives? Who dares to battle almost single-handedly, as it seems at times, the powers of darkness and the entrenched kingdom of evil? Who?

God the Holy Spirit! He is not intimidated by Satan and all the wrath of that roaring lion. He is not disheartened, no matter how long Satan has usurped control over a place, a situation, or a people. The Holy Spirit is God the Spirit. Satan is no match for God.

God has ordained to dislodge and defeat Satan by the prayers of His people. The triune God has chosen for the Spirit to empower and pray through you as He indwells and fills you. The Holy Spirit has been charged with the responsibility of engaging in conflict all the powers of darkness and enforcing Christ's victory. This is the age of the Spirit and also the age of battle. Age-long, all-out war exists between God and Satan.

In the mystery of God's purpose, He has chosen to conquer Satan by the cross of Christ and the prayer of God's children. Satan was defeated once for all at the cross. That victory Christ won alone—alone in the garden, alone on the cross. But that eternal victory must now be applied and enforced by the Holy Spirit working through the prayers and obedience of God's children.

The church today is the church militant, the church at war for God. It is God's will that the church be aggressive. We are not to rely passively upon Christ's total and eternal victory at Calvary. We are to launch our prayer battles from that triumph of Christ. From that mount of victory we are to keep a constant offensive against all the defeated forces of hell.

You are to prevail because Christ prevailed. You are to prevail by the Holy Spirit's power and by your prayer and obedience. The victory is sure if you maintain your position of victory won for you by Christ. You are to attack and dislodge Satan from one stronghold after another. You are to set free one captive after another. You are to go from victory to victory—not in yourself, but in the power of the Spirit.

Prayer warfare is of the very essence of New Testament Christianity. Prayer victories are your challenge and heritage as a believer. Arise to your holy privilege, your Christ-purchased, God-ordained role! Onward to victory after victory for Christ through prevailing prayer by the eightfold, Spirit-provided dynamics of prevailing prayer!

CHAPTER 9

The Dynamic of Desire

DESIRE HAS A tremendous motivating power in prevailing prayer. The deeper your desire to see God's answers, the deeper your hunger to see God at work, and the more urgent your heart-cry to see Christ triumph, the more powerfully the Holy Spirit can pray through you. Holy desire is a holy power that energizes prayer. It is a dynamic of the Spirit.

Fénelon wrote, "He who desires not from the depths of his heart makes a deceptive pray-er."[1] Heaven wants sincerity, not beautiful, polite words. Heaven wants depth of soul, not lukewarm mouthings. After hearing many of our family prayers or even pulpit prayers, God's angels, who see our souls through and through, must feel like uttering Solomon's words in Ecclesiastes 1:2, "Meaningless! Meaningless! ... Utterly meaningless!" We have said the same words so often that we can almost say them without thinking. There is nothing new because nothing is really desired.

Repetition is sweet in the ears of God when it is the heart-cry of the soul. Jesus repeated in the agony in Gethsemane, but repetition is lukewarm nothingness when it is unfelt words that are consciously or unconsciously intended as much for the ears of the people as for the ears of God. Such words may be a sedative for our own soul. They do not register with God.

You may have to prevail before God for some time before you reach total, deep sincerity in your praying. Fraser wrote, "Real supplication is the child of heartfelt desire, and cannot prevail without it; a desire not of earth nor issuing from our sinful hearts, but wrought into us by God himself. Oh, for such desires!" Urging the necessity of welcoming spiritual desire and turning it into prayer, he adds, "An earnest desire in spiritual things is a bell ringing for prayer. Not that we should wait for such desires. We should pray at all seasons, whether we are prayer hungry or not. If we have a healthy prayer appetite, so much the better."[2]

There is a sense in which your deep, holy desire is in itself prayer. "You hear, O LORD, the desire of the afflicted . . . you listen to their cry" (Ps. 10:17). Although your heart repeatedly cries out to God with deep desire, you will not be able to voice that desire constantly. But even when the prayer is not on your lips, the desire with which your whole being cries out to God burns as a continuing flame of prayer in God's sight.

Such was the unceasing prayer of Paul's heart, as he wrote, "I speak the truth in Christ—I am not lying, my conscience confirms it in the Holy Spirit—I have great sorrow and unceasing anguish in my heart. For I could wish that I myself were cursed and cut off from Christ for the sake of my brothers, those of my own race, the people of Israel" (Rom. 9:1–4).

Where did Paul get such constant deep desire that burned as a flame on the altar of his soul? He saturated his soul in the truth of the Old Testament. He saw Isaiah describe God as standing all day long with His hands outstretched to the people in longing (Isa. 65:2). He heard him plead through Ezekiel, "Turn! Turn from your evil ways! Why will you die, O house of Israel?" (Ezek. 33:11). He heard God plead through Hosea, "How can I give you up? . . . my compassion is aroused" (Hos. 11:8). Paul heard God in these Scriptures, and his heart-cry became one with God's.

Basic to our desire in petition and intercession is the recognition of need. Nothing is more essential. Says Andrew Murray, "Desire is the soul of prayer, and the cause of insufficient or unsuccessful prayer is very much to be found in the lack or feebleness of desire."[3] As long as it makes little difference to us whether our prayer is answered or not, we will not prevail.

Desire makes prayer specific. It focuses prayer and asserts priority. Desire makes prayer both vital and personal. Paul says of his deep prayer for unbelieving Israel, "Brothers, my heart's desire and prayer to God for the Israelites is that they may be saved" (Rom. 10:1). Again, to the Philippians he wrote, "This is my prayer: that your love may abound more and more" (Phil. 1:9). Paul focused his intercession in this way every time he thought of them.

Your intercession grows in prevailing power as you can begin to say with Paul that what you pray for is truly "my prayer"—the cry, the constant call of my heart to God. In the words of David, "One thing I ask of the LORD, this is what I seek" (Ps. 27:4). Desire makes your prayer very personal. It makes it your very heart-cry. Furthermore, it not only motivates your prayer, it helps you envision the answer and thus increases your faith. The half-hearted Christian is of little value to God or man. People consider him a hypocrite, and God is unable to use him greatly.

God has no use for insincerity or lukewarmness in prayer or other spiritual things (Rev. 3:15–16). Lack of heart and lack of heat are repulsive to Him. Christ wants fire-baptized followers (Matt. 3:11), a church that is aglow with the presence and power of the Spirit. Our God is a God of fire, and He wants us to share not only His presence and purity but His burning desire and zeal. The Spirit puts fire into our praying. According to Bounds, "This holy and fervid flame in the soul awakens the interest of heaven, attracts the attention of God, and places at the disposal of those who exercise it, the exhaustless riches of Divine grace."[4]

Desire refines and purifies your praying of many easily

mouthed, commonplace clichés. It strains out the generalities and the pious repetition of little-meant phrases. It distills away the learned prayer words that really express almost nothing of your inner soul and are but so many words before God. Desire boils away your almost hypocritical words that lull your own soul and the minds of the hearers to sleep and that rise little higher than your head. They are too meaningless to reach the throne of God.

HOW TO DEEPEN YOUR DESIRE

1. *Welcome God-given desires.* From one viewpoint, real desire is a gift of God. From another viewpoint, you must deepen your own desire with the help of God. Finney teaches that if you find a desire for the good of other people strongly impressed upon you, there is a strong possibility that the Holy Spirit is giving and deepening this desire so as to stir you up to pray. He adds, "In such a case, no degree of desire or importunity in prayer is improper. A Christian may come as it were and take hold of the hand of God."[5] Listen to Jacob pray, "I will not let you go unless you bless me" (Gen. 32:26). Did this attitude insult God? No! It made Jacob a prince with God, with a new name—Israel. Moses prayed with such a desire that God came face-to-face with him (Exod. 33:12–23; Num. 12:8).

2. *Do not quench or lose these holy desires.* They are a fire of the Holy Spirit. Do not put them out (1 Thess. 5:19). Do not let other things divert you or distract you. Let the Holy Spirit deepen your prayer more and more as you cherish these holy longings and hunger for them ever more deeply. Most things about you are so secular that they seek to intrude into your prayer time and to dissipate your holy desires and your awareness of God's presence.

God does not play games with you. The Spirit-born and Spirit-deepened desires indicate what God wants to do. He gives desires for what He longs to bring to pass. The Holy Spirit leads into the very heart-purpose of God and to the point of full prevailing.

3. *Surrender your own desires.* "The law is unchangeable: God offers himself, gives himself away, to the whole-hearted who give themselves wholly to Him."[6] Remember that in your humanity you may often wish for things and be more self-motivated than God-motivated. Your prayer may be colored more by self-interest than by desire for the glory of God. Prevailing prayer is normally possible only for things in the will of God. If you persist in willful self-desire and seek to demand your own will, you may live to regret your prayer. Israel cried before God till He gave them what they asked for, but they lived to regret it (Ps. 106:14–15). Such praying is not likely to happen if you surrender your own will and truly pray as Jesus taught us, "Your will be done" (Matt. 6:10).

You can be filled with "the knowledge of his will" (Col. 1:9). You can "test and approve what God's will is—his good, pleasing and perfect will" (Rom. 12:2). Those who live closest to God normally recognize God's will most surely and quickly. You can develop a listening ear to God.[7]

The Holy Spirit will faithfully teach you God's perspective, God's priorities, and God's process if you remain filled with the Spirit and selflessly committed to God's will. Then divine and human desires glow and merge together.

4. *Trust God for what you desire, and praise Him.* As you press on with deep, holy desires for God's will in the situation for which you pray, the Spirit will bring you to the place where faith will seize God's promise and the Spirit will give you the "garment of praise" (Isa. 61:3). Perhaps at this point your prayer has been granted, or perhaps the Spirit is leading you to the dynamic of faith and/or the dynamic of praise. (These levels will be further clarified in succeeding chapters.)

Desire is another word for hunger. Unless there is sighing, longing, hungering and thirsting, and perhaps even tears of desire, you have probably not yet reached prevailing prayer. Unless your heart cries out from its hidden depths, Satan's roadblocks seem at times unmoved, and Satan's captives remain bound.

It was unspeakable hunger that found voice in John Knox's

prayer, "Give me Scotland or I die!" John Smith in England cried out in almost identical words, "Give me souls or else I die." God gave him souls. That same prayer was prayed over and over daily by a young Korean evangelist, who is perhaps the reason I have given fifty years of service to OMS International. His face was aglow with the presence of God, and his heart constantly cried for souls. He won thousands to Christ in just a few years and began to be known as the D. L. Moody of Korea. Sadly, we later lost him to our OMS ministry, and God lost him to His service. Secular things robbed him of his hunger, and his lips turned to lips of clay. He ceased to prevail. He lost his power. He died in a foreign city practically unknown.

O fellow Christian! Cherish the hunger. Guard your hunger for God's answers to prayer. Pursuing hunger may cost you misunderstanding, even suffering. You may be considered an extremist or even a fanatic. Many churches experience very little prevailing prayer.

But must Jesus bear the cross alone? Again and again He has given of His soul passion to His children who walked in His footsteps. Where did John Wesley, George Whitefield, Charles Finney, William Booth, Praying Hyde, and Charles Cowman get that hunger for prayer answers, revival, and the salvation of souls? They learned the heartbeat of Jesus. Says Finney, "What must be the strength of the desire which God feels when His Spirit produces in Christians such amazing agony, such throes of soul, such travail—God has chosen the best word to express it; it is travail—travail of the soul."[8]

Learn to drink in the Spirit of Christ as He hungers to see the chains of evil habits, drugs, and Satan snapped and people set free. Learn to weep over your Jerusalem with Jesus if you would see Spirit-given revival come to your city or church. Mighty answers to prayer can be costly, but they are worth all the cost. Learn to hunger if you would prevail.

CHAPTER 10

The Dynamic of Fervency

THE DYNAMICS OF desire and fervency are closely related, yet each has something special to contribute to prevailing prayer. Each supports and strengthens the other; each is essential in its own right. Desire has more to do with hunger and urgency. Fervency has more to do with passion and zeal. Desire is born in need; fervency is born in love. We need eyes that see the need, and a heart burning with love.

Love opens your heart to God, who alone can meet all the needs. Love is the very nature of God. His heart is aflame with love for us and for His world. The flame that burns in the heart of God will set your heart aflame if you will draw close enough to Him. His love radiates to your heart. As you pray, His love places on your heart deep concerns for the needs He sees and wants you to see. His love, as it imbues you, makes your prayer a sweet perfume before Him (Ps. 141:2).

God's love is dynamic. It adds love, desire, and zeal to your praying. Said Charles Finney, "You must have so much of the love of God—a love like God's love for sinners—in your soul, that you are ready for any sacrifice or any labor. You need to feel as God feels . . . a love for souls." Unless you have this, he

73

asserts, your "prayers for this object will have little heart and no power with God."[1]

Andrew Murray insisted, "It is the very nature of love to give up and forget itself for the sake of others. It takes their needs and makes them its own, it finds real joy in living and dying for others as Christ did ... true love ... will become in us the spirit of intercession ... true love must pray."[2]

The dynamic of fervency has been called the law of earnestness. How many prayers fail for lack of it! Richard Watson, a theologian who lived about two hundred years ago, wrote, "Prayer without fervency is no prayer; it is speaking, not praying. Lifeless prayer is no more prayer than a picture of a man is a man." Acker adds, "Incense can neither smell nor ascend without fire; no more does prayer unless it arises from spiritual warmth and fervency.... Cold, lifeless, and idle prayers are like birds without wings ... mere lip prayers are lost prayers."[3]

Missionary pioneer Adoniram Judson knew how to prevail. He wrote, "A travailing spirit, the throes of a great burdened desire, belongs to prayer. A fervency strong enough to drive away sleep, which devotes and inflames spirit, ... belongs to wrestling, prevailing prayer. The Spirit, the power, the air, and the food of prayer is in such a spirit."[4]

Isaiah lamented, "No one calls on your name or strives to lay hold of you" (Isa. 64:7). Israel was in need, but no one was rousing himself to prevail in intercession for the nation. The Hebrew word means to rouse oneself, awake, incite. You must awaken and deepen qualities of concern, love, and zeal within yourself. You must wake yourself spiritually and prevail.

We need new mighty movements of the soul. We need to awaken and arouse our sleeping selves to take hold of God in mighty prayer. We need to marshal all our spiritual resources and sanctified energies to pray the prayer that prevails. Unless our prayer has fervent force, it has no power to overcome difficulties and win mighty victories.

Various Bible terms express fervor and passion in prayer. One term is *call*. It is used by Samuel, David, Elijah, and many of the prophets. The soul reaches out to God, calling out to Him with a force and intensity that expects to be heard.

Another term is *cry* or *cry out*. "O LORD, . . . day and night I cry out before you. . . . Turn your ear to my cry" (Ps. 88:1–2). Moses cried out at times in his impassioned prayer (Exod. 14:15). Samuel cried out on behalf of Israel (1 Sam. 7:8). So did Solomon (2 Chron. 6:19) and Ezekiel (Ezek. 9:8). Elijah cried to God to raise the widow's son, and God did (1 Kings 17:22).

Another Bible term is *pour out*. The psalmist describes how his soul pants for God as a deer pursued by hunters pants for water. He thirsts for God, longs to meet God, weeps day and night as he longs for God's answers, and pours out his soul (Ps. 42:1–4). In Psalm 62:8, David urges us, "Pour out your hearts to him, for God is our refuge." This verse is very expressive of the fervor and passion of the soul.

All of these godly people who pleaded in prayer, in the words of Finney, felt "the pressure of a great cause." There is no encouragement for feeble desires, listless efforts, and lazy attitudes in prayer. E. M. Bounds knew by experience prevailing prayer. He wrote, "Enflamed desires impassioned, unwearied insistence, delights heaven. . . . Heaven is too busy to listen to half-hearted prayers."[5]

The vision of the need for which you pray must become a burning passion to see God's answer. It must become a deep principle within you that dedicates itself to getting the answer. It must become a compelling drive. It must add fervency to your praying and put the iron of determination within your soul. You must not accept no for an answer!

Samuel Chadwick urges that prayer fervency alone makes ordinary intercession prevailing prayer.

There is passion in praying that prevails. Elijah was a man of passions. . . . All there was of him went into everything he did. . . . Listen to his praying in the death chamber. Watch him on Carmel. Hear him plead the honor of God and unto the Lord for the affliction of the people.

It is always the same: Abraham pleading for Sodom, Jacob wrestling in the stillness of the night, Moses standing in the breach, Hannah intoxicated with sorrow, David heartbroken with remorse and grief—Jesus in a sweat of blood. Add to that the list from the records of the church, personal observation and experience, and always there is the cost of passion until blood. It prevails. It turns ordinary mortals into men of power. It brings power. It brings fire. It brings rain. It brings life. It brings God. There is no power like that of prevailing prayer.[6]

The most important measure of prayer is not its length but its depth; not its beautiful words but its intensity. It is not necessarily a matter of how many hours you pray, but how intensely you pray when you do pray. There is a dynamic of perseverance—prayer must often be continued at some length, but whether short or long, let your prayer be fervent.

It is a law of prayer that those who seek with all their heart find. " 'Then you will call upon me and come and pray to me, and I will listen to you. You will seek me and find me when you seek me with all your heart. I will be found by you,' declares the LORD" (Jer. 29:12–14). Moses used almost identical words, specifying, "With all your heart and with all your soul" (Deut. 4:29).

Says Chadwick again, "Intensity is a law of prayer ... wrestling prayer prevails. The fervent, effectual prayer of the righteous is of great force. God hates strange fire. We must never try to work up an emotion of intensity. . . . If the spirit groans in intercession, do not be afraid of the agony of prayer. There are blessings of the kingdom that are only yielded to the violence of the vehement soul."[7]

Hebrews assures us that "during the days of Jesus' life on earth, he offered up prayers and petitions with loud cries and tears" (5:7). It is Christlike to be so burdened in prayer that we pray with a passion. Paul asked the saints at Rome to "join me in my struggle by praying to God for me" (Rom. 15:30). "Join me in my struggle" is two words in Greek—meaning literally, "agonize with me." That is prayer with a passion!

R. A. Torrey writes, "The prayer that prevails with God is the prayer into which we put our whole soul, stretching out toward God in intense and agonizing desire. . . . If we put so little heart into our prayers, we cannot expect God to put much heart into answering them. . . . When we learn to come to God with an intensity of desire that wrings the soul, then shall we know a power in prayer that most of us do not know now."[8]

Alexander Whyte, the great preacher and author from Scotland, pleads, "Let every man put his passion into his prayers."[9] James's description of Elijah, "he prayed earnestly" (James 5:17), is in the Greek "with prayer he prayed," an idiom that means he prayed with intensity or passion.

SUMMARY

Real prayer passion has these characteristics:

1. It grows out of the love of your soul.

2. It grows out of holy desire.

3. It may be a direct gift of God at a moment He wants to use you in prayer.

4. It may result from your new vision of a need.

5. It may result from gradually deepening conviction of the urgency of a need and God's will to meet that need. Finney advised, "If you find yourself drawn out in mighty prayer for certain individuals, exercised with great compassion, agonized with strong crying and tears, for a certain family or neighborhood or people, let such an influence be yielded to."[10]

6. It may become characteristic of your prayer life as you give yourself to intercession.

7. It quickens and strengthens your faith.

What prayer passion is not:

1. It is not synonymous with loud, vociferous praying. It may be quiet or even silent prayer. Many a person has prevailed so silently in the night hour that others sleeping nearby knew nothing about it.

2. It is not synonymous with physical exertion. Spiritual wrestling is not dependent on physical activity. Prayer passion

is not produced by lifting the hand, waving the arm, standing, kneeling, lying prostrate on the floor, walking back and forth, or any other form of prayer posture or action. The Holy Spirit may lead you to such change of posture, especially when you are praying alone in your secret place.

Sometimes use of such a posture for the time being harmonizes with or expresses the mood of your soul—humility before God, hungry pleas to God, waiting in His presence, or spiritual determination and urgency. Many mighty prayer warriors, like Brainerd and Finney, have had their bodies soaked with perspiration from the intense soul anguish in their prevailing prayer, even as Christ sweat the blood-sweat in Gethsemane. But do not try to work up spiritual intensity by your human exertion.

3. It is not synonymous with answered prayer. Many prayers are granted instantly or without your prolonged or intense praying. Many prayer desires are granted as you delight in the Lord (Ps. 37:4).

4. It is not a form of "works." It does not earn salvation or God's blessing. Fervency is, rather, an outworking of the Spirit's ministry within you.

HOW TO DEVELOP PRAYER PASSION

1. Ask the Holy Spirit to give you His love, passion, and zeal.

2. Welcome and cherish any drawing of the Spirit to prayer. Bounds assures us, "It is not in our power, perhaps, to create fervency of spirit at will, but we can pray God to implant it. It is ours, then, to nourish and cherish it, to guard it against extinction, to prevent its abatement or decline."[11]

3. Read and reread Scripture accounts or accounts in deeply spiritual books of how God has called people to prayer and answered their prayer.

4. Keep deepening your own prayer life by faithfulness in your prayer habits and prayer commitments.

5. Take several major prayer concerns or burdens on your heart and make them the special focus of your prayer: for

example, continuing prayer for revival, your church, your nation, youth ministry, prison ministry, ministry in Communist lands, ministry in Muslim lands. The burdens may include such special needs as pornography, drugs, child abuse, or AIDS. They may include a particular nation—India, China, Indonesia, Cuba, or another one God places on your heart. They may include radio ministry, TV ministry, or international or national ministries such as those of Billy Graham, Luis Palau, or Focus on the Family. You cannot pray at length for everything, but you can ask God to guide you to several special prayer concerns.

6. Keep a listening ear for any special prayer assignments that God may give you as a temporary urgent prayer burden. There may be special need on a particular day or hour for your prayer. As far as possible, go to prayer for that need immediately. Use every free moment possible until God lifts from your heart the prayer concern to pray for this need. Your prayer passion will be greatly increased as you obey this call from the Spirit.

Let us summarize in the words of Bounds: "Prayers must be red hot. It is the fervent prayer that is effective. . . . It takes fire to make prayers go. Warmth of soul creates an atmosphere favorable to prayer. . . . By flame prayer ascends to heaven. Yet fire is not fuss, not heat, noise. . . . To be absorbed in God's will, to be so greatly in earnest about doing it that our whole being takes fire, is the qualifying condition of the man who would engage in effectual prayer."[12]

CHAPTER 11

The Dynamic of Importunity

BESIDES FERVOR AND desire, intensity in prayer includes importunity. In some ways, importunity combines fervency, desire, and perseverance—but not always. Importunate prayer may be fervent, but it is something more than fervency. It may be clothed with the deepest desire, but it is something above and beyond desire. It usually includes perseverance, but it adds an important new dimension.

What is importunity? The Greek word used in Luke 11:8 is *anaideia*. It means utter shamelessness. It includes the concept of great boldness, of urgency, of pressing your request, claim, or demand to the very limits, and it includes determination to persist in that urgent boldness until it receives the answer.

Andrew Murray, a great believer in importunate prayer, describes the growth of importunity in these words: "It begins with the refusal to at once accept a denial. It grows to the determination to persevere, to spare no time or trouble, till an answer comes. It rises to the intensity in which the whole being is given to God in supplication, and the boldness comes to lay hold of God's strength."[1]

Importunity in prayer is prayer for God's will to be done. It must be wholly unselfish. It is usually shamelessness in pressing the urgency of the need of someone else. Wrestling in prayer may include some elements of self-benefit. When Jacob wrestled for God's protection for his family, he included himself and was himself also benefited.

But holy importunity is righteous and right as it pleads for others. Witness the Syrophoenician woman pleading for her demon-possessed daughter, the householder pleading for food for a friend at midnight, Moses pleading for forgiveness for Israel, Daniel pleading for the restoration of Israel and Jerusalem. Witness also Luther prevailing for the healing of his fellow reformer Melanchthon, and John Knox pleading for the soul of Scotland.

Importunate praying does not yield to discouragement, weariness, fear, or impatience. It is in dead earnest. Importunate prayer does not trifle with God in passive indifference to whether prayer is answered or not. Richard Sibbes wrote: "It is atheism to pray and not to wait in hope. A sincere Christian will pray, wait, strengthen his heart with the promises, and never leave praying and looking up till God gives him a gracious answer."[2]

The unembarrassed, shameless perseverance in prayer until God gives His full answer is described by George Mueller: "It is not enough to begin to pray, nor to pray aright; nor is it enough to continue for a time to pray; but we must patiently, believingly, continue in prayer until we obtain an answer."[3] Bengel, the Lutheran theologian in the 1700s who greatly influenced John Wesley, suggested we do not have God's permission to quit praying until He gives us some answer. Of course, these writers refer to prayer for significant needs for which God has burdened us.

P. T. Forsyth warns that we dare not reduce prayer to talking to God or even dialogue with God, "mere walking with God in friendly talk." We will not only lose the aspect of spiritual conflict, of wrestling and prevailing, but we may lose prayer's ultimate reality. We make it conversation, rather than the soul's great action.

As Forsyth concludes his book *The Soul of Prayer,* he urges us to wrestle in prayer in these words: "Cling to Him with your strength, not your weakness only, with your active and not only your passive faith, and He will give you strength. Cast yourself into His arms not to be caressed but to wrestle with Him. He loves that holy war. He may be too many for you, and lift you from your feet. But it will be to lift you from earth, and set you in the heavenly places which are theirs who fight the good fight and lay hold of God as their eternal life."[4]

Importunity is as essential in the spiritual realm as it is at times in secular life. It is probably even more effective with God than with man. When Abraham began his bold and respectful yet importunate intercession for Sodom, God did not resent it, even though Sodom was most sinful (Gen. 18:16–33). Every time Abraham pressed another point, God conceded. The merciful heart of Abraham blended with the merciful heart of God. Was the limit of God's mercy revealed when Abraham stopped interceding? Could Abraham have pressed further?

God longs to extend His mercy. How often He is limited by our inadequate importunity. Abraham became the friend of God in an even more intimate sense through his importunity. Press importunate intercession for others to the greatest spiritual bounds if you would be the friend of God.

We have yet such an incomplete vision of what God desires from our praying. God demonstrates His eagerness to be prevailed upon by bold, selfless intercession. Never does He rebuke one of His children for being inappropriately importunate at His throne of grace. God has given us immense spiritual responsibility and has placed tremendous initiative in our hands.

God put a limit on Moses' asking for himself (Deut. 3:26), but He put no limit on Moses' importunity in asking for sinning Israel. God cried out, "Leave me alone," to Moses, but this was a test of Moses' character (Exod. 32:10). Moses' desire and zeal for God's people was so strong that he refused to let God alone. He reasoned and argued and pleaded with God. He offered to expose himself vicariously to God's wrath and take Israel's place of punishment. Such substitution was, of course, impossible, but it demonstrated that Moses had the same passion as did our Lord when He took our place at Calvary. So Moses' importunity was not rude in the sight of God. It was holy, noble, and glorious before God. It confirmed him as a friend of God (33:11).

There are limits on importunity—the limits of the will of God. The more closely we walk with God, the more intimately we understand His unspeakable longing for the salvation of humankind and for all spiritual blessing for His people. He longs to bless with health and to supply essential needs and as much prosperity as is not spiritually harmful.

It is always God's basic will to bless. We do not persuade God to be merciful—He is already merciful. We do not need to persuade Him to manifest love—His very nature guarantees that He will always love to the limits of what is best. We only ask God to manifest what He so infinitely already is.

Yet God has ordained to limit much of His working to the intercession of His people. Our importunity is God's opportunity. He longs for us to give Him the opportunity to manifest His nature. God thus honored Moses' importunity and drew so near that Moses' face carried the radiance of God back to needy Israel.

Was the importunity of the heartbroken mother from Sidon an offense to Jesus? He did test her importunity by a seeming rebuff (Matt. 15:21–28), but when she passed the test by importuning even more boldly, Jesus responded, "You have great faith! Your request is granted."

Some commentators believe the main reason Jesus took His disciples to this area of Tyre and Sidon was to meet the need of this woman and to use this experience to train His disciples in the role of importunate prayer. Jesus tested her importunity but then commended her and made her an example for Christians of all time.

In Bounds's words, "He prays not at all, who does not press his plea. Cold prayers have no claim on heaven, and no hearing in the courts above. Fire is the life of prayer, and heaven is reached by flaming importunity rising in an ascending scale."[5]

God delights in your holy boldness that will not take no for an answer. God counts it "great faith," and He then counts you His friend, for you understand His heart.

Paul urges that "in him and through faith in him we may approach God with freedom and confidence" (Eph. 3:12). The Greek literally is, "We have boldness and access with confidence." *Parrēsia* is unreservedness of utterance, speaking plainly without fear, boldly but with cheerful courage.

"We have confidence [*parrēsia*—bold, confident courage] to enter the Most Holy Place by the blood of Jesus" (Heb. 10:19). "Let us then approach the throne of grace with confidence [*parrēsia*—bold, confident courage]" (4:16). Esther approached the throne of the emperor Xerxes with such boldness and was God's means to save her people.

How often our fear, timidity, and lack of faith have caused us to lose blessings and prayer answers God would have been delighted to grant. A. B. Simpson writes, "The secret of success in human affairs has often been audacity. There is . . . a holy audacity in Christian life and faith which is not inconsistent with the profoundest humility."[6] This was the audacity of Moses, Joshua, Elijah, Daniel, Luther, and a host of prayer warriors over the centuries.

The importunate prayer warrior presses beyond the bounds of friendship, almost beyond the bounds of sonship. There is a determination, a bold insistence that refuses to accept a negative answer or longer delay. Such importunity would not be appropriate for any situation other than that involving the glory of God. When God's will, name, and glory are at stake, nothing should stop us. Jesus taught that such praying gets answers that are obtainable in no other way. Holy importunity conquers all circumstances, defeats all darkness, and penetrates through demon hosts to the throne of God.

Laxity in prayer, timidity in intercession, and weakness in importunity are fatal to mighty prevailing prayer. "Awaiting the onset of our importunity and insistence, is the Father's heart, the Father's hand, the Father's infinite power, the Father's infinite willingness to hear and give to His children."[7]

Isaiah deplored the fact that "no one calls on your name or strives to lay hold of you" (Isa. 64:7). This sentence has been translated "no one arouses himself." God would have you take prevailing prayer seriously. He wants you to rouse yourself, to stir yourself up. God therefore says through Isaiah, "I have posted watchmen on your walls, O Jerusalem; they will never be silent day or night. You who call on the LORD, give yourselves no rest, and give him no rest till he establishes Jerusalem and makes her the praise of the earth" (Isa. 62:6–7).

"Importunate prayer is a mighty movement of the soul toward God. It is a stirring of the deepest forces of the soul toward the throne of heavenly grace. It is the ability to hold on, press on, and wait. . . . It is not an incident . . . but a passion of soul. . . . The wrestling quality in importunate prayer does not spring from physical vehemence or fleshly energy. It is not an impulsive energy, nor a mere earnestness of soul; it is an inwrought force, a faculty implanted and aroused by the Holy Spirit. Virtually, it is the intercession of the Spirit of God within us."[8]

You must rouse yourself, asking the Holy Spirit to help you, but at the same time, He will join in your importunity and intensify it by His mighty working within you. But you must take the initiative, and then the Holy Spirit will multiply your prayer by His inner groaning, zeal, and power. Listen to the psalmist take this audacious initiative with God: "Awake, O Lord! Why do you sleep? Rouse yourself! Do not reject us forever. Why do you hide your face and forget our misery and oppression? We are brought down to the dust; our bodies cling to the ground. Rise up and help us; redeem us because of your unfailing love" (Ps. 44:23–26).

In about A.D. 500, Bishop Avitus wrote, "You must clamor in the accents of supplication; and if while the danger increases He still remains deaf, you must knock with unsparing hands."[9]

CHAPTER 12

Importunity Prevails

THE ROLE OF IMPORTUNITY

GOD USES IMPORTUNITY to bring us into great spiritual blessing. Andrew Murray calls importunate prayer one of God's choicest means of grace.

1. *Importunity teaches the most Christlike aspects of character.* If for no other reason, God would reserve His special answers for the importunate intercessors because the very nature of importunity develops in you the highest Christian graces. W. E. Biederwolf called importunity "one of the instructors in God's training school."[1]

Moses' eighty days of communion and intercession, the last forty of which included much importunate intercession, left a lifelong seal of God upon his life. Afterward he was a more patient, forgiving, and humble man of God than he had ever been. The experience at Mount Sinai not only was vital for Israel, it was the vital preparation for the next thirty-eight years of Moses' leadership. Importunate praying makes us ever more godlike in character. Moses left that time of prevailing with God's glory radiating from his face and God's obvious seal upon his life—not just in outward miracles (which he had

86

experienced before), but in godliness of personality. More than ever, he became a partner of the very Spirit of God.

Importunity intensifies your desires for God's will and God's kingdom. It raises your will to its more godlike assertions for righteousness, holiness, and the realization of the will of God. It strengthens your faith till it believes not only because of what God can do but also because of who God is. Bounds explains, "Importunity . . . drives the prayer to the believing point. A persistent spirit brings a man to the place where faith takes hold, claims, and appropriates the blessing."[2]

God makes you strong spiritually by leading you to exercise your spiritual muscle. His love causes Him to delay your answers until you rise to the heights of His grace. R. A. Torrey wrote, "There is no more blessed training in prayer than that which comes through being compelled to ask again and again and again, even through a long period of years before one obtains that which he needs from God."[3]

2. *Importunity teaches the highest form of Christlike service.* There is no more Christlike ministry than intercessory prayer, and importunity is the highest form of intercession. Says Andrew Murray, "The highest exercise and the glory of prayer is that persevering importunity can prevail and obtain what God at first could not and would not give." Payne adds, "Intensified prayer . . . [is] the highest effort of which the human spirit is capable, and becomes an irresistible force."[4] God so desires that you become Christlike in spirit and Christ's partner in intercession that He reserves His choicest answers for you when you learn to importune in prayer.

3. *Importunity brings answers available in no other way.* It has often been said that nothing is beyond the scope of prayer unless it is beyond the will of God. Bold importunity succeeds where all other pleas and prayers fail. Importunity conquers impossible circumstances, drives back overwhelming forces of darkness, and overcomes a seemingly endless succession of hindrances. Importunity binds God to His promises, brings heaven's angels to your assistance, and scatters the demons from

hell. Importunity brings God's will into realization when all else fails.

IMPORTUNITY IS TOIL AND TRAVAIL

Importunity is no recreation. While it is exhilarating to prevail and see God's mighty answers, yet the securing of the answers is real work. Importunate prayer can be physically and emotionally exhausting, especially so when the soul travail extends over a long period of time. Prayer travail is primarily spiritual, but our spiritual nature is so interrelated with our mental and emotional nature that spiritual wrestling and spiritual warfare affect our whole being.

Let the biographies and journals of prayer warriors like John Knox, Martin Luther, Adoniram Judson, Praying Hyde, and John Smith testify. There is a physical toll from mighty prevailing prayer. Importunity costs. Jowett wrote, "All vital praying makes a drain on a man's vitality. True intercession is a sacrifice, a bleeding sacrifice."[5] But prevailing prayer is worth all it costs.

It takes determined exertion to prevail for Satan's defeat. Calvin said, "You will never aspire to pray until you urge and force yourselves." Zwemer called prayer "the gymnasium of the soul." One of the early church leaders wrote, "Believe me, I think there is nothing which requires more effort than to pray to God. . . . Prayer demands combat to the last breath." Martin Luther added, "Prayer is indeed a continuous violent action of the spirit as it is lifted up to God. This action is comparable to that of a ship going against the stream."[6]

All spiritual ministry done with burden, compassion, and holy zeal is both physically and spiritually depleting. During Jesus' importunate wrestling in the garden, His sweat became as blood (Luke 22:44).

If the prayer of a disciple is to "fill up" the intercession of the Master, the disciple's prayer must be stricken with much crying and tears. The ministers of Calvary must supplicate in bloody sweat, and their intercession must often touch the point of agony. . . . True intercession is a sacrifice, a bleeding sacrifice . . . a "filling up' " of the sufferings of Christ. . . . I am so often ashamed of my prayers. They so frequently cost me nothing; they shed no blood. I am amazed at the grace and condescension of my Lord that He confers any fruitfulness upon my superficial pains.[7]

REPETITION IN IMPORTUNITY

Some people have the mistaken impression that you should never repeat yourself to the Lord, that having told Him once, you can forget it. Perhaps God has at times given people such deep assurance that a particular prayer has been granted that they feel they would imply doubt if they reminded the Lord of it again.

There is nothing irreverent or unbelieving in telling the Lord the same thing repeatedly. A lover can tell the beloved "I love you" a hundred times, and it is not disrespectful; it is sweetly beautiful. Jesus is our most Beloved One. A young boy can repeat his need to his mother or father, unless he has been told to be quiet. God is our Father. He has not told us to be quiet, but to speak.

Jesus repeated Himself in the garden. The more intense your prevailing and the more urgent your importunity, the more likely it is that you will repeat some request or phrase many times. R. A. Torrey said that those who get beyond praying twice for the same thing have gone further in prayer than Jesus was able to go![8]

John Calvin wrote, "We must repeat the same supplication not twice or three times only but as often as we have need, a hundred and a thousand times. . . . We must never be weary in waiting for God's help." Oswald Chambers taught that "repetition in intercessory importunity is not bargaining with God, but the joyous insistence of prayer."[9]

Bounds adds, "We are to press the matter, not with vain repetitions, but with urgent repetitions. We repeat, not to count the times, but to gain the prayer. We cannot quit praying because heart and soul are in it. . . . We press our pleas because we must have them or die." Furthermore, he wrote, "Christ puts importunity as a distinguishing characteristic of true praying. We must not only pray, but we must pray with great urgency, with intentness and with repetition. We must not only pray, but we must pray again and again. . . . Jesus made it very plain that the secret of prayer and its success lie in its urgency."[10]

CHAPTER 13

The Dynamic of Faith

PRAYER IS NOT limited to the humanly possible. Prayer is a work of faith. The purpose of prevailing prayer is to bring to pass things that are divinely possible and that are in God's will. Our prayer is an essential condition to most of God's sovereign workings in redemption. Conditioning His works of power upon our prevailing in prayer does not limit God's sovereignty. He has chosen to make us His colaborers through our prayer and obedience.

In prevailing prayer you are asking God to do things you can accomplish in no other way. To prevail you need to desire and hunger deeply, to pray with fervor and passion. In addition, however, you need the dynamic of faith. "This is the victory," John assures us, to overcome the world—our faith (1 John 5:4). And equally, this is the victory in prevailing prayer—our triumphant faith.

Millions of prayers are prayed with almost no faith. James tells us that God is a generous giver, but we "must believe and not doubt" when we pray (James 1:6). He calls the doubter a double-minded person and states emphatically, "That man should not think he will receive anything from the Lord" (v. 7).

Henry Martyn was a great missionary of the cross and poured out his life in devotion to God. He lived sacrificially and died an early death because of his tremendous commitment, whatever the cost. He was a man of prayer but perhaps not a man of faith. He said he "would as soon expect to see a man rise from the dead as to see a Brahmin converted to Christ."[1] He translated the New Testament into Hindustani, Arabic, and Persian, and his journals are classics in devotional literature, but he did not see one Brahmin converted. Lack of a dynamic faith limits what God can do through us.

How often we are double-minded in our praying. We believe that God can answer our prayer. Obviously, we have some hope that He will answer it, or we would not pray. But oh, how often we do not really expect God to answer. If Jesus asked us, as He did the two blind men who came to Him for healing, "Do you believe that I am able to do this?" (Matt. 9:28), we would instantly reply, "Yes, Lord." We know He is able to do all things. If we are totally honest, however, we would admit we do not feel sure that God will answer the need for which we pray.

Perhaps there is no thing about which Jesus expressed so frequent disappointment as the lack of faith in His disciples. Five times He exclaimed, "O you of little faith." In three places we read the words, "unbelieving generation." Three times Jesus conditions the mighty work God will do by saying, "If you have faith."

Hear His words: "Where is your faith?" (Luke 8:25); "Do you still have no faith?" (Mark 4:40); "Because you have so little faith" (Matt. 17:20); "Stop doubting and believe" (John 20:27); "He was amazed at their lack of faith" (Mark 6:6); "He did not do many miracles there because of their lack of faith" (Matt. 13:58); "He rebuked them for their lack of faith" (Mark 16:14).

It is absolutely clear that our lack of faith limits God's freedom of working mightily. It stopped Jesus from using His miracle-working power (Mark 6:5). From the standpoint of omnipotence, God is almighty—His power is utterly unlimited. From the standpoint of His sovereignty, God can do what He will. But from the standpoint of His grace, He has chosen normally to limit His miracle answers to our believing. "According to your faith" (Matt. 9:29), said Jesus.

This limitation is just one of the many mysteries of God's will and grace. God desires to do many things for us, but His word is, "You do not have, because you do not ask" (James 4:2). Revival seems to come only when someone has prepared the way in prayer. God is pleased to work through His children. Again and again He premises much of His divine working in salvation and in kingdom advance on our obedience, faith, and prayer. What an awesome responsibility this places upon us!

It is amazing that Jesus said, "Your faith has made you well" (Luke 17:19); "your faith has saved you" (7:50); "your faith has healed you" (Mark 5:34; 10:52). Was it not Jesus' power? Jesus' act? Yes, but it would have been incomplete without their faith. The situation today is just the same: there is no substitute for faith. Hours and hours of praying do not eliminate the need for faith. They may help you to arrive at the position of faith, but without the dynamic of faith, prayer does not prevail.

Your need appeals to God's heart of love. Your prayer moves Him deeply. But without faith your prayer is incomplete. Talking to God without faith is not true intercession. Faith submits your need to the will of God and lays hold of the power of God. Faith honors God, and God delights to respond to faith.

In the process of prevailing intercession, faith proceeds step by step:

1. *Faith accepts God's revelation that you are created in the image of God, created to represent Him on earth and to rule on His behalf* (Gen. 1:26–28).

2. *Faith accepts Christ's redemption, making you a child of God with the spiritual right of access to God at any time for any need* (Eph. 2:18).

3. *Faith accepts your identity with Jesus, not only in His death,*

but also in His resurrection and exaltation, so that you now sit in the heavenlies with Christ at the right hand of the Father (Eph. 2:6). Faith accepts your role as a king and priest to God (Rev. 1:6; 1 Peter 2:5, 9; Exod. 19:6; Isa. 61:6; Rev. 5:10; 20:6).

4. *Faith recognizes the Spirit's aid as He indwells you and deepens your desires and guides your intercession* (Rom. 8:26–27). In the words of Andrew Murray, "Faith sees the intercession of the saints to be part of the life of the Holy Trinity—the believer as God's child asking of the Father, in the Son, through the Spirit."[2]

5. *Faith is overwhelmed by the amazing love of God to provide such a kingdom plan of your sharing in Christ's present rule through prayer.* You bow in humble submission to the will of God, boldly daring to exercise the role to which God has called and exalted you. Faith gives determination to be all that God wants you to be through Christ.

FAITH CONQUERS DOUBT

Doubt blinds your soul to the role and power of prayer, making you forget God's redemptive purpose and His good will. Doubt weakens your soul's confidence in God's availability, faithfulness, and active role in your life. It darkens your horizon, distorts your spiritual vision, and numbs your spiritual vitality. It robs your prayer of its power and effectiveness. In short, it dishonors God.

Faith focuses your eyes on God and His promises, faithfulness, and availability. Faith sees God present, deeply concerned, and active. Faith looks at the problems and needs from God's perspective.

Doubt, anxiety, fear, and worry focus primarily on circumstances, but faith focuses primarily on God. Anxiety looks at things and makes you concerned about, even obsessed, with things that seem impossible. It tries to get you to worry, to brood about your problems and needs. It gets your eyes off God. Murray says, "The beginning of anxiety is the end of faith."[3]

Faith is not blind to the needs. Faith faces reality but sees reality as measured by God, not as measured by man. Abraham exemplifies this God-focused faith. "Against all hope, Abraham in hope believed. . . . Without weakening in his faith, he faced the fact that his body was as good as dead—since he was about a hundred years old—and that Sarah's womb was also dead. Yet he did not waver through unbelief regarding the promise of God, but was strengthened in his faith and gave glory to God, being fully persuaded that God had power to do what he had promised" (Rom. 4:18–21).

Faith sees your empty hands but sees also the greater reality of the promise of God. On the basis of God's love and mercy, faith claims the promise of God. Faith is God-conscious, God-focused, and God-believing. Your love, prayer, and faith must always have an object. You do not have faith in faith; you say with Paul, "I have faith in God" (Acts 27:25).

Faith is a triumphing and prevailing grace. It overcomes the world and whatever opposes you, for it focuses your spiritual eyes on greater things than the world. Faith is highly specific. It claims definite answers from God. Prevailing faith does not just believe in God. It believes for God's answer for the need before you. God's answer will be as specific as your faith. Prevailing faith is as specific as prevailing prayer.

FAITH AND SIGNS

The purest, most simple faith does not demand signs. Abraham came to the place of faith where he believed God for a son, without demanding a sign. His faith was perfected to the point where he believed God would raise Isaac from the dead, even though no one had ever been raised from the dead up to that time (Heb. 11:19).

Yet God often stoops to our humanness and gives us a sign to strengthen our faith. God did not reprove Gideon but repeatedly granted him a sign (Judg. 6:16–23, 36–40). David prayed for a sign (Ps. 86:17). God told Ahaz to ask for a sign

(Isa. 7:10–14). He gave Hezekiah a sign that he would be healed (38:7–8).

Be open to God's confirming your prayer or obedience by signs if He so chooses. In a way, every miracle is a sign proclaiming God's presence, goodness, and power. A trembling faith can ask for a sign. Willful disdain and unbelief have no right to ask for a sign (Matt. 12:39; 16:4).

Our normal walk with God is to be a life of faith, not sight (2 Cor. 5:7). We fix our spiritual eyes on the unseen reality of God rather than on our visible surroundings (2 Cor. 4:18). We do not dictate to God or manipulate Him. Never demand signs from God, but welcome all He gives to strengthen your faith.

FAITH AND ASSURANCE

God does not despise your humanness. When you need some visible strengthening to assist your faith, God is often willing to help in this way. The witness of the Spirit to your new birth is an unseen but deep assurance that God grants to you (Rom. 8:16). Perhaps you can think of it as an assuring sign.

HOW TO KNOW GOD HEARS YOUR PRAYER

According to 1 John 5:15, "If we know that he hears us," then we have the confidence that "we have what we asked of him." But how can you have this knowledge, which is such a key condition of seeing prayer answered?

1. *You have the assurance that God is a prayer-hearing God.* David prayed with the assurance, "The LORD will hear when I call to him" (Ps. 4:3). Micah testified, "As for me, I watch in hope for the LORD, I wait for God my Savior; my God will hear me" (Mic. 7:7). This assurance upheld Moses, the prophets, and the heroes of faith of all ages. God always hears us! Such faith anchors your soul, fires prayer passion, and puts unwavering determination into your will.

2. *You may know that you are asking in accord with God's will.* Some prayers are always according to His will—the salvation of the sinner (2 Peter 3:9), the blessing and revival of the

church, the glorifying of God's name. I call these "always prayers." But there are some prayers we are not sure of—the healing of a particular sick person at a particular time, God's prospering a particular activity at a particular time (James 4:15).

3. *At times you know because of an inner assurance.* This sense is based upon God's clear guidance, answered prayer, providence in a related aspect of the situation, or a deep inner peace in regard to that for which you pray.

God grants a special inner assurance in your heart when you have been prevailing in prayer. Some people call this experience "praying through." Sometimes this assurance comes very quickly. You just know within your heart that God has heard and answered. At other times this inner assurance comes after long prayer or united prayer by several of God's children. Perhaps after hours or days of prayer, the Holy Spirit suddenly reveals that God has granted the request. It is as if God said in clear tones, "Your prayer is heard, and your request is granted." Such assurance is the experience of "most men to whom prayer is the basis of their life. . . . It occurs again and again." Goforth of China testified to the same clear assurances.[4]

Luther said of this assurance that though he did not understand it, "Sounding from above and ringing in my ears I hear what is beyond the thought of man."[5]

CHAPTER 14

How to Increase Faith

THE INCREASE OF FAITH

SPIRITUAL VISION IS based on natural eyesight but goes above and beyond material things. Spiritual vision sees what your eye cannot see. In a similar way, spiritual faith is based on natural faith but goes above and beyond it.

Natural faith is present in every human being, in greater degree in some than in others. Life would be impossible without faith. Buying and selling, the postal service, government in all its aspects, normal human relations with others, science, medical science, and even family life are dependent on faith. Faith in God, in God's Word, and in God's hearing and answering prayer is dependent on spiritual faith.

All Christians have some spiritual faith, or they would not be saved. We are saved by faith, live by faith, obey with faith, base our lives on God's Word in faith, and pray in faith. In some, faith is expressed more overtly, simply, or dramatically than in others. Faith can be increased as we grow in God's grace.

When the disciples asked Jesus, "Increase our faith" (Luke 17:5), it was in response to Jesus' instruction that if your brother sins against you he should be rebuked, and if he repents he should be forgiven. Jesus added that even if the offender were so unstable as to repeat his sin against you seven times in the short space of one day and each time profess to repent, you should still forgive. So when the disciples asked for increased faith, it was in relation to the salvation of a seemingly hopeless case.

But Jesus instantly expanded the application from faith for salvation to faith to cast a mulberry tree into the sea by using the command of faith. How can our faith be developed to that great degree?

SEVEN STEPS TO GREATER FAITH

1. *Recognize your own helplessness and need.* Hallesby testifies, "Helplessness united with faith produces prayer." Helplessness is the first step in the ladder of faith. Faith requires you to take the initiative, and strange as it may seem, a sense of helplessness, impotence, and total dependence upon God enables you to take faith's initiative. "The sense of our impotence is the soul of intercession."[1]

2. *Feed your soul on the Word of God.* "Faith comes from hearing the message, and the message is heard through the word of Christ" (Rom. 10:17). "Let the word of Christ dwell in you richly" (Col. 3:16). The more you read or hear God's Word—the whole Word—the more your faith grows. There are special accounts of God's mighty works in Scripture and wonderful promises that are special faith vitamins. But all of God's Word is faith building. Read it both extensively and intensively. Read, read, read. Fill your soul with the Word!

3. *Spend adequate time in prayer.* All forms of prayer help strengthen faith. Intercession for others, prayer warfare, and time communing with God and praising God in prayer are great helps in increasing faith.

4. *Read accounts of how God has answered prayer.* The biographies of people who were great examples of faith are a strong stimulus to faith. The accounts of great revivals, conversion stories, and accounts of answered prayer for healing,

protection, guidance, and the supply of financial and special needs all greatly strengthen faith.

5. *Obey God in everything.* You cannot trust God fully if there is light God has given you that you have not yet obeyed. Any controversy between your soul and God, any hidden sin, will block faith and effective prayer. God invited Israel to test and prove Him by obeying in tithing and then to see how He would answer and meet their material needs (Mal. 3:10–12). Be sure you are instantly obedient to all the light God gives you.

6. *Begin to trust God for specific answers.* The more you exercise your faith, the more it will grow. Some have compared faith to a muscle. The more you exercise it, the stronger it becomes. Begin trusting God for smaller specific needs. When an emergency comes, go to God first. Keep a diary of the answers to prayer you receive, and review it from time to time.

7. *Begin praising God.* God deserves our praise and always draws near as we praise Him. Build praise into your life whenever you have free moments. Love Him and praise Him. Sing silently in your heart praise choruses or praise verses of great hymns. Repeat praise verses from the Bible.

Make praise militant in the face of the Devil. I have seen militant praise cast out a demon that had resisted group prayer and fasting. Praise won a mighty faith victory for Jehoshaphat. He exhorted, "Have faith in the LORD your God," and then started militant praise. "As they began to sing and praise, the LORD set ambushes," and the combined forces of Ammon, Moab, and Mount Seir were totally defeated without Israel's having to fight (2 Chron. 20:20–23).

THE PRAYER OF FAITH

The prayer of faith is defined by Fraser as "a definite request ... made in definite faith for a definite answer"[2] Remember, God had promised Canaan to Israel. God led them by miracle to the borders of Canaan, and God parted the Jordan to help them enter the land. By miracle, God gave them Jericho, but from then on they had to fight for every additional section of

Canaan they occupied. Sometimes praying the prayer of faith is like securing God's general promise. Then you have to dislodge Satan from his strongholds one by one. The life of faith may often be a life of battles, but it is also a life of victories.

Fraser wrote, "We often have to strive and wrestle in prayer ... before we attain this great rest, restful faith. ... However, once we attain to a real faith, all the forces of hell are impotent to annul it. What then? They retire and muster their forces on this plot of ground which God has pledged himself to give us, and contest every inch of it. The real battle begins when the prayer of faith has been offered. But praise the Lord! we are on the winning side."[3]

The prayer of faith is a prayer that reaches through, consciously touches God's throne, and then rests unshakably in the assurance that the answer will come in God's time. Perhaps it can be called a special mighty form of believing prayer.

1. *It is prayer totally dependent upon the Holy Spirit.* You are sure of being guided in the subject of prayer, conscious of being energized in prayer (praying in the Spirit), and conscious of being quickened in faith during prayer. It does not arise from self-interest or self-will. Of course you are interested in the answer, but the Spirit confirms to you that the request is an essential prayer target.

2. *It is a prayer totally committed to seeing God's answer realized.* You must devote your whole person, your all to God, in a definite, intelligent vow, never to be broken. You must pray with an impassioned desire that commits itself. *Euchē,* the Greek word used in James 5:15, is a less used word for prayer and can be translated either "prayer" or "vow." Intense prayer in its highest form as a "prayer of faith" commits you to determination like a vow.

3. *It is a prayer willing to believe and prevail for God's answer in a situation that is utterly impossible.* Regardless of the difficulty of the situation, you require no external confirmation but believe God in spite of appearance. Your eyes are on God, not on the situation (Rom. 4:19-20).

4. *It is prayer that believes regardless of feelings or emotions.*

Faith trusts God in spite of contradictions and the absence of feelings or even in spite of your feelings. It has sometimes been called "naked" faith.

5. *It is prayer convinced that it is in accord with God's highest will.* You are totally submissive to God's will, but having been assured of that will, you can prevail until you have received God's promised answer.

6. *It is prayer so sure of God's will that it will not accept denial of the answer.* The longer the prayer battle, the more intense becomes your commitment to seeing the answer because you are sure it is God's will (Luke 11:9). You are aware that Satan is opposing so strongly because he so fears the answer.

7. *It is eager to obey God in any way He leads so as to help hasten the answer.* You rejoice in God's answer even before it is visible to you (Rom. 4:20). You are so sure of God's victory that you gladly invest time, possessions, and even life itself in the answer. You are alert to any guidance of the Spirit as to additional steps to be taken while you maintain the prayer of faith.

8. *It may include prayer warfare in resisting and routing Satan.* Satan is a usurper, a squatter. He tries to hold on to his territory or his slaves even after he has been defeated. Fraser said, "I like to read such passages of Scripture as 1 John 3:8 or Revelation 12:11 in prayer as direct weapons against Satan. . . . Nothing cuts like the word of the living God (Heb. 4:12)."[4]

9. *It is willing to pray through every detail of the answer or victory.* Detailed praying is always more definite and more helpful in prevailing and in believing. As far as you understand, you should prepare the way of the Lord point by point and countercheck Satan point by point. Fraser found detailed prayer exhausting but effective both in ascertaining the will of God and in securing total victories.[5]

CHAPTER 15

The Use and Command of Faith

TWO FORMS OF THE PRAYER OF FAITH

THE PRAYER OF faith at times has the quiet certainty and composure of an invincible commander in chief. At times it has the passionate determination of frontline troups blasting their way through the enemy's fortifications. Both are biblical. Both prevail before God. Each is as spiritual as the other. The Holy Spirit guides you in the form in which prevailing prayer is to be expressed. Let us illustrate this from the lives of Christians.

1. *The faith of quiet and absolute confidence.* Johann A. Bengel was a Lutheran theologian and commentator in the mid-1700s. A sudden devastating hailstorm swept across the fields, threatening total destruction of the crops. A person rushed into Bengel's room calling, "Alas, sir, everything will be destroyed; we shall lose all!" Bengel went quietly to the window, opened it, raised his hands toward heaven, and said, "Father, restrain it." Instantly the storm ceased.[1]

Mr. David Thomas, brother of one of our first OMS International leaders in Korea, was a well-known London merchant. As he left a church service on one occasion, his son came breathless, "Father, the store is on fire!" Mr. Thomas asked, "Are the firemen at work?" When assured that they were, Mr. Thomas turned to the evangelist, his hand on his shoulder, and said, "Let us pray about this." He then prayed, "Lord, it is not my store. It is thine. Put thy hand upon that fire, and do it now for Jesus' sake."

He then quietly said, "Now let us go to supper." Several accompanying friends protested, "What about the fire?" Thomas replied, "Didn't we commit it to the Lord? If we were to go, what more could we do? He will take care of it."

Halfway through the evening meal the son entered the room. "Well, what happened?" asked Mr. Thomas. "Happened! It seemed as though a miracle happened. . . . It looked as though nothing could save it from being completely burned out, but when I returned, in some mysterious manner the flames had been arrested. The firemen themselves cannot understand it. It looks like an act of God."[2]

2. *The faith of passionate determination.* D. McIntyre tells of a boy who fell in the flood-swollen Wupper River. His Christian father called out, "Lord, teach me to swim!" as he leaped in. He swam successfully in spite of the raging water, reached his son, and rescued him. He had never tried to swim before![3]

A friend of mine, M. B. Case, disinherited by his wealthy English family in Britain because of taking his stand for Christ, came to America and began to hold evangelistic meetings. Once during the 1920s he was staying with a very poor family. He wanted to be helpful, so he went out to the woodpile to split some wood for the stove. He had been accustomed to being waited on by servants in Britain and had never used an ax before. As he tried to split the wood, he inadvertently split the sole of his foot. As the blood gushed out, he stomped his foot on the ground, shouting, "Praise the Lord!" Instantly his foot was healed without a scar.

The great revival in Kilsyth, Scotland, under the ministry of William Burns, began Tuesday morning, July 23, 1839. Praying people of Kilsyth had been longing, prevailing, and wrestling in prayer for a new visitation of God. The night before, many gathered and spent the whole night travailing in prayer for souls to be born again. They were given such assurance of faith that they came to the morning meeting expecting a glorious work of God. As the young preacher spoke, the power of God came upon him. The whole audience broke down and began to weep. Many found peace with God. At once revival services began that continued night after night for months in the church and in the marketplace. At times three to four thousand people met to hear Burns. The whole town was cleansed of vice, the drinking of alcoholic beverages was abandoned, and home and loom shops became places of prayer.[4]

Before the Diet of Nuremberg, Luther continued in intense earnestness of wrestling prayer. The Spirit enabled him to lay hold of God's throne of grace with such faith and power that he prevailed with God. He felt sure, even before the diet took action, that those who composed it would stand firm in reformation principles. And they did.[5]

THE COMMAND OF FAITH

At times the Spirit has led God's people to a level of faith called the command of faith. Spurgeon urged God's people to rise to this level of faith and be daring with God. Its illustrations are found in the Old and New Testaments and in the lives of God's prayer warriors over the centuries. While we usually think of prevailing by prayer and the prayer of faith, at other times the Spirit guides to take an act of faith or to give the command of faith.

In some of the Egyptian plagues, Moses cried to the Lord before the plague was stopped. But the plague in each case began by Moses' obedient act of faith. He did not need to pray. At the Red Sea, God told Moses to stop praying and act in faith and cross. God commanded Moses, "Speak to that rock." He did not need to pray any longer but was to command in faith (Num. 20:8). Jericho fell by Joshua's act of faith. When he fought the five Amorite kings, he commanded that the sun "stand still" (Josh. 10:12). Nature obeyed.

Elijah did not pray the Lord to multiply the food of the

widow of Zeraphath. He commanded in faith. When Elisha and Elijah needed to cross the Jordan, Elijah smote the water. So did Elisha on the return trip. Elisha said, "If I am a man of God, may fire come down from heaven" (2 Kings 1:10). The fire instantly fell. When the son of the widow of the prophet was about to be sold for debt, Elisha commanded and the oil multiplied. When he needed to feed the hundred with a small quantity of food, he commanded and it multiplied.

Jesus spoke the command of faith when He said to the man with the shriveled hand, "Stretch out your hand." He was instantly healed (Matt. 12:13). Jesus commanded, "Lazarus, come out!" (John 11:43). The dead man came out.

Jesus usually gave a command of faith to those needing healing. He clearly taught that if we have faith like a grain of mustard seed, we can command in faith, and mountains will be moved from our way (Matt. 17:20–21).

Peter combined the act of faith and the command of faith in the incident with the crippled beggar. "'In the name of Jesus Christ of Nazareth, walk.' Taking him by the right hand, he helped him up" (Acts 3:6–7). He combined prayer and the command of faith for Dorcas. "He got down on his knees and prayed. Turning toward the dead woman, he said, 'Tabitha, get up'" (9:40). She was instantly brought back to life.

At Derbe, Paul saw the man crippled from birth and commanded, "Stand up on your feet!" He was instantly healed (Acts 14:10). The command of faith is repeatedly used in the casting out of demons. At Philippi, Paul turned to the girl with the spirit of fortune-telling: "'In the name of Jesus Christ I command you to come out of her!' At that moment the spirit left her" (16:18).

This truth of the command of faith is so important that Jesus repeated His teaching about it three times. When the apostles asked Jesus, "Increase our faith," Jesus did not tell them to pray more. His instant response was, "If you have faith as small as a mustard seed, you can say to this mulberry tree, 'Be uprooted and planted in the sea,' and it will obey you" (Luke 17:6).

On another occasion when Jesus had rebuked a demon and

cast it out, He said to His disciples, "I tell you the truth, if you have faith as small as a mustard seed, you can say to this mountain, 'Move from here to there' and it will move" (Matt. 17:20).

When the disciples marveled that the fig tree Jesus cursed was dead overnight, Jesus explained, "I tell you the truth, if you have faith and do not doubt, not only can you do what was done to the fig tree, but also you can say to this mountain, 'Go, throw yourself into the sea,' and it will be done" (Matt. 21:21).

There are mountains of difficulty for which much prayer has been made. It may be that a command of faith from the throne is what is needed. The Holy Spirit can give guidance when to take this step. Satanic opposition often has to be commanded to stop. Jesus commanded Satan to get behind Him (Matt. 16:23). Frequently in prevailing prayer we may need to take the courage of our throne position and rebuke Satan to his face.

R. Arthur Mathews wrote, "Many mountains obstruct the progress of God's work in the world today. They are there by default and the blame is on us. As long as the mountains persist we will never be able to see what God has for us on the other side. . . . Our calling and function is not to replace God, but to release Him. Nor do we have to overcome any reluctance on His part. It has been rightly said, 'Without God man cannot; without man God will not.' "6

"It is very apparent from the sequence of this teaching (Matt. 11:20–23)," writes Huegel after years of missionary experience, "that 'the command of faith' is given the same place that ordinary prayer has in the life of the believer."7

When you are on the throne, you do not need to wait to win the victory. Christ has already won the victory, and Satan is already defeated. From that position of power and authority, command Satan to leave. By virtue of Christ's victory, bind Satan, your enemy, by using the power of Jesus' name.

"Have faith in God" (Mark 11:22) is literally "have the faith of God." There is a sense in which God-given faith is made available to us by God, but we must act on it or command because of it. True faith is primarily a matter of the will. It becomes creative by the Spirit's power. You take your stand with God, look down on the problem from the perspective of God's throne, and dare to speak on behalf of God from the throne, where you sit enthroned with Christ.

CHAPTER 16

The Dynamic of the Spirit
Part 1

ALL THE DYNAMICS of prevailing prayer that we have discussed are dependent on the dynamic of the Holy Spirit. He helps, enables, and coordinates all. He is the Lord of prevailing prayer. We listen to His voice, respond to His touch of power, and offer ourselves in total surrender to His active lordship so that He may indwell us, infill us, and pray through us.

The Spirit's lordship is, in effect, the lordship of Christ, who has sent the Spirit to be our other Helper-Counselor (John 14:16). He receives from Christ and reveals and imparts to us (16:14). Through prayer the Spirit places all the powers of the heavenly world at our disposal.

Archbishop Trench wrote, "We must pray in the Spirit . . . if we would pray at all. Lay this, I beseech you, to heart. Do not address yourselves to prayer as to a work to be accomplished in your own natural strength. It is a work of God, of God the Holy Ghost, a work of His in you and by you, and in which you must be fellow-workers with Him—but His work notwithstanding."[1]

Andrew Murray adds, "It is only as we give ourselves to the Spirit living and praying in us, that the glory of the prayer-

109

hearing God and the ever-blessed and most effective mediation of the Son can be known by us in their power."[2] Spurgeon preached that it is not true prayer to God except as the Spirit is in total lordship of the praying. The Holy Spirit Himself "must be present all through it, to help infirmity, and give life and power."[3]

Real prevailing prayer is born of the Spirit, in the Spirit is prevailed in, and by the Spirit is made effective. To pray most truly is to pray in the Spirit. He is the Spirit of grace and supplication (Zech. 12:10). This phrase, says Andrew Murray, means "grace for supplication" (Hebrew: grace and seeking for grace). He is the Spirit of sonship that enables you to say, "Abba, Father," thus making your prayer acceptable to God (Rom. 8:15).

The Holy Spirit breathes the spirit of prayer within you; power in prayer comes from His empowering within. He will not continue to empower for prayer unless you use that power in prayer. Prayer weakness usually results from spiritual weakness, and itself contributes to spiritual weakness. Andrew Murray called prayer "the index of the measure of the Spirit's work in us." Only those who are Spirit-filled can repeatedly prevail mightily in prayer.

When the Spirit works in you only feebly, then your prayer life will be weak and powerless. The more mightily the Spirit works within you, the more mighty will be the results of your praying. The main reason for prayerlessness is that the Spirit indwells you only minimally, almost nominally, and not in His fullness.

God can work through your prayers only as He is truly Lord of your praying. That lordship is exercised entirely by the Holy Spirit. Prayer vision is Spirit-given vision, prayer hunger is Spirit-given hunger, and prayer power is the mighty power of the Spirit pouring through your whole spiritual being. Says Bounds, "Would you pray with mighty results? Seek the mighty workings of the Holy Spirit in your own spirit."[4]

The New Testament standard for the Christian is to be filled with the Spirit. But remember, He is the Spirit of power.

Leonard Ravenhill questions whether any claimed experience of the fullness of the Spirit that does not result in "extended periods of prayer" can be regarded as biblical.[5]

Living on this side of Pentecost, we have far greater availability of the Spirit's ministry than had the saints of the Old Testament. We should know in a far greater degree the power and reality of prayer and the life of prevailing prayer through the Spirit. By sending the Holy Spirit, God has made available to us "the incomparably great power for us who believe" (Eph. 1:19). Paul thus prayed constantly that the church might know God better and know His power better (vv. 17–21). It is all waiting for us to discover and appropriate through prevailing prayer.

"The gift which He so freely bestowed has never yet been exhausted. The skies are still full of Pentecosts. The great need is for men who know how to prevail with God so as to bring down the showers upon the church and the world. Here lies the ... secret of carrying forward the Apostolic prayer-life in full operation, as well as all the other ministries of the Spirit."[6]

In prayer, as in all else in our spiritual life, it is "'not by might nor by power, but by my Spirit,' says the LORD Almighty" (Zech. 4.6). It may well be that Jesus had this promise in mind when He said your faith could move any opposing mountain, for the very next verse in this passage in Zechariah says, "What are you, O mighty mountain? ... You will become level ground."

When God called the church to supernatural work for Him, He provided supernatural power. That supernatural dynamic of the Spirit operates through prayer, faith, and obedience. Why do we depend almost exclusively on our best wisdom, the perfecting of our own methods, and our psychological and managerial training? We have been so busy depending on our own natural strengths, our good training, and our busyness for God that we are near spiritual bankruptcy.

We hardly know what it means to pray in the Spirit and to have our words accompanied by "a demonstration of the Spirit's power" (1 Cor. 2:4). Mighty prevailing prayer will

111

accompany a mighty spiritual revolution in our soul. God's overwhelming presence in our worship services and His almightiness making our evangelism and missionary endeavor effective are waiting for us to have a new dimension of prayer life by the dynamic of the Spirit.

THE SPIRIT HELPS US PRAY

Jesus promised to send us another Helper (possible translation of John 14:16), and Paul assures us the Spirit helps us in our weakness in prayer (Rom. 8:26). Ravenhill writes, "The Holy Spirit as the Spirit of life ends our deadness in prayer . . . as the Spirit of wisdom delivers us from ignorance in this holy art of prayer . . . as the Spirit of fire delivers us from coldness in prayer . . . as the Spirit of might comes to our aid in our weakness as we pray."[7]

About A.D. 400, Bishop Ambrose taught, "This helping of the Spirit is very emphatic in the original; as a man taking up a heavy piece of timber by the one end cannot get it up till some other man takes it up at the other end. . . . The Spirit of God comes at the other end, and takes the heaviest end of the burden, and so helps the soul to lift it up."[8]

Let us examine a number of ways in which the Spirit helps you so that you are enabled to prevail in prayer:

1. *The Spirit fills you so that He can be Lord of your praying.* You never truly become a person of prayer, mighty in prevailing prayer, until He fills you. His filling you, in the words of Payne, "brings Pentecost up to date." The apostles were not outstandingly men of prayer until Pentecost. Then their perspective, commitment, and spiritual experience were transformed. They made it their first priority to give "attention to prayer" (Acts 6:4). Says Chadwick, "those who pray in the Spirit must be in the Spirit." J. Stuart Holden adds that being filled with the Spirit is "the only secret of a real prayer life."[9]

2. *The Spirit makes you spiritually healthy.* He makes Christ your very life (Rom. 8:2; Col. 3:4). Living in the Spirit gives you spiritual health and vitality so that you can pray and serve

God as you ought. Living in the Spirit equips you to pray in the Spirit. As you abide in Christ, you have the right to ask what you will (John 15:7).

That great teacher on prayer, Andrew Murray, wrote, "The connection between the prayer life and the Spirit life is close and indissolvable." He also wrote, "Prayer is one of the most heavenly and spiritual of the functions of the Spirit-life; how could we try or expect to fulfill it so as to please God, except our soul is in perfect health and our life truly possessed and moved by God's Spirit."[10]

One more quotation from Murray: "The extent of the abiding is the exact measure of the power in prayer. It is the Spirit dwelling within us that prays, not in words and thoughts always, but in a breathing and a being, deeper than utterance. Just so much as there is of Christ's Spirit in us there is real prayer. . . . Oh, let our lives be full of Christ, and full of His Spirit, and the wonderfully unlimited promises to our prayer will no longer appear strange."[11]

3. *The Spirit draws you to prayer.* As guardian of your soul and as steward of your spiritual life, He draws you to prayer again and again. Sometimes He draws you to prayer by showing you how great is some need and how helpless you are to meet that need. Sometimes He draws you by giving you a vision of all God longs to do. Only the Spirit can convey to you the heartbeat of God, the priority of God, or the spiritual battle in which He calls you to fight.

You do not know when some friend or loved one is in need of your prayer, is facing danger, is ill, is facing temptation, or is seeking an urgent answer from God in which he or she needs your prayer partnership. But the all-knowing Spirit can call you to prayer and fix that person upon your mind so that through the Spirit you know you are to pray.

Spurgeon preached,

Whenever our Lord gives you the special inclination to pray, then you should double your diligence. . . . When He gives you the special longing after prayer, and you feel a peculiar aptness

113

and enjoyment in it, you have over and above the command which is constantly binding, another command which should compel you to cheerful obedience. At such times I think we may stand in the position of David, to whom the Lord said, "When thou hearest a sound of a going in the tops of the mulberry trees, then shalt thou bestir thyself." That going in the tops of the mulberry trees may have been the footfalls of angels hastening to help David.[12]

Thank God, you can depend on the Spirit to give you desires, drawing, and hunger to pray at the very time your prayer is strategic to the advance of Christ's kingdom.

Says James McConkey, "Never disobey this drawing of the Spirit to prayer. It is a special call of God to the individual who is conscious of it. . . . Tremendous issues may hang upon obedience to that call to prayer."[13] It is always tragic to neglect prayer, but it is doubly so when the Spirit thus calls you. Some person in a crisis may need your prayer just then, or some danger may be averted if you pray just then. Often only eternity will cast full light on the importance of obeying such a call to prayer.

4. *The Spirit gives special access to God.* "Through him we . . . have access to the Father by one Spirit" (Eph. 2:18). "In him and through faith in him we may approach God with freedom and confidence" (3:12). Who are you and I that we should have access to the throne room of heaven? No ruler of any nation gives instant, constant access to anyone. But through Christ you and I have been made kings and priests to God by virtue of Christ's redemption.

The Spirit, as it were, ushers you into God's presence. This image suggests a court official who introduces people who desire an audience with a king. You know not how to approach God or how to express your deepest requests, but the Holy Spirit expresses your heart-cry and perfectly interprets your deepest need. "Let us then approach the throne of grace with confidence, so that we may receive mercy and find grace to help us in our time of need" (Heb. 4:16).

CHAPTER 17

The Dynamic of the Spirit Part 2

THE SPIRIT HELPS US PRAY (continued)

5. *THE SPIRIT TEACHES you to pray.* At the beginning of every prayer period, you should commit yourself to the Lord and ask that the Holy Spirit deeply possess you in your praying, enabling you to pray in the Spirit. "In the Spirit" (Eph. 6:18) is literally "in spirit." This wording has been interpreted to mean completely surrounded by the Spirit. He is the transforming atmosphere of prayer. You are to breathe in the atmosphere of the Spirit and breathe out the spirit of prayer.

You are to "walk in Spirit" (Gal. 5:16, Greek), "live in Spirit" (v. 25, Greek), and walk "according to the Spirit" (Rom. 8:4). The atmosphere and lordship of the Spirit must characterize all of your living but, above all, your praying. The Spirit exercises His lordship by teaching you to pray, calling you to pray, strengthening you to pray, guiding you in prayer, and giving faith as you pray.

Charles Finney counsels, "If you would pray in faith, be sure to walk every day with God. If you do, He will tell you what to pray for. Be filled with His Spirit, and He will give you objects enough to pray for. He will give you as much of the spirit of prayer as you have strength of body to bear."[1]

You are totally dependent on the Spirit, which anyone who has longed to prevail in prayer knows. He must touch your emotions, giving you deep desire; your faith, giving you boldness in prayer; and your will, giving you persevering insistence. He must both teach you and enable you to put His teaching into praying. He is the giver of all praying in the Spirit, as Spurgeon has well said.

The Holy Spirit is the Master Intercessor within you, even as Jesus is the Master Intercessor at the Father's right hand. The Spirit is your infallible, all-wise Teacher, but He also enables you to do as He teaches. He not only teaches you the need and the manner of prayer, but He opens to you the mysteries of prayer. He is the Helper in all your spiritual life, but especially in prayer.

The Spirit is the *paraklētos* Teacher (John 14:26). The *paraklētos,* or paraclete, went to the courtroom with a man on trial as his helper or counselor. He gave the person courage as he stood beside him. The defendant was not alone, but his paraclete was with him. He helped the defendant understand the issues before him, helped him see clearly the statements he needed to make, suggested action to take, and was constantly available at his side.

Even so, the Holy Spirit is your paraclete when you pray. He is both by your side and within you. He pleads for you, and He pleads within and through you. He works mightily within you so that He can pray mightily through you.

The Spirit so sanctifies you to the will of God, so yearns within you for the will of God, so illumines for you the will of God, and so believes through you for the will of God that He sanctifies your intercession until the intercession of God the Son, God the Spirit, and your heart-cry are as one. In this holy and irresistible unity of intercession, heaven and earth can be moved as necessary.

You and I do not know how to intercede as we ought. We could pray amiss. Prayer could become dangerous! God would have to say to us again and again, in the words of Jesus to Peter, "You don't know what you are asking" (Matt. 20:22). What would we do without the Spirit to teach us and guide us in prayer?

The Holy Spirit teaches you the love of prayer, the wise and appropriate content of prayer, and how to pray in the Spirit. These spiritual things are Spirit-taught and spiritually discerned by those who are Spirit-filled (1 Cor. 2:14). Spiritual sensitivity, spiritual perception, spiritual longings, and spiritual warfare are all deep things of God that are taught by the Holy Spirit (2 Cor. 2:10).

But the Spirit teaches only what is in the will of God. He never gives holy hunger for anything outside God's will nor prays through you for anything but what is God's best for you.

If you pray for carnal desires, the Spirit lapses into silence within you. Spirit-filled persons suddenly realize that something is wrong. They are praying on their own. There comes an inner hesitation, a gentle restraint of the Spirit. The Paraclete is saying by His silence, "I can't endorse that prayer. Jesus can't 'amen' that prayer. You may mean well, but you are missing My purpose and will. Wait, wait, and I will help you see a better way, a better prayer."

As you delight yourself in the Lord, you begin to understand more and more clearly what pleases the Lord and what is His will. The Holy Spirit, your loving Teacher, will help you to know God's will, rejoice in God's will, long for God's will, and pray for His will. You would not truly or deeply desire anything that you knew was contrary to God's will. God can then give you the desires of your heart because they are one with His desires (Ps. 37:4).

Without total commitment to the will of God, known and unknown, we cannot be filled with the Spirit. Until we are filled with the Spirit, He cannot exercise His full role as Teacher in our praying.

In a very real way, the deepest prayers of the Spirit-filled person come from the Father, by the Spirit, to the praying one and then are returned from his or her heart back to the Father by the Spirit and are "amened" by God the Son. Christians are never in closer unity with the Trinity than when they pray. It is the joy of heaven to hear believers praying in the Spirit.

When praying in the Spirit, you are always praying in harmony with God's Word, for the Spirit guiding you in prayer is the One who inspired the Word. There is blessed unity of the Spirit, the Word, and you as you pray. The Spirit always teaches you to love and be guided by the Word and to lay hold on God's will and purpose as revealed in the Word. Thus, nothing excels prayer in the Spirit in bringing glory to God. God's glory is your primary desire; God's goodness for others and for yourself is secondary.

The carnal Christian and the natural man are comparatively untaught by the Spirit. Prayer often seems so baffling to them. Sadly, self-will, self-centered desires, unwise requests, and shallow praying are about all that many people know of praying. They can never enter into the Spirit-taught life of mighty prevailing prayer until they make the total consecration and commitment that can lead to the Spirit-filled life.

6. *The Spirit burdens you to pray.* No Christian has fully understood the burden on the heart of the Holy Spirit as He longs for, loves, and identifies with all the suffering, heartaches, and heart-burdens of Christians across the world. There is never a discouragement, a hidden tear, or an unspoken pain that the Holy Spirit does not feel completely and personally. Never an injustice, a sorrow, or a heartbreak that the tender Holy Spirit does not suffer with us.

In addition, however, the Holy Spirit yearns and longs for all the broken lives, broken homes, hurting unsaved millions of the world. He feels their tragedy. He suffers from their hatred and violence. He carries the suffering of our world upon His holy heart. God the Father, God the Son, and God the Holy Spirit share the same love and the same longings and compassion.

The Holy Spirit longs to flood your heart with the holy, yearning agape love of the triune God. Romans 5:5 explains that God pours out His love into your heart by the Holy Spirit.

What love is this? It is the love that caused Jesus to come to earth, go to the cross, and die for you (v. 8). The love that the Spirit longs to pour and flood into your being is the self-giving, longing love of God that we see in Jesus (8:39).

The Spirit does not want just a minimum portion of that love somehow to rub off or seep into your nature. He longs to pour and pour that love into your being and through you out to the hurting world. He wants this love to be manifested in your words and your actions, but more constantly and perhaps more powerfully than all else, in your praying.

You can love more people through prayer than any other way. You can love, by your prayer, people who avoid or resist you. You can love people anywhere in the world by your prayer. The more you pour out God's love through your prayer and actions, the more the Spirit will pour in as you ask Him. God gives the Spirit to those who ask (Luke 11:13).

The Spirit longs to share His burden, compassion, and travail of soul with you. God has ordained that the power to change things, to restrain evil, to calm human hatred, and to heal the world's wounds is released by the prayer of His people. You and I are expected to be priests to the hurting world. But how can we fulfill this role?

It has to begin with our hearts. We must feel before we can heal. We must see before we can prevail. One of the chief roles of the Holy Spirit in relation to the world's need is to place prayer burden on our hearts. How much do you share and carry on your heart the burden of our world? You are failing your people, city, nation, and world unless you are a priest of God carrying their burden on your heart.

We are not just saved to be happy. We are saved to bless. What greater way can we bless than through our prayers? In what other way can we bless so many? God is a God who blesses, but much of that blessing can be mediated and manifested only through your intercession.

The Holy Spirit longs to help your eyes to see, your heart to feel, and your prayers to carry a burden of prevailing prayer for people and for society. How can Christians be carefree in a hurting world and think they have the heart of Christ? How can Christians be tearless in a broken world and think that they are representing Jesus? How can you and I be so often free of prayer burden and still be prayer partners with Jesus?

Open your heart to the hurting, the brokenness, the tragedy all about you and across our world. Open your heart to the Spirit to burden you. Learn to rejoice with those who rejoice and to weep with those who weep (Rom. 12:15). Ask the Spirit to teach you burden-bearing through prayer. You can make a difference in many lives if you let the Spirit burden you for intercession. What greater joy could you give to your triune God then to share their burden for our world?

The story has often been told about a visitor who came to see Robert Murray McCheyne's church and pulpit after his death. The sexton took him to the pastor's office and, pointing to McCheyne's chair, said, "Sit there. Now put your elbows on the table." The visitor obeyed. "Now put your face in your hands." Again, the visitor complied. "Now let the tears flow. That was the way Mr. McCheyne used to do."

He then led the visitor to McCheyne's pulpit, where he had blessed the people by his ministry. "Put your elbows on the pulpit," said the old sexton. The visitor complied. "Put your face in your hands." Again, the visitor obeyed. "Now let the tears flow. That was the way Mr. McCheyne used to do." Ah, that was the secret of his ministry. He carried the burden of his people and of his nation and of God's cause upon his heart. Let the Holy Spirit burden you.

7. *The Spirit empowers you to pray.* Do you feel you have so little prayer power? Of course, you do. None of us has prayer power in ourselves. The role of the Holy Spirit is to empower. He wants to express His power through you as you prevail for the burdens on His heart.

Power and love belong to God (Ps. 62:11–12). And power and love He imparts to you as you share and express His heart. Just as He increases your love, so He increases your power as you use it in intercession. He as the breath of God will breathe His power into your soul. The more you prevail, the more you will be filled with prevailing love and power. The Spirit longs to equip you to be a mighty intercessor. He rejoices to make you what you need to be as His prayer channel of blessing.

God longs for you to prevail. He longs to use your prayer. He will gladly empower any Spirit-filled person in prayer if he or she will only pray. The more you prevail, the more you will be empowered to prevail. Heaven rejoices when you love as God loves and when you prevail as Christ prevails. Make yourself available—respond to the Spirit and take up the burdens of others. Ask God to place His priority burdens on your heart. He has specific prayer assignments for you. As you prevail, He will give more to you. Your role will grow, the more you fulfill it. The Spirit is waiting to use you more and more.

8. *The Spirit multiplies your faith.* There is much talk about faith that is little more than pseudofaith. R. A. Torrey insists, "Trying to believe something that you want to believe is not faith. . . . In no case does real faith come by simply determining that you are going to get the thing that you want to get."[2]

Bounds wrote, "What a world of natural praying there is, which is selfish, self-centered, self-inspired! The Spirit, when He prays through us, or helps us to meet the mighty 'oughtness' of right praying, trims our praying down to the will of God and then we give heart and expression to His unutterable groanings. Then we have the mind of Christ and pray as He would pray."[3]

The Holy Spirit, as He indwells you, strengthens and multiplies your faith for those areas where you are praying in accordance with the will of God. He multiplies faith by giving you a new revelation of the greatness and power of God, by giving you a vision of how God longs to act on your behalf, and by impressing upon your heart particular promises from the Word. As you prevail in prayer, He kindles a joyous expectancy in your heart that God's answer is on the way.

The Spirit affirms your faith through the Word and through the assurance in your heart that He is praying through you. The Spirit does not lead you to pray for useless goals. He burdens you because God desires to work. His assistance in your prayer undergirds your confidence in His promise. Just as Abraham was strengthened in His faith and gave glory to God and became fully persuaded (Rom. 4:20–21), so the Spirit guides, encourages, and affirms your faith till you too give glory to God and rejoice in faith's victory even before you see it with your eyes.

Jean-Nicolas Grou prayed in 1750, "O my Savior, I say to thee again with more insistence than ever: Teach me to pray; implant in me all the dispositions needful for the prayer of the Holy Spirit. . . . Of what use is my prayer if the Holy Spirit does not pray with me? Come, Holy Spirit, come to dwell and work with me! Take possession of my understanding and of my will; govern my actions not only at the moment of prayer but at every moment."[4]

CHAPTER 18

The Dynamic of Uniting in Prayer

THERE IS UNUSUAL power in united prayer. God has planned for His people to join together in prayer, not only for Christian fellowship, spiritual nurture, and growth, but also for accomplishing His divine purposes and reaching His chosen goals.

In unity there is strength, a principle that is true in all of life, in the family and nation and among the people of God. The principle of Ecclesiastes 4:12 applies in spiritual life and prayer warfare: "Though one may be overpowered, two can defend themselves. A cord of three strands is not quickly broken."

Jesus built upon this truth. He is present with any one of His children wherever they may be—present always, and certainly so during prayer. But Jesus is specially present where two or three gather in His name. Jesus stated this fact as a concluding part of His promise for the power of prayer, specifically for united prayer, for agreement in prayer (Matt. 18:18–20).

The New Testament teaches the importance of the Christian church and community. When we are born of the Spirit, we are born into a family. God purposed this interrelationship for our spiritual good. We need each other. We specially need each

123

other in prevailing prayer and prayer warfare. Often we must fight spiritual battles humanly alone. God has adequate power and grace to make us victorious even when we feel very alone.

Many times, however, we need the prayer of our brothers and sisters in Christ. The exhortation "pray for each other" (James 5:16) is important not only for healing but for all of life. Note that the assurance "the prayer of a righteous man is powerful and effective" is stated in conjunction with praying for each other.

The greatest demonstrations of the power of prayer are usually given in prayer for others and prayer for Christ's kingdom. God does answer prayer for our own needs, but the primary role of prayer, apart from communion, is intercession. The priority of Jesus is not just communion with His Father but intercession for us and for the world.

From one viewpoint, all prayer of intercession in the will of God is united prayer. So important is united prayer that all intercession in the Spirit is intercession of the Son, the Holy Spirit, and you—a kind of intercessory trinity seeking the glory of the Father. But above and beyond this basic united prayer, God is pleased to honor in a special way the united intercession of two or more of His children. Most powerful of all is agreement in prayer.

Chrysostom, around A.D. 400, wrote, "What we cannot obtain by solitary prayer we may by social . . . because where our individual strength fails, there union and concord are effectual." Thomas Payne wrote, "While it is true that one man who knows how to pray and make intercession in the Spirit has far more power with God than a host of half-hearted ones, it is nevertheless a glorious fact that the prayers of a sanctified host, when of one heart and soul, become irresistible."[1]

GOD BLESSES WHEN YOU UNITE IN PRAYER

Perhaps we should distinguish between being united in prayer and being in united prayer. When a call for prayer is issued, people can join in praying for the same need or request

124

wherever they are. All whose hearts cry out to God are thus united in prayer.

Thank God, we can unite with others in prayer whatever our circumstances. Here are examples of how this has been done:

1. *Make the Lord's Day a time of prayer.* Even if circumstances prevent us from joining in public worship, we can and should be uniting with God's people by our prayer on the Lord's Day. His day should always, as far as humanly possible, be a day when extra time is set apart for prayer. Those imprisoned for Christ's sake, though very alone, have reported being specially blessed as they prayed on the Lord's Day, knowing that millions of God's children were praying around the world.

John received the visions recorded in the book of Revelation in such a time of prayer. Pastor of the church at Ephesus, John was banished to the small island called Patmos, probably to work in the mines at slave labor. He was separated from his beloved congregation, but on the Lord's Day he knew they would be meeting for prayer in Ephesus and he, although banished from them, joined them in prayer, when suddenly the Lord revealed Himself to him in a wonderful and dramatic way (Rev. 1:9–10).

2. *Make available a prayer list or prayer requests to as many Christians as possible.* Then all can join in daily prayer or prayer at set times for the needs listed. During World War II, Christians throughout South Africa stopped wherever they were, in streets or stores, for a moment of silent prayer at noon.

3. *Use prayer chains.* A congregation can organize one or more prayer chains among its members. Each person in a prayer chain can inform the next person on the list. Thus in a short time the church can all be uniting in prayer for the same urgent request. Most prayer chains are done entirely by phone.

4. *Pray around the clock.* People can pledge to pray for half an hour or an hour and be assigned particular times of prayer so that prayer continues for an urgent need all night or even twenty-four hours around the clock. It is reported that the Moravian Pentecost that God gave in a prayer meeting at

Herrnhut in 1731 resulted in unbroken prayer day and night for a hundred years and was part of the key to God's tremendous blessing upon the Moravians as they scattered the message of Christ around the world.

5. *Become prayer partners.* There is tremendous blessing in being a prayer partner with one or several others. Each prayer partner can agree to uphold the other specially in prayer. For years R. Stanley Tam and his prayer partner have sat in his car in a city park and spent an hour in prayer together at the same time each week. Some meet together regularly in prayer by telephone. Many missionary organizations enlist people to spend some time each day praying for their ministry and supply prayer requests regularly to all these intercessors.

Some husbands and wives have a very effective prayer partnership together. Couples in their retirement have been able to give an hour or more each day in united prayer partnership together using prayer lists.

We should remember that Christ is always our prayer partner. We are never alone. This truth I very blessedly realized during a time of ministry in a village in India. I was supervising our students in village evangelism, and we were all living in a rented village mud house for several weeks.

I came down with malaria but had no medicine with me, and there was no shop of any kind in the village where we were staying. Each day I expected to be better the following day but, instead, became more ill. One day the students were gone for the day in their evangelism, and I was alone in the house. Toward noon, my fever rose so high that I became concerned.

I longed in my heart for someone to pray for me and anoint me for healing, according to James 5:14–15. I had no olive oil but noticed standing in a window a bottle of coconut oil that one of the students used on his hair. I went and got it and prayed, "Lord Jesus, You and I are the only two here. I have no one but You to join me in prayer. I anoint myself in Your name. You join me in prayer for my healing." Instantly I was healed of malaria and, during the many succeeding years in

India, never had a recurrence. Jesus, my prayer partner, had prevailed for me.

George Whitefield, who was so mightily used in evangelism across the British Isles, always took with him a little crippled man who was a prayer warrior. Frank Laubach says, "His prayers, even more than Whitefield's peaching, were the cause of the wonderful results."[2] Charles G. Finney, in his greatly blessed evangelism, which brought several hundred thousand to Christ, often had with him two ministers, Clary and Nash. They would rent a room and give themselves to day after day of prevailing prayer. Sometimes these prayer partners began praying in a community before Finney's meetings began.

It is reported that after Finney had gone to Bolten, England, to minister but before he actually began, these two men came to the door of a woman, asking if she could rent accommodations to them. She had a rather dark and damp cellar that she rented to the men for about twenty-five cents a week. There these two men, Nash and Clary, interceded in prevailing prayer, battling the forces of darkness with their prayer wrestlings, tears, and invincible faith. God worked mightily.[3]

Mrs. Goforth in China had a Chinese Christian lady who often accompanied her. The two worked, prayed, and wept together and were mightily used of God. The Goforths also frequently attributed God's blessing on their ministry in China to their prayer partners who so faithfully interceded for them at home.[4]

6. *Call for a special day or week of prayer.* Sometimes a special call has gone out nationwide for a specified day or week to be spent as much as possible in prayer for an urgent need.

7. *Prepare for God's revival working by a call to prayer.* Sometimes groups in a local church, city, or nation issue calls to prayer for God to prepare hearts and visit the group or nation with repentance, spiritual awakening, and revival blessing. At times these calls have preceded special meetings arranged for the deepening of spiritual life. At other times they have been general calls for prayer for a mighty visitation of God's Spirit at God's own time. All those responding have then given priority

daily to such prayer. They have prayed as often as possible and also have assembled in meetings for earnest prayer.

All of the above illustrate the many ways in which God's children can unite together in prayer, even when they cannot attend a united service of prayer.

CHAPTER 19

God Honors United Prayer

WE HAVE DISCUSSED uniting together for the same request. Now we consider united prayer. United prayer can occur in the regular services of the church at periods when all join in intercession. Alas, often so little time is given during worship services for united intercession. No part of the service has greater potential for blessing than when the congregation takes time for united prevailing intercession for definite needs.

It is a tremendous responsibility to lead God's people to God's throne and into God's presence in public prayer. God can so strongly anoint the one who leads in prayer that all present are brought into consciousness of God's presence until the one praying is forgotten and the people as one in heart and soul unite and agree in the prayer.

Special united prayer meetings can be convened. Prayer meetings have been held from the earliest days of the church. The ten days between Christ's ascension and Pentecost were largely given to united prayer. The believers then met together daily for prayer (Acts 2:42). When Peter and John were brought before the Sanhedrin and threatened because of the healing of the crippled beggar, they returned to the group of believers, who engaged in such united prevailing prayer that the place where they were meeting was physically shaken, and again the believers were "all filled with the Holy Spirit" (4:31). From then on, prayer times characterized the early church. Christ planned to build and extend His church through prayer meetings.

Many churches have traditionally had a midweek prayer meeting. In all too many of these meetings most of the time is given to singing, testimony, and Bible study or exposition, and a comparatively small amount of time is actually spent in intercession. Many churches have a variety of midweek church activity alternatives. Various good subjects are taught, and perhaps only one of these groups is designated a prayer group. Even there, the danger can be that so much time is spent talking about the listed needs that tragically little time is actually spent interceding.

United prayer can continue at much greater length at times specially set apart primarily for prayer. Special prayer services have been called for the express purpose of prevailing in prayer. Usually, thank God, such services are given almost entirely to prayer. One after another leads the group in prayer, or a larger group may divide up into small groups so that more people are actively praying the entire time set apart for prayer.

BLESSINGS FROM UNITED PRAYER

Tremendous answers to prayer have resulted from gatherings for united prayer. In addition to the specific answers received, there are always great spiritual benefits, as all those praying learn to prevail more effectively.

1. *The spirit of prayer is deepened.* When one believer prays in the Spirit, God's holy fire and prayer passion works more deeply in others who are joining in prayer. By hearing the prayers of others, we can become more deeply convinced that we are praying in the will of God. Said Finney, "Nothing is more calculated to beget a spirit of prayer than to unite in social prayer with one who has the Spirit himself."[1]

130

The two most effective ways to learn to prevail in prayer are by spending much time prevailing in prayer yourself and by praying with someone who truly prevails in prayer.

2. *Love of the brethren and unity are intensified.* The more you pray together, the more you sense each other's heartbeat, burdens, joy in the Lord, and Christian experience. To quote from Finney again, "Nothing tends more to cement the hearts of Christians than praying together. Never do they love one another so well as when they witness the outpouring of each other's hearts in prayer."[2]

Apart from personal sin, nothing is more certain to hinder prevailing prayer than disunity. Disunity in a home hinders the prayer of the members of the home (1 Peter 3:7). Disunity in a church hinders the prayers of the church. There are many scriptural injunctions to maintain unity in the church (Rom. 12:16, 18; 14:19; 15:5–7; 1 Cor. 1:10; 7:15; 2 Cor. 2:11; Heb. 11:14).

Many a church has experienced revival when God brought members of the church into unity. Many years ago in the central section of India, a missionary was praying to God to send revival to the work where he was involved. As he prayed earnestly day after day, the Holy Spirit brought to his mind another missionary in his own organization with whom he had had a serious disagreement. Every time he got down on his knees to pray, the other missionary's face came before him. Finally, he boarded the train and went to the town where the other missionary lived. He walked from the train station to the missionary's house and knocked on the door. The other missionary came to the door, surprised to see him.

Falling on his knees outside the door, the first missionary began to ask forgiveness from the other. "Come on in," the second missionary pleaded. "I'm the one who needs to ask your forgiveness." They prayed together and wept together and were fully reconciled. Then each prayed for God to send revival to the other's work. As they separated, each began to pray daily for God to send revival to his own work and to the work of the other. Within twelve months both churches experienced mighty revival.

God will not be mocked. We cannot prevail in prayer while disunity festers. As much as is in our power, we must seek to humble ourselves, take the blame, and restore unity (Matt. 5:23–24; Rom. 12:18).

3. *Faith is strengthened.* The more you hear others joining in prayer for the same needs, the stronger your faith tends to become. You become encouraged by the way God is giving faith to them. You become more persevering and more constant in prayer for the need as you find others persevering for the same concern. Heart warms heart. Prayer kindles prayer. Faith strengthens faith. Courage and expectancy rise, and you are able to plant your feet on God's promises with new firmness and determination. Others "amen" your prayer, and you "amen" theirs, and step by step you both grow in assurance, lay hold of the throne of God, and are able to agree in prayer (Matt. 18:19).

4. *Spiritual power is multiplied.* As you pray together, the prayer of each helps deepen the hunger for God's answer and helps fan into flame the spirit of prayer. Love and unity are intensified, purified, and made more blessed. Faith for God's answer is strengthened. All who unite in prayer begin to sense God's power coming upon them and anointing their praying in a new way.

As others reach out to God, you are helped to reach out more effectively. As you realize how heartbroken others are over the need, your compassion is moved, and your desire deepens to see God meet the need. As you realize how others are prevailing, you are so blessed that you too prevail more effectively. Very often God's refreshing, blessing, and power come in a new way, collectively, to a group, an experience the believers had at Pentecost and in Acts 4.

There is a spiritual dynamic hinted at in the Bible that when two or more people prevail together in faith, praying in the Spirit, their prayer power not only is added together, it seems multiplied. Moses referred to one of Israel's people, by God's help, chasing a thousand of their enemies, and two, ten thousand (Deut. 32:30). Again, he promised that five would chase a hundred, and a hundred, ten thousand (Lev. 26:8).

The shout in united faith of Gideon's three hundred, although they were armed with nothing but flaming torches, completely routed the vast armies of Midian. By the same principle, united faith, singing, and praise so confused Satan and the combined forces of Ammon, Moab, and Mount Seir that they were completely annihilated without a physical battle being fought by Israel (2 Chron. 20).

United prayer backing was what Paul so much desired. In his letters he pleads that the believers unite with him in prayer for his life and ministry. To the Romans: "I urge you, brothers, by our Lord Jesus Christ and by the love of the Spirit, to join me in my struggle by praying to God for me" (Rom. 15:30). To the Corinthians he expressed his confidence: "He will continue to deliver us, as you help us by your prayers. Then many will give thanks on our behalf for the gracious favor granted us in answer to the prayers of many" (2 Cor. 1:10–11).

To the Philippians Paul wrote, "I know that through your prayers and the help given by the Spirit of Jesus Christ, what has happened to me will turn out for my deliverance" (Phil. 1:19). To the Colossians: "Devote yourselves to prayer . . . and pray for us, too, that God may open a door for our message" (Col. 4:2–3). And to the Thessalonians: "Finally, brothers, pray for us that the message of the Lord may spread rapidly and be honored" (2 Thess. 3:1).

EXAMPLES FROM CHRISTIAN HISTORY

William Carey and a small praying band in Kettering, England, prayed monthly for nearly eight years before mighty revival came. William Wilberforce was used of God to bring moral and spiritual awakening to England. He had the backing of a group in his church that covenanted together to pray three hours a day.[3]

John Livingstone and a group from his church in Shotts,

Scotland, spent all of Saturday night in prayer, and the next day five hundred were saved as a result of his sermon.[4]

Jonathan Edwards had a group of his members at Enfield, Massachusetts, who were deeply burdened that God not pass them by while He was sending revival to other places. They became so burdened that they met one Saturday evening and spent the whole night in prayer.[5] The same night Jonathan Edwards was so burdened that he spent the whole night in prayer. The next day his sermon "Sinners in the Hands of an Angry God" was greatly anointed by the Holy Spirit. God gripped some so strongly that they grabbed the pillars of the church, feeling that their feet were slipping into hell. Edwards then issued a call for Christians to join in meetings of united prayer across New England until God visited them with revival. God sent revival.

George Whitefield, so mightily used of God in the early 1700s, called for people to join in united meetings of prevailing prayer. Spurgeon led a prayer meeting every Monday night, which usually had at least 1,000 to 1,200 in attendance.[6] Charles Finney repeatedly spent one or more days in fasting and prayer. He was used by God mightily in Boston in 1856 and in various New England cities in 1857–58. Noon united prayer meetings, usually without preaching, began in Boston and spread across the country in almost every major city and in many smaller cities. Over a million were won to Christ and joined local churches in two years' time.

During D. L. Moody's campaigns in Oxford and Cambridge, he was opposed by such lawless rowdyism of the university students that it was impossible to hear the gospel singing of Sankey or the messages of Moody. Moody gathered three hundred godly women of Cambridge in Alexander Hall for a time of nothing but prevailing prayer. One after another pleaded with tears for "some mother's son." That night the tide turned, as a hush from God came upon the service. Scores of students humbled themselves before God, confessed their sins, and found salvation. Moody referred to this as the greatest victory of his life.[7]

A number of years ago it seemed that Communism was going to take over Mexico. Education was based on atheism. Night after night radio stations poured blasphemy over the land. Tension gripped hearts. Then a group of Christian leaders met together to seek God's answer. They decided to meet each morning at 6:30 for prayer and to hold on until deliverance came. For months this group of prayer warriors prayed every morning.

"They found themselves in a mighty conflict with the powers of darkness. They wrestled not with flesh and blood, but with principalities and powers." They represented many denominations, but all were united in seeking God. For six months they prayed with strong crying and tears. Then one morning while they were praying, a pastor came into the room with a newspaper. Its headlines told that the president of the country had dismissed the Communists from the cabinet—the nation was being turned right about face. God had changed the course of a nation by united prayer.[8]

The Friends Missionary Prayer Band movement in India is reported to have five hundred weekly prayer bands, most of which fast and pray all night one night each week for God to move in India. More than twenty thousand lay Christians are involved in this prayer movement.[9]

David Bryant reports that Korean pastor Yonggi Cho spends an hour and a half in private prayer each morning and that from 10:30 P.M. till 6:00 A.M. Saturday at least fifteen thousand of his members meet for united prayer. The rest of his members meet in twenty thousand prayer cells across Seoul.[10]

J. Edwin Orr, historian of revival worldwide, stated, "No great spiritual awakening has begun anywhere in the world apart from united prayer—Christians persistently praying for revival."[11]

CHAPTER 20

The Prayer of Agreement

JESUS PLACED A tremendous value on agreement in prayer. Matthew quotes Christ's words on prayer agreement in the context of the way you should react when your brother sins against you and any disciplinary action of the church that may be involved. In this context Jesus states three general principles, very broad in their application and impact. They are all interrelated in this teaching concerning prayer (Matt. 18:18–20).

1. God's people have been given power of binding and loosing (v. 18).
2. God's people have special power by agreement in prayer (v. 19).
3. God's people are assured of Christ's presence when they meet together for prayer (v. 20).

These principles are laws of the kingdom and laws of prayer that far transcend dealing with an erring brother. They are true for all of prayer as it relates to the total interests of Christ's kingdom.

United prayer is probably the most powerful expression of Christian unity, and to agree in prayer is the most specific and powerful form of united prayer. It is the crowning activity in group prayer. It does not replace private prayer but builds upon it. United prayer does not necessarily lead to it, but it is always possible.

There is cumulative power in united praying, as the Bible and Christian experience prove. Prayer reaches its climax when it becomes a prayer of accord, a prayer of agreement. This form of prayer either may be chosen and used directly under the guidance of the Spirit, or it may be reached through a process of prevailing prayer by a smaller or larger group of God's people.

Jesus placed solemn emphasis on this teaching by saying, "Amen" (or "I tell you the truth," NIV). "Whatever you bind on earth will be bound in heaven" (Matt. 18:18). "Again [implying a second amen], I tell you [emphasizing the significance of what He is about to say] that if two of you on earth agree about anything you ask for . . ." (v. 19).

Jesus is emphasizing many wonderful truths in the short space of three verses:

1. *This is momentous truth.* He says, in effect, "Amen, amen"—which has been translated "Verily, verily, I say unto you," or "I tell you the truth."

2. *It is for practical life and God's kingdom activities.* "On earth" is repeated twice. It is for you and me living day by day for the glory of God and concerned about the extension of His kingdom.

3. *It is for believers as part of His body, the church.* It is so simple that it is available wherever God's people are. It will even hold true if only two believers are involved together.

4. *It is accomplished through prayer.* Whether binding or loosing, or any other kind of Christian concern, it is a guaranteed method for God's results in prayer.

5. *It is for every practical matter of kingdom business.* Jesus used the word *pragma,* from which we get our word *pragmatic.* The phrase *pantos pragmatos* we could translate "every practical matter."

6. *It is specially done by uniting in prayer.* Any number of

people from two to ten thousand might be involved. It makes use of the cumulative effect of united prayer.

7. *It requires total unity, harmony, and agreement in prayer.* The Greek verb is *symphōneō* (lit., "sound together"), from which we get our word *symphony.* When the many and diverse instruments of a great orchestra all sound as one in perfect harmony, we call it a symphony. We must pray till there is a total symphony of agreement among those praying.

8. *Jesus Himself is present.* Not only is He there in His omnipresence, He is there in a very personal way as Head of the church. He does not promise to come and join His believers, for He is already there waiting for them (note "there am I" in v. 20). He is specially, significantly, and purposely present in an even more wonderful way among His people whenever they meet to agree in prayer.

9. *This is a special prayer of beautiful harmony, total agreement, and sweet symphony.* It is made possible and guaranteed effective by Christ's own presence. He is the great, eternal, and moment-by-moment Intercessor. He lives to intercede (Heb. 7:25). He is thrilled that we are joining to pray and desires us to agree fully in prayer. He instantly, moment by moment, joins our agreement, our symphony of prayer. How can such prayer fail to be effective? Whenever two meet together, there are really three. When three meet together, there are really four. When twenty-five meet together, there are twenty-six. Jesus Himself is always there, joining in the united prayer, and especially so in the agreement of prayer.

THE POWER IN PRAYER OF AGREEMENT

If everyone who asks receives and everyone who seeks finds, and if to everyone who knocks, the door is opened (Matt. 7:7), then how much more can be expected when two, five, or ten unitedly ask, seek, and knock? Spurgeon preached, "If one Jacob can prevail over a wrestling angel, what can two do? What victory would come to two joined in the same wrestling! 'One of you shall chase a thousand and two put ten thousand to flight!' There is accumulated power in united intercession; two do not only double the force, but multiply it tenfold." He then added, "God grant to each of us a praying partner."[1]

If Jesus is present with every believer, adding His amen to each prayer in the will of God (Rev. 3:14), how much more is Jesus fully present in adding His amen when His children unite in prayer.

To Jesus, the prayer of agreement is the most meaningful of all prayer. The prayer of two or three in real symphony far outweighs the normal praying about the same request by thousands who have no true unity of heart-cry, no determination to see God's will effected, and no really prevailing intercession.

Jesus referred to two gathering "in my name" (Matt. 18:20). The Greek is literally, "into my name." This wording implies entering into all that the name of Jesus includes. We not only believe in Christ, we pray together in commitment to Christ, sharing His love, sensing His heartbeat and the priorities of His will.

The name of Jesus, when we are sure we are praying in accordance with God's holy will, gives us confidence in prayer, authority in prayer, and special boldness in spiritual battle. The name of Jesus should help draw us into the close unity needed in the prayer of agreement, and it should be our spiritual missile to blast through Satan's hindrances and blockade. There is power and authority in the name of Jesus.

The Holy Spirit longs to work in power, but except for deliberate sin, nothing grieves Him more than disunity, and nothing gives Him the liberty He needs to work in and through us like unity. The closer our unity, the more fully His presence can be manifested and His power appropriated by us. When the Spirit sees God's children united in the tremendous unity of the prayer of agreement, with hearts beating as one, with longings, tears, hopes, and faith blended together in holy oneness, He puts Himself into our praying. He is power, all power. He enforces the authority of Jesus. He glories in bringing victories in Jesus' name.

HOW TO AGREE IN PRAYER

When two or more Christians are willing to agree in prayer for a need, what steps can they take to make their unity in praying true agreement in heart and soul, the kind of agreement that fulfills the conditions Jesus gave in Matthew 18:19? Please do not get legalistically bound to take consciously each of these steps or to follow this exact sequence. Rather, these are aspects that the Spirit will use and in which you can seek the Spirit's help as you seek to agree in prayer that prevails.

1. *Agree in the assessment of the need.* Seek to unite in seeing the need for which you pray, the reasons for the need, and the urgency. The more you unitedly understand and feel the need, the more your spirits cry to God as one as you intercede. Seek God's perspective on why it is important to Him. Seek to be completely unbiased, to see it as God's sees it.

2. *Agree in deep hunger for God's answer.* Perhaps God has already given each of you a real hunger to see God move in answering this prayer. But as you face it together before God's throne, each helps deepen the hunger of the other as you agree together and "amen" each other. God may see fit to deepen your hunger until you are moved to tears as you pray. Do not hesitate to pray with tears if the Spirit gives you that depth of hunger. Tears can be precious in God's sight (Ps. 56:8). Jesus prayed with such hunger that He was moved to "loud cries and tears" (Heb. 5:7).

3. *Agree in giving God full liberty to work.* Agree with each other that God's ways are higher than your ways, that God may have a far better answer than you have even thought of (Isa. 55:8–9). Agree together that God's time is the best time, the perfect time. Agree that God does not need to show you in advance just how He plans to answer your prayers.

4. *Come to agreement in God's will in the matter.* Sensing what God desires to do regarding a need is very helpful in effective praying. You can agree in the deepest sense much more totally and powerfully when each of you is assured of God's will in the

matter. As I have indicated elsewhere, some things are always God's will. Other prayer requests are for matters about which we will not know God's will until He discloses it to us.

It is always God's will to save the lost, bless His people, revive the church, and extend His kingdom. It may or may not be God's will to give a person employment at the exact time you suggest. The person prayed for may be out of God's will in some matter, and God may be teaching a specific lesson that takes time to learn. God may need to teach that person faith. God may have a better opportunity a little later, and a host of other possibilities may be involved. Success in a particular matter, such as healing, the election of a particular person, or matters of settling a church dispute, involves many possibilities of God's having a plan that you are unaware of.

But as you pray unitedly, you can come to an increasingly clear awareness of God's will or steps you should take. As you continue praying together, His Spirit may begin to witness to you what God's will is in this matter, giving you new deep peace or joyous anticipation. You can reach a place of assurance, of real spiritual agreement.

5. *Agree in claiming an appropriate promise.* Unite in making your very own a specific promise for the specific needs. You need more than mental assent that the promise is indeed God's word. Peter said at Pentecost, "The promise is for you" (Acts 2:39). Seek to arrive at deep, united conviction that the promise is really for you, appropriate, and God's clear word for this situation about which you pray. Mental agreement is not sufficient. Pray till you get heart agreement.

You need to be united not only that the promise is available to you but that you are now firmly standing upon it. You have made it your own. Rejoice together that God has the whole world in His hands, that God has known about the need before you realized it, and that He has been working even before you began to pray.

6. *Agree in holy determination to see God's answer realized.* Is this prayer request important enough to you and to God's cause that once you unite in prayer for it, you will not give up until

you obtain the witness of God's answer? Sometimes God gives assurance that the answer has been granted before we see it actualized before our eyes. Agree that you will unite in prayer for the answer until you receive it, receive an even better answer, or until you have "prayed through" to clear assurance that God's answer is on the way.

7. *Agree in steps of obedience.* Often as you pray, God guides you to take certain steps. It may be to involve more people in praying or to set apart special prayer times or increased prayer times for the request. Perhaps God will show you something that hinders your praying. He may show you things that you must do or that the person or group you are praying for must do. Every act of obedience to which God guides you will increase your faith. You often need to prepare the way of the Lord by obedience.

8. *Agree in giving God all the glory.* It may not be essential for others to know that you were praying. Sometimes that knowledge is important to a person being prayed for, but often it is better to say nothing. The answer is God's answer. Don't touch the glory that belongs to God alone. Stay in the background. Don't seek glory for your church, organization, or family or have any selfish motive. It is very easy for self to enter so subtly into your praying that you are unaware of it. Much prayer for success is more concerned for self than for God. Agree together that God shall have all the glory.

CHAPTER 21

Mighty Answers Through Agreeing in Prayer

THERE ARE THRILLING biblical examples of agreement in prayer. When Moses faced the problems of disobedient, unbelieving Israel, he and Aaron repeatedly agreed in prayer. We first see it when the Amalekites attacked Israel at Rephidim. Moses, Aaron, and Hur climbed a hill, and Aaron and Hur upheld Moses' hands in prayer. This action symbolized their agreement in prayer (Exod. 17:8–16). Moses reported afterward, "Hands were lifted up to the throne of the LORD" (v. 16). Primarily, they were the hands of Moses, but united with Moses were the hands of Aaron and Hur.

At Kadesh-Barnea when Israel wanted to turn back to Egypt, "Moses and Aaron fell facedown" in prayer before the Lord (Num 14:5). When God was about to destroy the whole community of Israel who had rallied with Korah in rebellion, Moses and Aaron again fell facedown before the Lord (16:22). The next day (v. 45) and when Israel grumbled from thirst (20:6), we see them again on their faces agreeing before God.

During Jesus' ministry on earth we have no proof that His disciples ever agreed in prayer with Him. No doubt Christ often longed for such prayer, especially in Gethsemane (Matt.

26:38–45). Most probably much of the ten days in the Upper Room were spent in united prayer. But as their prayer time continued, they most probably came to the place where they were united in the prayer of agreement for the promised Holy Spirit. It may well be that the Spirit delayed His coming until the 120 were totally agreed in prayer (Acts 1:14; 2:1). Certainly in Acts 4:24–31 the now Spirit-filled Upper Room group was praying in agreement.

Peter and John prayed the prayer of agreement in Samaria (Acts 8:5–17), and many of the church did when Peter was in prison (12:5, 12). It seems the early church missionary movement of Paul and Barnabas was launched through such a prayer meeting (13:2–3). Though absent in body from the church in Corinth, Paul may have been praying the prayer of agreement with them (1 Cor. 5:4).

The Methodist Pentecost in London was obviously a time of prayer of agreement. Wesley's journal of January 1, 1739, records how he, his brother Charles, George Whitefield, and more than sixty others were praying. "About three in the morning, as we were continuing instant in prayer, the power of God came mightily upon us, insomuch that many cried out for exceeding joy, and many fell to the ground. As soon as we were recovered a little from that awe and amazement at the presence of His majesty, we broke out with one voice, 'We praise Thee, O God, we acknowledge thee to be the Lord.'"[1]

REVIVAL IN INDIA

Pandita Ramabai, who died in 1922, was born in a very religious Hindu home. By the time she was twelve years old, she could recite eighteen thousand verses of the Hindu scriptures. She was wonderfully converted to Jesus Christ and set up a boarding school in 1899, later expanding it into a women's home. Her settlement at Kedgaon near Pune, India, grew to a community of over 1,300. In 1901 God sent much blessing, and 1,200 were converted and baptized in two months.

In 1904, when God sent tremendous revival to Wales, a

Welsh missionary in India wrote home, begging the people to pray that God would send revival to India. A large group of coal miners began to meet daily at the entrance to the mine for a half-hour before dawn, agreeing in prayer for revival in India. After some weeks of prayer, they received the message, "Revival has come to India."

In the meantime, news of the revival in Wales reached Ramabai, and she started daily prayer meetings for revival in India. By June 1905, there were 550 meeting twice daily to agree in prayer for revival. One day one of the girls was filled with the Holy Spirit and was so transformed that soon girls all over the grounds were on their knees weeping and confessing their sins.

The next evening during the evening prayer, the Holy Spirit came in power upon the girls with the spirit of repentance and a spirit of intercession. Little children, teenage girls, and young women were weeping and confessing. Two little girls prayed for hours for revival. One day some of the girls asked a staff member what Luke 12:49 meant, where Jesus said, "I have come to bring fire on the earth." They determined to pray for this fire. As they agreed in prayer, revival deepened, "the work went on, and a spirit of prayer and supplication for a revival in India was poured out like a flood. . . . Waves of prayer go over the meetings like the rolling thunder; hundreds pray audibly together." Seven hundred girls and women gave themselves to prayer.[2]

Each day about sixty went out by turns to help evangelize. One party of these girls came to a town where there was a missionary and asked him for permission to stay and pray for his work. They asked for a hall or shed, any place where they could pray. He gave them permission.

That evening an Indian pastor came to his door, began to weep, and said that God had convicted him of sin and that he felt he had to come and confess his wrongdoing. After he received assurance of God's forgiveness, another Christian arrived under deep conviction of sin. Then followed a succession of one after another, people coming under deep conviction of sin. No meeting had been announced, but it was the Holy Spirit working in answer to the prayer of agreement of these children and girls. "There was a remarkable time of blessing. Backsliders were restored, believers were sanctified, and heathen brought into the fold."

One group of Ramabai's girls went to northwest India to Rawalpindi, which is now a part of Pakistan. They began immediately to have meetings of united prayer. One prayer meeting lasted six hours. A missionary lady looked out about midnight and was surprised to see a light burning in one of the girls' tents, which was contrary to rules. She went to correct the girl and found a girl of fifteen kneeling in the farthest corner with a little candle in one hand and a list of five hundred girls' names in her other hand. She was interceding one by one, hour after hour, before the Lord. Again, God poured out His blessing.

The Holy Spirit, through agreement in prayer by coal miners in Wales, coordinated with the united prayer of Ramabai's girls, sent revival to place after place and brought hundreds to Christ. In the meantime, revival fires broke out hundreds of miles away in other parts of India, in the Khasi hills in northeast India, where Welsh missionaries were laboring and praying.

OTHER EXAMPLES

At the beginning of this century there was a member of Congress from New England who had been reared in a godly family but who later became an infidel and lectured against God and the Bible.

His wife was a nominal Christian but was led to make a full surrender of her life to Christ. God then gave her a great desire for the salvation of her husband. She and other Christians made an agreement to intercede each day for her husband until he became a Christian. One night as she knelt beside her bed praying for her husband's salvation, God asked her, "Are you willing for the results that will come if your husband is converted?" Three times this question came. She told God she was ready to pay the price if only her husband would come to Him.

That very night her husband was sitting in Congress. It was during a presidential election, and excited and heated speeches were being made in Congress. Suddenly he got the feeling that the God he had been trying to disprove was just above him, looking down on him, and displeased with him. He thought to himself, "This is ridiculous; I guess I have been working too hard. I'll go get a good meal and take a long walk, and shake myself and see if that will take this feeling away." He did, but when he resumed his seat in Congress, he felt that God was right above him, looking down on him with displeasure. This feeling continued for some days, and day after day he took walks trying to shake it off.

He went back to meet his constituency because he had ambitions to be the next governor of his state and seemed to be in line for the position as candidate of the dominant party. He had hardly entered his home when his wife announced to him that she and a group of ladies had made a covenant of prayer that he would become a Christian. He casually asked, "When did this thing begin, this praying of yours?" She told him the date, and he knew it was the very day when he began to feel God was looking down upon him. He was tremendously shaken. That night he went to a little Methodist church where special meetings were in progress. The second night he went back and was converted. God called him to preach, and he gave up politics and entered the ministry.[3]

An Anglican church in Britain many years ago had a prayer meeting each Sunday morning before the eight o'clock Communion service. As the people arose from their knees one Sunday, a man asked the pastor, "I wish you would pray for my boy. He is twenty-two years old now and has not been to church for years." The pastor proposed that they stop immediately and pray for five minutes. They earnestly united together in prayer. Nothing was said to the young man, but that night he came to the church, was deeply convicted by the message, stayed behind brokenhearted, and received Christ as his Savior.

The next morning one of the church staff said to the pastor, "That conversion last night is a challenge to prayer—a challenge from God. Shall we accept it?" "What do you mean?" asked the pastor. "Well," he said, "shall we single out the worst man in the parish and pray for him?" After discussion, they all decided on a Mr. K. as the most sinful person they knew. They all agreed together in prayer for his conversion and began to hold on in prayer each day. At the end of the week, during a Saturday night prayer meeting, while someone was actually praying by name for this man, the door swung open, and in he staggered in a very intoxicated condition. He had never been inside the building before. Without removing his cap, he sat on a chair and buried his face in his hands. Before the prayer meeting was over, God had sobered the man and saved him, and he later became a Christian worker.[4]

Is there someone you hunger to see come to Christ who is now rejecting God? Do you hunger deeply enough to pray a costly spiritual price, if need be, to see God's answer? Do you have one or two or perhaps more people so united in spirit with you, so sharing your burden, that you can agree together in prayer? Be sure there is nothing in your life or any matter of obedience that is blocking you. Be sure that your motive is for God's glory and not to be known that you prayed the prayer that was answered. Then prove God's promise. It is there waiting for you to claim.

CHAPTER 22

The Dynamic of Perseverance

"JESUS TOLD HIS disciples a parable to show them that they should always pray and not give up" (Luke 18:1). He told the parable of the unjust judge who was not interested in justice but became so tired of a widow's coming to him and bothering him by asking for justice that he finally said, "I will see that she gets justice, so that she won't eventually wear me out" (v. 5). Jesus did not teach that God was like the judge. Far from it. He taught that we should be like the widow, who would not give up till she got her answer. Jesus was teaching persevering commitment and persevering faith.

The dynamic of perseverance is essential in most prevailing prayer. In George Mueller's autobiography we read his formula for prevailing prayer. "It is not enough to begin to pray, nor to pray aright; nor is it enough to continue for a time to pray; but we must patiently, believing, continue in prayer until we obtain an answer."[1]

When you are sure that you know the will of God concerning a matter that God has placed upon your heart, do not give up till you know you have prevailed and God has lifted the prayer burden from you. Bengel wrote, "A Christian should not leave off praying till his heavenly Father gives him leave, by permitting him to obtain."[2]

Emotions are useful in prayer. We pray best when we feel deeply, but our emotions should not guide our praying. Discouragement in prayer is usually an emotional condition. It does not indicate the will of God. Once you have discerned God's spiritual goals in your circumstances and in the lives of those about you, persevere till you receive God's answers.

GIVE GOD TIME TO ANSWER

Many prayers are granted by God but given up by the ones praying because they stopped praying before the answer arrived. Undelivered prayers help no one. Without the dynamic of persistence much prayer remains unanswered.

Daniel prayed with fasting until, on the twenty-first day, the angel Gabriel finally delivered him the answer. He said, "Since the first day that you set your mind ... to humble yourself before your God, your words were heard, and I have come in response to them" (Dan. 10:12). But the angel revealed that a demonic ruler "resisted me twenty-one days" until Michael, another archangel, came to help him (v. 13). Then the answer granted three weeks earlier was delivered. What if Daniel had stopped praying on the twentieth day? He would have missed the answer God desired to give him.

There are important reasons why you need to give God time:

1. *Sometimes demonic resistance delays God's answer until you and heaven prevail.*

2. *Sometimes it takes time for separate parts of complex situations to fit together.* God knows the perfect time to give maximum results.

3. *Sometimes it takes time for God to coordinate circumstances to bring pressure on a person* until that one becomes willing to do what God wants him or her to do.

George Mueller began praying for five unsaved friends. After five years, one came to Christ. After ten more years of prayer, two more were converted. Once Mueller said in

Chicago, "I have prayed for two men by name every day for thirty-five years; on land or sea, sick or well, I have remembered them before God by name. . . . I shall continue to pray for them daily, by name, until they are saved, or die." After thirty-five years of prayer, the fourth was saved. Mueller prayed almost fifty-two years, and the fifth was saved just after Mueller's death.[3]

John Newton's mother was a very godly person. Because of her tuberculosis she knew she would soon die. Every day she prayed with and for John and taught him the Scriptures. When he was seven years old, she died. Neither his father nor his stepmother was interested in spiritual things. He first went to sea at the age of eleven on his father's ship. He became very wicked, constantly blaspheming the name of God. He repeatedly escaped death by the narrowest margin.

Newton tried to get as far away as he could from any sacred influence. He became involved in the slave trade and was employed by a Portuguese man married to an African woman. While the man was gone, his evil wife chained John, made him her slave, and gave him almost no food or clothing. After fifteen months he escaped but went deeper and deeper into drunkenness, revelry, and blasphemy. At the age of twenty-eight a severe illness prevented him from going to sea again.

He later was won to Christ and had fellowship with Whitefield, Wesley, and others. He began to study Greek and Hebrew and in six years had become a preacher of the gospel. He later became the most famous minister in London. Among those he led to Christ were Thomas Scott, the commentator, and William Wilberforce, who led in the eradication of slavery from the British Empire. His numerous hymns still bless the church, including "Amazing Grace," his autobiographical hymn.

John Newton won thousands to Christ, and when he died, Parliament closed, London shops closed, and several thousand followed his body to the cemetery. His mother's prayers had prevailed in spite of all Satan's efforts to destroy her son and keep him from becoming God's instrument. After twenty-two years, during which he faced death again and again, God's individualized, providential circumstances finally brought him to Christ, answering his mother's persevering prayers.

William Carey labored and prayed for seven years before he baptized his first convert in India. Judson prayed, prevailed, and suffered for seven years in Burma before he won his first disciple. Morrison prayed and labored for seven years before he brought his first Chinese person to Christ. Moffatt prayed, persevered, and prevailed for seven years before the Holy Spirit moved upon the Bechunanas of Africa. And Richards labored and prayed for seven years in the Congo before the first convert was found. Their prayers were heard all those years. But they had to persevere until God answered.[4]

4. *Sometimes it takes time for God to prune from your own life things that are hindering your prayer.* Study John 15:2. Of all fruit-bearing plants, vines, and trees, none requires so much pruning as does the vine, which must be pruned each year. Abraham, Moses, Elijah, Paul—all became very fruitful as God pruned their lives. You may have attitudes, activities, friendships, habits, possessions, spiritual idols, or other things that are hindering your prayer. Perhaps it is taking time for God to get you to the place where He is first in your life and prayer is first in your lifestyle. When you reach the place of fruitfulness, you will be amazed at your answers to prayer.

5. *Sometimes time is needed for the cumulative effect of a great amassing of prayer.* When a dam is erected in a mountain valley, its construction may take many months. Then the water begins accumulating behind the dam, which can take months or even a year or longer. But when the water level reaches the right height, the sluice gates are opened, water begins to turn the generators, and there is tremendous power.

Perhaps at times something similar happens in the spiritual realm. As more and more people unite in prayer or as the prevailing person prays on and on, it seems as if a great mass of prayer is accumulated until suddenly there is a breakthrough and God's will is accomplished. Revelation 5:8 and 8:3–5 assure us that prayers prayed in the will of God are never lost but are stored until God gives the answer. J. Oswald Sanders states, "There is a cumulative effect in prayer. The focusing of many prayers on one life or on a situation can change defeat into victory." And again, "Both Scripture and experience unite to indicate that there is cumulative power in united praying."[5]

Frank Laubach has said, "Prayer is the mightiest power on earth. Enough of us, if we prayed enough, could save the world—if we prayed enough!"[6] God has not promised that the whole world would be saved by prayer, but undoubtedly there are many situations that could be totally changed by the amassing of the prayer of God's persevering intercessors.

A Christian young lady was a very loving, faithful, and earnest Sunday school teacher. As she taught her class for a period of time, one by one the children gave their hearts to Jesus. She was requested to give that class over to someone else and take another class. Again, one by one the students in that class committed their lives to Jesus. After some time, she was persuaded to give up this class and take a third class of children. Again there were the same results, and every one of the children was converted.

She was very faithful in keeping a daily diary, and after her death friends discovered three entries in the journal. First, "Resolved that I will pray once each day for each member of my class by name." A later entry added the words, "and agonize in prayer." Sometime later in the journal were these words: "Resolved that I will pray once each day for each member of my class by name and agonize in prayer and expect a blessing."[7]

Fraser, who saw the victories of persevering, prevailing prayer in China, wrote, "The longer the preparation, the deeper the work. . . . I do not believe that any deep work of God takes root without long preparation somewhere."[8]

There is always a mystery in the timing of God's answers. It is a mystery to us because we cannot see as God sees. If we saw as completely as God does, we would understand what God means by "the proper time." "Let us not become weary in doing good, for at the proper time we will reap a harvest if we do not give up" (Gal. 6:9).

Monica, the mother of Augustine, prayed fervently day after day as she prevailed for her sinful, rebellious son. It seemed to her that Augustine was like a man asleep in a boat that was nearing the edge of a cataract and that he might at any time be dashed to his death. He was wasting his mind and his body, showing no spiritual concern. But she followed him with her prayer wherever he went. We are told, "Sleep went from her." After twenty years of prevailing intercession, God wonderfully saved Augustine and made him one of the great leaders of the early church.

The father of John G. Paton, the famous missionary to the Hebrides, was mighty in prevailing prayer as, night after night in his little Scotch home, he audibly interceded for the unsaved of his village and the world. The most immoral, sinful woman in the village repeatedly said that the only thing that kept her from suicide and hell was that at times in winter nights she would creep close to the window of the Paton home, where she could hear Mr. Paton interceding in prayer. She heard him ask God that He would convert "the sinner from the error of his wicked ways and polish him as a jewel for the Redeemer's crown." She realized that she was a burden on the heart of Mr. Paton and believed that God would not disappoint him. That thought, she said, was what kept her out of hell and at last led her to repentance and the forgiveness of sin.[9]

6. *Sometimes the answer is delayed because Satan is so entrenched.* Jesus taught that some cases of demon possession required more prayer and fasting than others, commenting once, "This kind can come out only by prayer" (Mark 9:29, many ancient manuscripts add "and fasting"). Whether "this kind" refers to a special kind of demon or a demon in a special level of authority, or whether it refers to a special kind of situation, it is a call for increased prayer.

Some people are possessed by more than one demon (Matt. 12:43–45). Luke, the physician, describes a man with a host—a legion—of demons (Luke 8:30). A legion in the Roman army

154

was composed of three to six thousand soldiers. Obviously, this symbolizes a very large number.

Spiritually sensitive people have sometimes been aware of greater spiritual darkness and resistance in certain geographical areas. Satan seems more entrenched, particularly in areas where there has been much Satan worship in its various forms, occult practices, or idolatry. It often requires prolonged prayer or amassed prevailing prayer before spiritual breakthrough comes in such places.

Similarly, the pioneer missionaries in a number of countries had to pray and sacrificially labor for some years before the first convert came to Christ. Satan does not want Christ to get a foothold in any place that he stubbornly claims for himself.

CHAPTER 23

How Long Must You Persevere?

1. *PERSEVERE IN PRAVAILING prayer as long as Christ does.* You are chosen to be Christ's prayer partner. He has seated you in the heavenlies beside Him on His throne. You are to join His rule of intercessory grace by joining your prayers with His. He still loves. He still longs. He still intercedes. You dare not give up while He is praying. Don't fail Him by stopping to pray while He is still interceding. As far as Scripture reveals, prayer is Christ's major work today. "If we then are to have fellowship with Jesus Christ in his present work, we must spend much time in prayer; we must give ourselves to earnest, constant, persistent, sleepless, overcoming prayer."[1]

2. *Persevere in prevailing as long as the Holy Spirit gives you desire.* Charles Finney taught that whenever you have a desire for the good of another one, "there is a strong presumption that the Spirit of God is exciting these very desires, and stirring you up to pray for that object."[2] A holy concern, desire, or hunger in your heart for the welfare of another person, particularly for their salvation or a similar hunger to see God work in any particular situation, is always an evidence that the Holy Spirit is

156

conveying to you the heartbeat of God. You can be sure it is the will of God the Father to grant that prayer in accordance with the intercession of God the Son and with the infinite desire of God the Spirit. Don't become weary. Pray on.

3. *Persevere in prevailing as long as Satan keeps resisting and hindering.* If what you are praying for is of little importance to Satan, he will give up more easily and concentrate on what is important to him. But the more strategic a prayer answer is to the kingdom of God, the more Satan will fight to keep you from the answer to your prayer.

Satan fears prayer more than almost anything else we could ever do. Prevailing prayer is potentially the greatest continuing threat to Satan that there has been since Calvary. Nothing will please him more than to get you to stop or neglect a strategic prayer request. Hold on. If Satan is fighting, your persevering in prayer is worth all that it costs.

Paul urged, "Devote yourselves to prayer, being watchful and thankful" (Col. 4:2; or, "persevere in prayer," NEB). Martin Luther said, "To pray diligently is more than half the task."[3] But half the answer is not an answer. We must pray until.

PERSEVERE UNTIL

Don't give up at the very time God's answer is nearing, at the very time the angels have almost delivered to you the answer for which you have been praying. Instead, your prayer then should be strongest. What is the great difference between Luther, Knox, Wesley, Finney, Edwards, Brainerd, Praying Hyde, and a host of other prevailers, and so many who pray casually today? Those people of God refused to give up till God's answer came. "Whether we like it or not, asking is the rule of the kingdom," said Spurgeon.[4]

How long were the disciples to tarry in Jerusalem? "Until you have been clothed with power from on high" (Luke 24:49). How long did Moses keep his hands raised to God in prayer? Until Amalek was totally defeated (Exod. 17:13). How long did Joshua hold out his javelin toward Ai while the army attacked?

Until Jericho was destroyed (Josh. 8:26). How long did Elijah stay on his knees in prevailing prayer after the three years' drought? Until rain clouds formed in the sky (1 Kings 18:44). How long did Jesus pray in Gethsemane? Until Satan was defeated. How long did the disciples continue in prayer in the Upper Room? Until the Holy Spirit came upon them. No matter what our prayer request, if God has led us to pray for a need that we believe is the will of God, how long should we pray? Until the answer comes!

PREVAILING INVOLVES TIME

Prevailing in prayer until God's answer is given involves the investment of time. Any prayer answer worthy of prevailing prayer is worth all the time that you can invest in it. It may involve time spent in prayer on repeated occasions as well as a priority on your heart, so that you return to this special petition whenever you have free time.

Persevering prayer takes time. Alexander Whyte said, "Prayer worth calling prayer, prayer that God will call true prayer and will treat as true prayer, takes far more time by the clock than one man in a thousand thinks."[5]

Bounds adds, "Prayer which is felt as a mighty force is the mediate or immediate product of much time spent with God. Our short prayers owe their point and efficiency to the long ones that have preceded them. The short, prevailing prayer cannot be prayed by one who has not prevailed in a mightier struggle of long continuance.[6]

Samuel Chadwick emphasized, "To pray as God would have us pray is the greatest achievement of earth. Such a life costs. It takes time."[7]

When Jesus said, "Give . . . to God what is God's" (Matt. 22:21), He surely included a major portion of our time as due to God. The Lord's Day belongs to God, and it is a great day to spend in prevailing prayer for the church, the community, loved ones, unsaved friends, and God's work on the mission

158

field. How much time do you average alone with Jesus on His day?

So often we let the good rob us of the best. Our days are so filled with church activities that we do not have time to cover these activities adequately with prayer. Probably if we had half the activities we do but prepared for each one by hours of prayer by our people, we could see far greater results. We even let the television, newspaper, and casual, almost meaningless, social conversation rob us of time on the Lord's Day. We fail to make it a day of prayer. It would probably be far more spiritually profitable for you now—and for those you pray for, in eternity—if you watched one or two less Christian telecasts on Sunday or any other day and spent that time in intercession.

Let me urge you to set apart a period of hours on the Lord's Day to prevail for your prayer priorities. Perhaps God will often guide you to fast for one or more meals to add more time and intensity to your prevailing. If we are really serious about prevailing, there is a way to find time. But a person unwilling to sacrifice some good things in order to have time to prevail with God should not expect great answers from God.

E. M. Bounds teaches, "God does not bestow His gifts on the casual or hasty comers and goers. Much with God alone is the secret of knowing Him and of influence with Him."[8]

Jacob prayed all night when he prevailed in prayer. Elijah prayed seven times in succession before he prevailed for rain out of a cloudless sky. Daniel, a busy minister of state in the capital of the Persian empire, had to schedule his time in order to go home and pray three times a day. David, though king, prayed morning, noon, and night.

We do not know how long these Bible saints prevailed in prayer. We do not know how long our Lord prayed when He got up early in the morning to get alone with the Father. He seems to have spent some three hours in Gethsemane on the night of His arrest. But it is suggested that He had gone there night after night for similar prayer time (Luke 22:39). He prayed for our world because He loved our world. He still prays today because He still loves us and our world today.

We cannot really love our unsaved friends very much if we are unwilling to pay the price of prevailing for them in prayer. The "Unknown Christian," who blessed many by his writings during the early decades of our century, wrote, "The wonder is ... that we can ever get up from our knees if we realize our own need; the needs of our home and our loved ones; the needs of our pastor and the church; the needs of our city—of our country—of the heathen and Mohammedan world!"[9]

PLAN YOUR PRAYER TIME

We will never have enough time for prevailing prayer unless we deliberately plan for it. Our days will become as crowded as we permit. The time we give to prayer by deliberately planning is the measure of our value of prayer. It is the measure of our love for those for whom we pray. It is the measure—perhaps the truest measure—of our love for Jesus. It is cheap to sing about our love for Jesus and then not take time with Him in joyous communion and tearful burden sharing of His intercession.

Obviously, you do not engage in prevailing prayer for a large number of requests at the same time. Usually you will seek to prevail for one main priority request, or at the most for two or three main heart-cries. You may have many items on your prayer list and may carry a continuing burden for many items on your heart. But true prevailing focuses on one or two priorities at a time, seeing them through to the assurance of victory. You need not neglect your continuing requests to prevail specially for one or more urgent needs.

Just as prayer should be a major priority in your life, so in prevailing prayer you must seek the Spirit's guidance as to what your priorities are during the time of prevailing. Normally when the Spirit guides you to a priority, you keep major focus on it until you know you have prevailed and have the Spirit's inner assurance that your prayer is granted by God. Many people have referred to this experience as "praying through."

PERSEVERE TILL YOU "PRAY THROUGH"

During my college years one of my fellow students was out witnessing in a slum area one cold night. As he witnessed to a drunk outside a tavern door, the derelict said, "Oh, yes! It is all right for you to stand there in your warm coat and talk about Jesus. What has Jesus ever done for me?" Instantly the student took off his warm overcoat and put it around the shoulders of the shivering, coatless drunk.

When he came back to college, he prayed until he prayed through for another coat. He testified to the rest of us students that God had given him a new coat. For several days, however, he was without an overcoat but was always cheerful. Then God gave him a new coat, and he praised God for it before us all. But he added, "I was already wearing this coat (by faith) for several days before I actually received it."

Parents have prayed through for the salvation of a wayward child and rejoiced in God's answer to prayer for some time before their son or daughter actually submitted their life to the Lord. They were able to rejoice in the assurance of answered prayer before they had any visible evidence of it. In fact, sometimes the child seemed more rebellious and wayward just before the visible answer to prayer came.

Charles Blanchard, who was president of Wheaton College for forty-three years, shares this testimony, which he heard in person and later verified.

Friends, about two and a half or three years ago I was in the hospital in Philadelphia. I was an engineer on the Pennsylvania Lines, and although I had a praying wife, I had all my life been a sinful man. At this time I was very ill. I became greatly wasted. I weighed less than one hundred pounds.

Finally the doctor who was attending me said to my wife that I was dead, but she said: "No, he is not dead. He cannot be dead. I have prayed for him for twenty-seven years and God has promised me that he would be saved. Do you think God would let him die now after I have prayed twenty-seven years and God has promised, and he is not saved?" "Well," the

161

doctor replied, "I do not know anything about that, but I know that he is dead." And the screen was drawn around the cot, which in the hospital separates between the living and the dead.

To satisfy my wife, other physicians were brought, one after another, until seven were about the cot, and each one of them as he came up and made the examination confirmed the testimony of all who had preceded. The seven doctors said that I was dead. Meanwhile my wife was kneeling by the side of my cot, insisting that I was not dead,—that if I were dead God would bring me back, for He had promised her that I should be saved and I was not yet saved. By and by her knees began to pain her, kneeling on the hard hospital floor. She asked the nurse for a pillow and the nurse brought her a pillow upon which she kneeled.

One hour, two hours, three hours passed. The screen still stood by the cot. I was lying there still, apparently dead. Four hours, five hours, six hours, seven hours, thirteen hours passed, and all this while my wife was kneeling by the cotside, and when people remonstrated and wished her to go away she said: "No, he has to be saved. God will bring him back if he is dead. He is not dead. He cannot die until he is saved."

At the end of thirteen hours I opened my eyes, and she said, "What did you wish, my dear?" And I said: "I wish to go home," and she said: "You shall go home." But when she proposed it, the doctors raised their hands in horror. They said, "Why, it will kill him. It will be suicide." She said: "You have had your turn. You said he was dead already. I am going to take him home."

I weigh now 246 pounds. I still run a fast train on the Pennsylvania Lines. I have been out to Minneapolis on a little vacation, telling men what Jesus can do, and I am glad to tell you what Jesus can do.[10]

CHAPTER 24

God's Will and Prevailing Prayer

ONE SECRET OF prevailing prayer is the inner assurance that we are praying in the will of God. The Holy Spirit is our Counselor, Father-sent and Christ-given. The Greek word *paraklētos,* used repeatedly by Jesus for the Holy Spirit (John 14:15, 26; 16:7), is very full of meaning. It is variously translated as Comforter, Helper, or Counselor.

He is our Counselor in all of life. He is specially our Helper-Counselor in prayer (Rom. 8:26–27). The Spirit always prays in accordance with God's will. He will never guide and empower us to pray contrary to the Father's will.

It gives us tremendous confidence and strength to prevail in prayer when we know God's will in the matter about which we pray. God rejoices when we unite our will with His in prevailing prayer. This is what we actually pray for in the Lord's Prayer when we pray, "Your will be done on earth."

What are the steps to assurance that you are praying in harmony with God's will?

1. *Be totally surrendered to God's will for the remainder of your life.* This position requires a definite act of absolute surrender of your whole being—your personhood, ambitions, desires, and

possessions and your present and future. Make the commitment so total and so permanent that hereafter you need only reaffirm the full surrender you have already made.

Can God do with you whatever He likes? Can He change your plans, goals, or ambitions? Can He veto your plans without explaining to you? Can He move you from one situation to another without your protesting? Is your will so surrendered that God can ask of you whatever He will? If you can answer yes to all these questions, then in the words of Bengel, you are "the Lord's property." That is what Bengel always called himself.[1]

McConkey urges, "To know the will of God we must will the will of God. Self-will is the surest and densest vale which hangs between us and the knowledge of God's will. . . . We will be amazed . . . to discover how much of our prayer life is an effort to win God over to assent to, and carry out, our own will rather than asking according to His will."[2]

Some people will have God's second best through much of their life because they failed to make and maintain full surrender. God prefers His first plan for us. But if we insist on our own will, there will be place after place where God has to give us second or third best. The more unsurrendered we are, the less we will be able to prevail in prayer.

2. *Be active in your daily surrender.* Once you have made your total surrender, do not resign yourself passively to whatever God may bring to pass. Seek actively to discover His will and to endorse His will in each situation. When you pray, "Your will be done on earth" (Matt. 6:10), you are committing yourself to seek to enforce God's will actively by prayer and obedience. You are reaching out to God's will so that you can join your will with His. After full surrender, we are not spineless, indifferent creatures. We become militantly involved in bringing God's will to pass on earth. Eagerly grasp God's will for you. Eagerly surrender to God's will in you, and eagerly give yourself to God's will through you. God's will is not done automatically by a surrendered person. It must become the passion of your soul to do and ratify God's will in everything.

164

3. *Be expectant of God's revealed will for your prayer life.* When you live in the sphere of God's will, you can expect the Holy Spirit to unfold to you step by step the acts of obedience He desires from you and the prayers He desires to pray through you. Harry Jessop says, "The will of God is a sphere with distinctive boundaries within which souls consciously dwell."[3] God wants us to understand what that will is (Eph. 5:17). "Test and approve what God's will is—His good, pleasing and perfect will" (Rom. 12:2).

Samuel Chadwick wrote, "The humblest follower of Jesus may know the Divine Will first hand. It is every man's privilege to be fully assured in the will of God. . . . Come straight to God. Do not bother other people. Lay all questions naked before Him, and He will make plain to you what is His will. When God speaks, His speech is easily understood."[4]

4. *Make God's priorities your prayer priorities.* Day by day God has a highest choice in each situation and for each life. As God shows you the prayers He wants you to pray, trust the Spirit to guide you to special urgent priorities at moments of need. You do not know who most needs your prayer or for what need God most needs your prayer at any given time.

Live in an unbroken communion with the Lord. Cultivate a listening ear. Whenever He brings a person, situation, or need vividly to your attention, make that your prayer priority for as long as God keeps the concern on your heart. If at all possible, find free moments or a quiet place where you can pray for this priority. You need not know the details—just obey the Spirit's guidance to pray at the time He suggests the need vividly to your mind.

S. D. Gordon wrote, "The Spirit . . . is the Master Pray-er. He knows God's will perfectly. He knows what best to be praying under all circumstances. And He is within you and me. He is there as a prayer-Spirit. He prompts us to pray. He calls us away to the quiet room to our knees. . . . God listening above . . . recognizes His own purposes and plans being repeated in this man down on earth by His own Spirit."[5]

5. *Through prayer, deliberately will God's will.* Now that you

know God's will in the matter you pray about, you must deliberately commit your whole self, including your will, into prayer insistence. Dare to pray militantly in regard to the situation, "Your will be done!"

Do not meekly submit to Satan's delays or to his evil workings and opposition to God's will. Boldly lay hold of God's power through prayer and resist Satan (James 4:7). Place your feet on God's promises and stand on them. Take your stand with God. Advance against Satan with God. Take the prayer offensive with Christ.

"He waits for our ministry of willing according to His will to free Him to work that will. And while we know that everything in prayer depends on God, He would have us realize that everything also depends on us."[6]

Pastor Johann Blumhardt, mightily used in prayer for the sick and in casting out demons more than a century ago in Germany, knew his power in this ministry depended upon praying according to the will of God. In his early years he often spent many hours in prayer before he knew whether it was God's will to heal a particular person for whom prayer was requested. But he testified that "after about two years he came to be so familiar with the inner voice of God that often he would scarcely have lifted his heart to God in communion ere the mind of God in the matter was clearly revealed to him."[7]

Never insist on your own way or the way of some other person. A mother insisted God heal her dying baby boy. God seemed to say to her, "Are you sure that it is best for your boy to live?" She replied, "I want him to live whether it is best or not!" The baby lived, but the mother lived to see her boy hanged as a criminal.[8]

Dr. Goodell was requested by telegram by an Anglican bishop to pray for the healing of his son who was dying. After some days a second urgent wire came requesting more earnest prayer. Dr. Goodell prayed with great earnestness but heard no result. After some years he met the bishop and asked how the son was. "I fear I did wrong in insisting. It would have been better had the Lord taken my boy at the time. He is grown now, and, oh, what sorrow is mine to see him walking in sin and wickedness."[9]

CHAPTER 25

The Dynamic of Praise

GOD HAS PREDESTINED that our Christian lives bring praise and glory to Him (Eph. 1:5-6). We are to be to His praise now and eternally (v. 14). Therefore, our lips and our lifestyle should constantly praise God. God rejoices in our praise. We are to begin His worship with praise (Ps. 100:4; Isa. 60:18). We are to praise Him with our voice (Ps. 34:1), with song (147:1), and with music (150:3). We are to be clothed with praise (Isa. 61:3), and our very lives are to be a praise to God (1 Peter 2:9).

What does praise have to do with prevailing prayer? Praise both prepares for prevailing prayer and is itself a holy means of prevailing during our prayer.

1. *Praise focuses our hearts on God.* Praise lifts our hearts to God in adoration, worship, and love. The most important fact of prevailing prayer is that it is made to God. To pray worthily, we must be supremely conscious of God. The problem or need about which we pray may seem overwhelming, but we must see God infinitely greater than our problem, able to meet all our need. Praise focuses our whole being on God.

Hallesby writes, "When I give thanks, my thoughts still

167

circle about myself, but in praise my soul ascends to self-forgetting adoration, seeing and praising only the majesty and power of God, His grace and redemption."[1]

2. *Praise cleanses our hearts of cares, fears, and earth-centered thoughts.* We need to enter God's presence and shut the door behind us on the outside world. To prevail effectively we must forget all other duties, activities, involvements, and concerns. Praise pulls the curtain over all extraneous things. Praise shuts the door on intruding ideas, our normal thought life, and satanic suggestions. It shuts you in with God and His angels.

3. *Praise begets and increases faith.* The more you praise God, the more you become God-conscious and absorbed in His greatness, wisdom, faithfulness, and love. Praise reminds you of all that God is able to do and of great things He has already done. Faith comes through God's Word and through praise. Faith grows as you praise the Lord.

Praise gives you the spirit of triumph and overcoming. Praise fires you with holy zeal. It lifts you above the battles to the perspective of God's throne. Praise cuts the enemy forces down to size. "If God is for us, who can be against us?" (Rom. 8:31). What can man do when God is with you? (Ps. 118:6; Heb. 13:6). God's angel hosts with us are more than all who oppose us (2 Kings 6:16).

August H. Francke, Lutheran minister around 1700 and founder of the orphan homes at Halle, Germany, tells of a time when he needed a large sum of money. His treasurer came to him for the money. Francke told him to come after lunch, all the while praying earnestly. After lunch the treasurer came again for the money, and Francke asked him to come in the evening. In the meantime, a friend of Dr. Francke came to see him. The two men prayed together. When Francke began to pray, God led him to recall God's goodness to humankind, going back all the way to Creation. Francke praised God over and over for His goodness and faithfulness over the centuries but felt restrained from mentioning his urgent petition. When the friend left, Francke accompanied him to the door. There stood the treasurer waiting for the money, and beside him a man who then handed Dr. Francke a very large sum of money that fully met the need.[2]

4. *Praise invokes God's presence, God's power, and God's forces.* God manifests His presence in the midst of His praise. God is enthroned among His praising creatures. God's praise seems in a special way to call Him to be active among His people, calling forth the manifestation and use of His almighty power. Nothing unites us more with the angels of God than joining in praise of God, and perhaps our worshiping and militant praise unites them in our endeavor and in the answering of our prayer. The angels ceaselessly minister to us (Heb. 1:14), but surely never more than when we prevail in prayer, even as they ministered to Jesus in Gethsemane.

Huegel tells of a pastor who longed for new awakening in his church. He convened a week's meetings of nothing but praise. At first the people did not understand and kept asking and begging God for things. But the pastor kept explaining that he wanted nothing but praise. By Wednesday the service began to change. Thursday saw much praise, and even more was evident on Friday. By Sunday "a new day had dawned. Sunday was a day such as the church had never seen. It was genuine revival. God's glory filled the temple. Believers returned to their first love. Hearts were melted. . . . It was wonderful. Praise had done it."[3]

5. *Praise confounds, terrifies, restrains, and thwarts Satan.* Praise beats back the powers of darkness, scatters the demon opponents, and frustrates Satan's strategies. Praise takes the initiative out of Satan's hands. It is a tremendous means of resisting Satan and causing him to flee. A Spirit-filled, anointed, and empowered believer can assault the strongholds of Satan by praise. Hezekiah, Isaiah, and the Israel of their day are not the only ones who have routed the enemy by praise.

During my missionary days in India, students and staff of the girls' Bible school of another society were praying and fasting for a demon-possessed student to be delivered. I was called to help but felt so helpless. As I prayed, I was impressed to go to the struggling, semiconscious girl being held down by several adults as they tried to control her thrashing and jerking.

I called into her ear, "Jai Masih Ki" (victory to Christ), the idiomatic way to say "Praise the Lord" in her language. As I called this sentence into her ear, she began to respond, as if she could hear what I was saying. Then she struggled to control her locked mouth, and when she finally forced it open, called out after me, "Jai Masih Ki." Instantly she was delivered. Prayer and fasting probably helped prepare the way, but praise was the Spirit's weapon to set her free.

Huegel, an experienced missionary to Mexico, has said that often when prayer does not bring the answer, adding praise will lead to victory. He states, "There is power in praise which prayer does not have. Of course, the distinction between the two is artificial. . . . The highest expression of faith is not prayer in its ordinary sense of petition, but prayer in its sublimest expression of praise."[4]

CHAPTER 26

Levels of Intensity in Prevailing Prayer

SCRIPTURE SUGGESTS SEVERAL levels of intensity in prevailing prayer. In order to help you prevail, the Holy Spirit may lead you to use any of these levels of prayer. Some prevailing prayer is very brief. Thank God, often we prevail in a few moments of intercession. These times are not necessarily predictable. In many emergencies, when we have been living the life of an intercessor, we will be able to pray the prayer of faith in a moment of need or in the short space of time available.

Thank God also that when there are needs that require the united prayer of prayer partners, a local church, or even larger groups, the Holy Spirit can guide you to take the necessary steps. Similarly, when a need is not met by simple asking, the Spirit may lead you step by step into very intensive forms of prayer.

LEVEL ONE: ASKING

Asking is the most simple, most basic form of prayer. A new believer, a small child, a seriously ill person—anyone can ask. Intercession and prevailing prayer begin with asking. God

171

always hears when we ask. Jesus Himself commanded us to ask and assured us our asking would be answered. "If you believe, you will receive whatever you ask for in prayer" (Matt. 21:22). God gives the Holy Spirit to those who ask (Luke 11:13). "I will do whatever you ask in my name. . . . You may ask me for anything in my name, and I will do it" (John 14:13–14). "If you remain in me and my words remain in you, ask whatever you wish, and it will be given you" (15:7).

This confidence is not surprising, for Jesus assures us God our Father knows what we need even before we ask Him (Matt. 6:8). Far more than any human father can do for his children, our heavenly Father can and will give good gifts to us if we ask (7:9–11).

Asking is the level where most all intercession begins. We ask when we seek and when we knock. We ask when we agree in prayer (Matt. 18:19). We ask when we intensify our intercession by fasting. We ask when we carry a prayer burden, when we wrestle in prayer, and when we engage in prayer warfare. It is always the right time to ask God, for He loves to be asked.

Abraham asked God for a son, an heir (Gen. 15:2). Moses asked God to heal Miriam of her leprosy (Num. 12:13). Nehemiah prayed repeated brief prayers of asking and received God's answers (Neh. 1:4; 4:9). Elijah, on Mount Carmel, had only begun to ask God when God sent fire from heaven (1 Kings 18:36–38). Hezekiah asked God to heal his people, and God did (2 Chron. 30:18–20). Peter and John asked that the Samaritan converts be filled with the Holy Spirit, and God answered (Acts 8:15–17).

God may lead you to ask for things you had not thought about. Amy Carmichael was a missionary to India whom God greatly used in prayer and faith. God at times impressed her to ask for things for which she saw no immediate need. But when she asked, God provided, and they proved of great value in her ministry. God knows the things we need even before we ask Him (Matt. 6:8).

Praise God, often we can prevail in prayer by merely asking.

Always we can claim the promises given for those who ask. Asking is the foundation of all prevailing in prayer.

LEVEL TWO: SEEKING

Seeking is a more intensified form of prayer than asking. Seeking implies greater earnestness, continued perseverance, and often deeper hunger and desire. Many prayers are in the will of God, but they are not instantly granted when we ask. Perhaps repeated asking will lead us to making a special priority of this need. We become so convinced that the answer is important to God's kingdom that we are willing to give ourselves more fully and with more determination to prevailing prayer. Being convinced it is the will of God, our asking now intensifies to seeking.

Seeking is prayer that is willing to hold on in intercession until the answer comes. It searches to find any possible reason why the answer to prayer may have been hindered. Is there some hindrance in my life that hinders my answer? Have I really understood God's will in the matter? Is my faith what it should be? Is there some step of obedience I can take that will speed the answer? Seeking often involves heart searching.

Seeking may involve intense heart yearning, desires that burn in the soul like a flame, a heart that cries out in tears to God. God said through Jeremiah, "You will seek me and find me when you seek me with all your heart" (Jer. 29:13). Moses had given Israel the same assurance: "You will find him if you look for him with all your heart and with all your soul" (Deut. 4:29). The psalmist added, "Blessed are they who . . . seek him with all their heart" (Ps. 119:2).

Serious intercessors will gladly intensify their asking into seeking when this is needed. They know that as a by-product of their seeking for God's answer as they wait on God, their own strength will be renewed and their own walk become closer to God. Their hearts agree with David, who said, "My heart says of you, 'Seek his face!' Your face, LORD, I will seek" (Ps. 27:8). Their hearts do what David said in verse 14, "Wait for the

173

LORD; be strong and take heart and wait for the LORD." David realized that prolonged prayer is sometimes required, so he said, "Wait patiently for him" (37:7).

David's seeking in prayer is repeatedly mentioned in the Psalms. Can you feel David's heart-cry as he says, "O God, you are my God, earnestly I seek you; my soul thirsts for you, my body longs for you. . . . Because you are my help, . . . my soul clings to you" (Ps. 63:1, 7–8). The unknown writer of Psalm 123 prays, "I lift up my eyes to you, to you whose throne is in heaven. As the eyes of slaves look to the hand of their master, as the eyes of a maid look to the hand of her mistress, so our eyes look to the LORD our God, till he shows us his mercy" (vv. 1–2).

Can you see the pleading intercessor of Psalm 130 as this faithful servant prevails and waits for God's answer for His people? "I wait for the LORD, my soul waits, and in his word I put my hope. My soul waits for the Lord more than watchmen wait for the morning, more than watchmen wait for the morning" (vv. 5–6).

Moses prayed a seeking prayer as he held on until God again promised to accompany Israel (Exod. 33:12–23). Hezekiah and Isaiah prevailed in seeking intercession for deliverance for the nation (2 Chron. 32:20–21). Nehemiah sought and prevailed in prayer for Jerusalem till God sent him and used him to rebuild the city (Neh. 1:4–11). Then upon reaching Jerusalem, he led the whole nation in seeking intercession until God sent national revival (chap. 9).

Daniel too prevailed in seeking prayer as he sought God's answer so that the exiles could go back to their homeland. Israel was restored as God's nation through the seeking, prevailing prayer of Daniel and Nehemiah (Dan. 9:1–23; 10:2–14).

The early church used seeking, prevailing prayer for the outpouring of the Spirit at Pentecost. Any intercessor who has learned to prevail with God has used the prayer of earnest seeking again and again. God gladly hears and answers such prayer yet today.

R. A. Torrey believed that few people who are converted to Christ without someone praying for and seeking their salvation. He gives the example of his own conversion in the middle of the night. He was not converted in church, Sunday school, or in personal conversation with anyone. He went to bed without any thought of God or salvation. He awoke in the night, God spoke to his heart, and he surrendered his life to Jesus in perhaps five minutes. He writes: "A few minutes before, I was about as near eternal perdition as one gets. I had one foot over the brink and was trying to get the other one over.... I thought no human being had anything to do with it, but I had forgotten my mother's prayers, and I afterwards learned that one of my college classmates had chosen me as one to pray for until I was saved." Torrey adds, "Oh, the power of prayer to reach down, down, down where hope itself seems vain, and lift men and women up, up, up into fellowship with and likeness to God."[1]

General Charles Gordon, brilliant British military leader from 1855 to 1885, always had a list of people on his heart for whom he prayed. He not only kept them on his list until they were saved, he prayed for them earnestly and then lovingly, wisely, and earnestly sought to lead them to Christ. He was famous for his prayer life and won scores to Christ.

Many years ago a zealous layman in Springfield, Illinois, formed a band of praying people. One day he suggested to them that that evening they write down the names of all the people in Springfield that they would like to see saved. Then he suggested that three times a day they pray for the salvation of each one on their list. In addition, they should do what they could do to win to the Lord those on their list.

An almost helpless invalid Christian woman who had been bedridden for seventeen years was told of this challenge. She had been praying in a general way for the salvation of people for years. When her family told her of this praying band, she determined to do similarly. She made a list of fifty-seven unsaved people in Springfield that she knew and began to pray for the salvation of each three times a day. She also urged her

Christian friends to pray for these and do their best to get them to repent and believe. With humble spirit but unquestioning faith she interceded day after day. In time, every one of the fifty-seven received Christ as Savior. She sought and she found.[2]

LEVEL THREE: KNOCKING

Jesus' words to us are, "Ask and it will be given to you; seek and you will find; knock and the door will be opened to you. For everyone who asks receives; he who seeks finds; and to him who knocks, the door will be opened" (Matt. 7:7–8). Jesus followed up this challenge with one of His "how much more" promises (v. 11).

At times your seeking becomes so urgent, your soul so desperate, that you actually begin to knock at heaven's door. When the need is crying for God's answer but the answer is still not forthcoming, and when your soul is also crying out to God in holy desperation, it is not irreverent to knock at the entrance to heaven's door.

Jesus Himself went beyond asking and seeking in Gethsemane. He cried out with loud crying and tears, as He no doubt often had done (Heb. 5:7). He was knocking until He was heard. He taught us to knock in His parable of the friend at midnight (Luke 11:5–8). When the unexpected traveler arrived, the householder had urgent need and went at midnight to the home of another friend and begged at first unsuccessfully for bread for his unexpected guest. It was not for himself—it was for a man in need.

Jesus showed that when your relationship as a friend is insufficient to get your need supplied by ordinary asking, your continuous knocking will finally get the answer. Jesus is not telling us that God is like that sleepy man who did not want to be bothered. No, God always welcomes us. He was teaching us that some prayer answers demand a holy boldness. We should be like the man who persisted until he got the bread.

See the picture as Alexander Whyte visualizes Christ's nights of prayer. "He continued all night. Do you see Him? Do you hear Him? Can you make out what He is asking? He stands up. He kneels down. He falls on his face. He knocks at the thick darkness. All that night he prays, and refuses to faint, till the sun rises, and he descends to His disciples like a strong man to run a race. . . . No—we have not an high priest who cannot be touched with the feelings of our infirmities."[3]

A. B. Simpson wrote:

> This is more than seeking. . . . It is not so much the prayer that knocks at the gates of heaven and extorts an answer from an unwilling God, as the prayer which, having received the answer and promise, carries it forth against the gates of the enemy and beats them down, as the walls of Jericho fell before the tramp and shout of Israel's believing hosts. . . . It is faith putting its hand on the omnipotence of God and using it in fellowship with our own omnipotent Head until we see His name prevail against all that opposes His will, and the crooked things are made straight, the gates of brass are open, and the fetters of iron are broken asunder.[4]

Do you see Moses on Mount Sinai? God is so angry with idolatrous Israel that He is ready to blot them out. Moses asks, seeks, pleads, and knocks; he throws himself into the breach as a mediator: "Please forgive their sin—but if not, then blot me out of the book you have written" (Exod. 32:32). Do you see Moses instantly cast himself facedown before God again and again in the succeeding years as he prevails till Israel is spared God's wrath, as Israel repeatedly insults God to His face?

Do you see Elisha at Jordan? Elijah has just gone to heaven in a triumphal chariot of fire. Elisha has Elijah's mantle. He comes to the Jordan and calls out as he strikes the Jordan with it, "Where now is the LORD, the God of Elijah?" (2 Kings 2:14). Both the Berkeley and the Knox translations indicate that "as he struck the waters again, it parted." Elisha was knocking. He struck the Jordan once, but nothing happened. He called out, asking where God was, and nothing happened. So he struck the

Jordan a second time, and the waters parted before him. I believe if necessary he would have struck it even more times. He prevailed because he knocked.

Look at the church prevailing for the release of Peter. The Greek word used in Acts 12:5 to describe their praying is *ektenōs* (stretched, stretched out). They must have been storming the gates of heaven, knocking.

Thomas Payne tells the story of a godly mother who prevailed in general prayer for years for her unsaved husband and nine children. Finally she was led to focus on her children one at a time with intensified, earnest prayer. One by one, God began to answer her pleading prayer. First her oldest daughter was converted, then her two oldest sons. In time, all of her children were won to Christ. But in spite of her intense intercession and tears, her husband remained unmoved.

She determined to make one last all-out effort. She spent a whole night in intense prayer of pleading earnestness beyond anything she had ever known. Her heart was almost breaking. In the morning she said to him, "God has given me all my nine children, but you are still without God and without hope. I have but one more request to make, and then I must leave you to God. Will you now at this moment seek the salvation of your soul?"

She had asked, sought, and knocked all night in agony of soul. Her husband stood speechless, almost as if paralyzed. Suddenly, he began to sob, "I will." That morning he was saved, and so remarkable was his changed life that the whole surrounding district was greatly impressed.[5]

Such was Martin Luther's prayer for his great friend and fellow reformer, Philip Melanchthon. Luther heard that Melanchthon was dying, and he went at once to see him. All the usual signs of death were present—the cold, clammy sweat; the fixed eyes; the semicoma state. He could not eat or drink or seemingly be roused. Luther was deeply moved, turned away from the bed, fell upon his knees with his face toward the window, and agonized in prayer for an hour, praying with earnestness and holy boldness, knocking on heaven's door.

Listen to Luther's words: "This time I besought the Almighty with great vigor. . . . I attacked Him with His own weapons, quoting from Scripture all the promises I could remember and said that He must grant my prayer if I was henceforth to put faith in His promises! I said, 'Be of good courage, Philip. You will not die. . . . Do not give way to grief and do not become your own slayer, but trust in the Lord who can destroy and bring to life, who can strike and heal again!'"

Then Luther arose from his knees and went quietly to the bed. He took Melanchthon by the hand. The sick man roused, recognized Luther, and said, "O dear Luther, why don't you let me depart in peace?" "No, no, Philip, we cannot possibly spare you from the field of labor yet!" Luther then requested the nurse to go and bring some nourishment. When it was brought, Melanchthon had no desire for it and asked again to be allowed to go home and be at rest.

Again Luther replied, "Philip, we cannot spare you yet." Upon Luther's insistence a third time, Melanchthon relented, tasted a bit of food, began to get better, was restored to complete health, and for many years continued to labor, battling with the powers of darkness for the Reformation that God sent across Europe. Reformation came to Europe because of men who knew how to prevail in prayer, even when it required knocking on heaven's door.

CHAPTER 27

Jesus Said We Would Fast

LEVEL FOUR: FASTING

JESUS, SPEAKING OF you and me, said, "Then they will fast" (Matt. 9:15). He was referring to His followers during the period between His ascension and His return. Jesus expects all His children to fast. Why? It is an even higher level of intensity of prayer, level four. Ask, seek, knock, fast. John Wesley preached many sermons on fasting and prayer. He said, "The man who never fasts is no more in the way to heaven than the man who never prays."[1]

When prevailing in prayer for needs that are very urgent or resistant, fasting is often used by the Holy Spirit to give the extra power to bring Satan's defeat and Christ's victory into view. Since Jesus expects us to fast, He set the example for us, just as He set the example in prayer. His forty days of prayer after His baptism were days of fasting prayer.

The early church, following Christ's example, put great emphasis upon fasting. We know that at least for four hundred years after Christ, the faithful Christians everywhere fasted twice each week. Epiphanius, the writer of perhaps the first Christian encyclopedia on the Bible, asked rhetorically, "Who does not know that the fast of the fourth and sixth days of the week (Wednesday and Friday) are observed by Christians throughout the world?"

Since fasting was a part of normal Christian devotion, it naturally was the next step in intercession after asking, seeking, and knocking.

The great leaders of the Reformation, in their spiritual warfare to restore purity to the church, naturally made great use of the biblical means of fasting. Martin Luther not only maintained the spiritual discipline of fasting one day a week but additionally fasted so often along with his three hours' daily prayer that he was often criticized for fasting too much. But he blessed the whole evangelical church and impacted the world for God by his prayers, fasting, and holy boldness.

John Calvin was called an inveterate faster—and lived to see God's power sweep Geneva. The Moravians fasted, as did the Hussites, Waldensians, Huguenots, and Scottish Covenanters. Except for prevailing prayer that included fasting, we would have had no Reformation and no great awakenings over the centuries.

John Knox impacted the whole of Britain and moved the world toward God as he wrestled day and night in prayer and fasted regularly. Heroic Archbishop Cranmer and equally heroic Bishops Ridley and Latimer were known for regular fasting as well as for bold preaching of the truth. Jonathan Edwards was a regular faster. Charles G. Finney, probably the greatest and most anointed soul-winner since the apostle Paul, fasted every week. Whenever he sensed the work of God slowing down or less of the power of God on his ministry, he would spend another two to three days in fasting and prayer, and he testified that the power was always renewed.

From the time of Moses to our own century, great prayer warriors have regularly intensified and empowered their prevailing prayer by fasting. No one boasts of one's prayer life, and all hesitate to reveal the details of their personal walk with God. Heaven's record will reveal how again and again the great victories of the church have been won by prevailing prayer intensified by fasting.

Rev. Seth C. Rees, father of Dr. Paul Rees, was greatly used in the early decades of this century. He never held an evangelistic campaign without setting apart one or two days for fasting prayer. Pastor C. Hsi, noted Chinese scholar-saint, fasted constantly. Often when some difficult matter arose, he gave himself to a day of fasting prayer. Even while he was traveling, he waged a mighty spiritual war with the powers of darkness, confronting Satan almost hand-to-hand in conflict. At such times he would give himself to "days of fasting and prayer."[2]

Fasting as Self-Denial

Fasting is a God-ordained form of self-denial. The very nature of intercession calls for as much or more self-denial than any other form of spiritual activity. The major work of prayer and fasting from food is normally in secret. We think of fasting as abstaining primarily from food. However, fasting may include abstaining from such normal activities as sleep, recreation, and other special enjoyments. As far as possible, it should include abstaining from social relations with others while you fast. You may need to fast while still discharging family responsibilities or your regular work, or you may be able to get completely alone for the fast period (1 Cor. 7:5).

Andrew Bonar defined fasting as abstaining from anything that hindered prayer. Though himself an avid reader, he had to fast at times from his excessive love for reading to find time to commune with God. Phillips Brooks described fasting as abstaining from anything innocent in itself in order to grow more spiritually or serve God more effectively. Perhaps for our generation fasting should often be from radio and TV in order to give ourselves more totally and intensely to prayer.

The purpose of fasting is (1) to subject the physical to the spiritual and to give priority to spiritual goals; (2) to disentangle oneself for a time from one's environment, material things, daily responsibilities, and cares; and (3) to devote one's whole spiritual attention to God and prayer. We do not imply that daily duties and life's necessities are unholy or unspiritual; rather, we subject permissible things, even profitable things, to greater spiritual priorities.

Andrew Murray taught, "Prayer is the one hand with which we grasp the Invisible; fasting the other, with which we let loose and cast away the visible." Fasting added to prayer makes our communion more precious to the Lord and our intercession more powerful in its ministry to the Lord (Acts 13:2), as He royally intercedes from heaven's throne (Rom. 8:34). What, then, is the role of fasting?

Fasting is integral to a life of deep devotion and intercession. Anna the prophetess is a beautiful example of such a lifestyle (Luke 2:37). Fasting is essential to a life of personal spiritual discipline, and such discipline greatly enhances and empowers prevailing prayer.

When you long to strengthen and discipline your prayer habits and to add a new dimension to your prevailing in prayer, add fasting. When you seek to humble yourself before God in total submission to His will and in total dependence on His almighty power, add fasting. When you face an overwhelming need, a human impossibility, and your soul hungers to see God intervene by supernatural power, add fasting.

In such situations you may well find such a powerful drawing to fasting that you are sure you will fail the Lord unless you set apart time for fasting prayer. Scripture is clear in this point: God does call His people to fasting (Isa. 22:12–13). Tragically, so many are not walking closely enough with the Lord to feel His holy drawing and to hear His gentle voice. How shocked many Christians will be in heaven to see what blessings they missed and how often they failed all that God intended to do through them just because they did not add fasting to their prayer.

But you are more likely to hear God's voice calling you to fast if you already have been making fasting a regular part of the spiritual discipline of your life. Jesus said of us today,

"Then they will fast" (Matt. 9:15). You and I have no more right to omit fasting because we feel no special emotional prompting than we have a right to omit prayer, Bible reading, or assembling with God's children for lack of some special emotional prompting. Fasting is just as biblical and normal a part of a spiritual walk of obedience with God as are these others.

Why don't we fast more? For the same reason we hesitate to deny ourselves and take up our cross in other ways! Yet Jesus said so emphatically, "If anyone would come after me, he must deny himself and take up his cross and follow me" (Matt. 16:24). You are an incomplete disciple unless you do. But denial of self is seldom preached and all too seldom practiced. What more biblical and Christlike way is there to deny self than to fast as we pray?

How do you take up your cross? To take up a cross is not to have someone place the cross upon you. Sickness, persecution, and the antagonism of other people are not your real cross. To take up a cross is a deliberate choice. We must purposely humble ourself, stoop down, and pick up the cross for Jesus. Fasting is one of the most biblical ways to do so.

You can indeed deny yourself some expenditure and give the money saved to missions or to some other aspect of God's work. Such an action could be taking up your cross. You could identify with an unpopular cause for Jesus' sake and thus take up your cross. But no way is more God-approved and more constantly available than to add fasting to your prayer. In what form of self-denial have you found most blessing? Or don't you practice self-denial?

There may be times when physically you cannot fast more than one or two meals, rather than a full day or more. Perhaps your responsibilities demand that you eat, alone or with others. But you can still fast. Do like Daniel. He fasted partially for three weeks, and God wonderfully honored his fast. As a prime minister he had to attend some functions. He had to preserve his strength and could not hibernate for three weeks. So Daniel fasted from choice food (i.e., he ate only the bare essentials) and from the use of lotions (Dan. 10:3).

God is not a slave driver. He understands your health and your situation. He wants to keep you well and effective. Ask the Spirit's guidance, and He will show you how and when to fast. But as far as possible, spend the fast mealtimes in prayer. Set apart a period of hours for prayer, especially if you are in a prayer battle.

Satan does not want you to fast. He did not want Jesus to fast. He will try to tempt you with the thought of food. He will try to get you to forget your commitment to fast, just as he tries to keep you from prayer. Satan tries to make you hesitate to fast, to procrastinate about fasting. Why be surprised? He fears tremendously lest your prayer be empowered by fasting. He may even temporarily try to battle you all the more if you fast. He may become desperate. You are greatly endangering his work when you fast and pray.

Watch Your Motive

Remember, the motive in your fasting is all-important. Remember what fasting is not:

1. *It is not a way to earn God's blessing and God's answer to your prayer.* You are never worthy of His help and blessing. You implore His love and mercy. You do not earn any aspect of His grace.

2. *It is not a way to bypass obedience.* Prayer and fasting do not change your need to be obedient to God and His clearly revealed will. God will not hear your prayer, even if you add fasting, if you are out of His will in some regard. Take the steps of obedience, and then begin to fast and pray.

3. *It is not an automatic way to miracle.* Fasting is not some spiritualized form of magic. It does not work by itself. Fasting may do you physical good quite apart from your spiritual condition, but fasting is not some secret of power available to just anyone. Fasting has power only as it is added to your humbly seeking God's face. The more closely you are walking

with God, the greater can be the spiritual values from your fasting.

You may not be able to stop all of your other activities while you fast for twelve hours or for a day. But if your soul is constantly crying to God as you go about your work, if every moment you are reaching out to Him as you fulfill your responsibilities, then whatever fasting you can do adds tremendous power to your seeking God's answer.

4. *It does not accumulate power to your credit, so that you can display it at will.* You do not use the Holy Spirit—He uses you. The moment you parade your power, it is gone. The moment you flaunt your fasting, it does you no good, a warning that Jesus made very clear. If you want God's reward for your prayer, fasting, and good works, keep them as hidden as possible.

Jesus took it for granted that you would do all three, so He does not say, "Pray," but "when you pray." He does not say, "Fast," but "when you fast" (Matt. 6:2, 5, 16). Jesus tells you to let your fasting, as far as possible, be known only to God, and He will reward you (v. 18).

CHAPTER 28

Fasting Strengthens Prayer

FASTING IS SO CLOSELY related to prayer that it adds its blessing in many ways. Much of your praying will be without fasting, just as much of your prayer does not involve prayer wrestling or prayer warfare. But fasting always has this twofold capacity:

First, it can bless and deepen your regular prayer. It is a blessed component of a deep devotional life, of a close walk with God. My father often pleaded when he exhorted his congregations to fast, "Try it! Try it!"

Second, it can intensify your power to prevail in prayer. For those occasions when Satan is long-entrenched and needs to be driven back and expelled, fasting added to prevailing prayer may be imperative. For those battles where Satan has resisted thus far much militant intercession, add fasting to your prayer. If possible, add collective fasting and prayer.

Let us detail some of the wonderful ways that fasting adds to your prayer.

1. *Fasting deepens humility.* Ezra humbled himself with fasting (Ezra 8:21). David humbled himself with fasting, "when my prayers returned ... unanswered" (Ps. 35:13). Earnest

seeking of God always involves humbling oneself before God. "Humble yourselves . . . under God's mighty hand, that he may lift you up in due time" (1 Peter 5:6; see also 2 Chron. 7:14; James 4:10; 1 Peter 5:5). The least bit of pride or self-related ambition can block prevailing prayer. Fasting is a biblical way to deeper humility.

2. *Fasting can deepen hunger for God to work.* Spiritual hunger and fasting have reciprocal power. Each deepens and strengthens the other. Each makes the other more effective. When your spiritual hunger becomes very deep, you may even lose the desire for food. All of the most intense forms of prevailing prayer—prayer burden, prayer wrestling, and prayer warfare—can be deepened, clarified, and greatly empowered by fasting.

Fasting is natural when you are burdened sufficiently, wrestling with mighty prevailings, and warring in hand-to-hand conflict with Satan and his powers of darkness. Fasting becomes sweet and blessed as your hunger reaches out to God. Your hunger gains tremendous power as you fast and pray— particularly if you set apart time from all else to give yourself to fasting and prayer. It can become a spiritual joy to fast.

3. *Fasting intensifies prayer concentration.* Fasting strengthens your prayer priorities, focuses your prevailing, and enables you to give more uninterrupted concentration to prevailing intercession. Satan wants to bring a hundred distractions to disrupt your prevailing prayer. Fasting helps your spiritual nature master your wandering thoughts and helps you triumph over sight and sense.

Fasting helps unclutter and unburden your mind from life's activities, problems, responsibilities, and associations. It permits the wind of the Spirit to blow away your mental and spiritual fog, freeing you and, as it were, cleansing you from much of the external world. Then it is more easy to be truly alone with God, face-to-face in communion and intercession.

Fasting can lead to great calm and peace of soul. On the other hand, it may clear the way for dynamic wrestling in prayer and mighty prayer warfare. Jacob's night of prayer was a fasting from sleep and from family as he wrestled alone with God (Gen. 32:22–30). Jesus' forty days in the desert included fasting from food, normal work, social contacts, and, probably part of the time, sleep.

Said R. A. Torrey regarding fasting prayer, "There is a peculiar power in such prayer. Every great crisis in life and work should be met in that way." Andrew Murray stated, "Prayer needs fasting for its full and perfect development."[1]

4. *Fasting solidifies determination.* Satan always wants to suggest that we give up and stop interceding. He comes with many forms of attack—lethargy, battle weariness, and discouragement. He wants to divert you from prevailing until the answer comes. Fasting helps inject iron into your soul, feeds your inner nature with new boldness and single-mindedness, and gives you holy determination. Fasting helps and nerves your importunity and helps express it.

Andrew Murray writes, "We are creatures of the senses: fasting helps to express, to deepen, and to confirm the resolution that we are ready to sacrifice anything, to sacrifice ourselves, to attain what we seek for the kingdom of God."

5. *Fasting feeds your faith.* When you add fasting to your prayer, you know you are following the example of prevailing prayer in both Old and New Testaments. Your confidence begins to deepen. Your hope begins to rise, for you know you are doing what pleases the Lord. Your willingness to deny self and voluntarily to take up this added cross kindles an inner joy. Your faith begins to lay hold of God's promise more simply and more firmly.

6. *Fasting opens you more fully to the Spirit's working.* Fasting is a letting go of your natural desires, refusing to be bound by the visible and tangible, and makes it easier to lay hold of heaven's resources. It helps transcend the natural and helps keep your body your slave (1 Cor. 9:27) when you are denying your physical nature. It perhaps opens your nature more fully to the Spirit's touch. It is easier to hear the Spirit's voice, as fasting helps shut out the world about you.

We do not manipulate or command the Spirit, but we

become increasingly available to Him as we fast and pray. He is able to say new things to us, to have new access to us. I can never thank God enough for what He said at such a time. He can clothe us more fully and prepare us to be used more freely. It just seems to open us anew to the Spirit's presence and power. Jesus returned "in the power of the Spirit" when He had won His forty-day battle of prayer and fasting (Luke 4:14).

7. *Fasting fires earnestness and zeal.* As fasting feeds our faith, solidifies our determination, and opens us to the Spirit's inner working, it fires us with increasing earnestness and zeal. Shortly after Jesus' forty-day fast we see Him burning with zeal for God's will in God's house (John 2:17). Fasting kindles all kinds of holy earnestness and zeal—to give oneself totally to and for God, to pray until we prevail, to see Satan defeated and God's will brought to pass, and to do everything possible for the honor of Christ's name. Such earnestness and holy zeal greatly empower prevailing prayer. They fire your soul to see Christ prevail in every life and in every situation.

To summarize, fasting prepares the way of the Lord. It empowers prayer to push back and repel Satan's darkness, to remove Satan's roadblocks, and to defeat Satan's attacking forces. Fasting prayer prepares your heart to prevail more powerfully, believe more trustingly, and hold on perseveringly until Christ's will visibly triumphs. Fasting adds tremendously dynamic power and effectiveness to all forms of prevailing prayer.

Isaiah rebuked Israel for assuming that fasting without obedience had any value whatever. He said, "You cannot fast as you do today and expect your voice to be heard on high" (Isa. 58:4). He was not condemning fasting per se, but hypocritical fasting. The implication is clear: biblical fasting does help your voice to be heard on high and helps your prayer prevail for God on earth.

UNITED FASTING

Just as there are situations that call for united prayer, so there are needs that can be met only by adding united fasting to united prayer. Unity in seeking God by fasting confers the same multiple dimensions of effectiveness as unity in seeking God by prayer alone, only more so.

When a multination foe assembled to attack Israel, Jehoshaphat proclaimed a fast for all of Judah. People came from every village and town to Jerusalem for united prayer and fasting. While they stood before the Lord, the Holy Spirit came upon one of the Levites, and he prophesied they would not need to fight this battle. The people fell on their faces and worshiped and praised God.

The next morning they sent out a choir to lead the army, singing the praises of Jehovah. As they began to sing and praise, the armies of the three nations began attacking and destroying each other. It took Judah three days to collect the loot. On the fourth day they had a praise assembly by the battlefield, where they had not had to shoot even one arrow. Then they marched triumphantly back to Jerusalem, led by the king, playing trumpets, flutes, and harps, singing and praising all the way to the temple—the most amazing war in history (2 Chron. 20).

When Ninevah united in repentance, prayer, and fasting, God spared them (Jonah 3). When Esther called the Jews at Susa to three days of united prayer and fasting, Haman's plot was foiled, and the Jewish nation was spared.

The New Testament missionary movement began through the united prayer and fasting of the Antioch church (Acts 13:2). Paul and Barnabas convened meetings of fasting and prayer in every church they established (Acts 14:23). From then on, the appointment of elders in the churches was always accompanied with fasting. Church history tells us that whenever someone wanted to be baptized, the baptizer, the one to be baptized, and as many of the church as possible united in prayer and fasting.[2]

Church history in recent centuries gives many glowing accounts of how God honored united prayer and fasting by ending drought, protecting nations, and sending revival to God's people. In this century, the Korean church has become specially known for both its personal and united fasting.

PRACTICAL SUGGESTIONS

Begin to incorporate fasting into your prayer life. If you have never practiced biblical fasting, begin at least occasionally to set apart some hours, a half day, or longer for a personal prayer retreat, and include fasting.

1. *Fast for a meal occasionally, and spend the mealtime (and, if possible, additional time) in prayer.* Sometimes God so burdens your heart that you lose normal desires for food and sleep. At other times, He wants you to fast by faith, rather than by feeling.

2. *Pray about planning for fasting as a regular part of your devotional life*—once a month or perhaps one day a month. Or you may want to plan to fast one or two meals each week. Remember to get alone with God for the time that you spend in fasting so that you will get the full spiritual benefit.

3. *Spend the first part of your time feasting on God's Word, worshiping, adoring, and praising the Lord.* Then concentrate on one or perhaps two major prayer concerns for your prayer and fasting time.

4. *Be flexible in your fasting.* Avoid legalistic bondage, and don't take a vow concerning fasting. Rather, set a fasting goal that you seek faithfully to fulfill by God's help. If circumstances make impossible a time when you had planned to fast, choose another time as soon afterward as possible. If for medical reasons it is inadvisable to have a total fast, then, like Daniel, fast from "choice food."

5. *Do not attempt long fasts* (twenty to forty days) unless you have been informed how to do it and how to break the fast at the close. Our OMS churches in Korea know of more than twenty thousand of their people who have completed a forty-day fast—usually at one of their "prayer houses" in the mountains. Perhaps most of their pastors have engaged in such a fast on behalf of their church and ministry. But they are well informed on health cautions in their fasting.

Be sure to keep someone informed where you are in a longer fast. Keep drinking liquids, for the body needs water. The long fasts without food or water in the Bible were special miracles. If you plan an especially long total fast and you are an older or unwell person, be sure and check out the plan with your doctor.

6. *Keep a listening ear for the Lord's guidance when He calls you to a special fast for a particular need.*

7. *Keep your fasting a matter between you and God alone.* If someone asks you, you may feel free to answer questions. If God gives a tremendous victory as you fast alone or in unity with others, you may feel God wants you to share the testimony of how He has honored the fasting prayer. But be sure to give God all the glory. You may sometimes feel led to confide in some close Christian friend concerning the joy you have found in fasting.

Full-souled seeking of God by prayer with fasting enables God to do things in answer to prayer that He cannot do without the level of praying that is reached by the added fasting. God has ordained that fasting help release His power to work in a more decisive and sometimes more immediate way. We therefore have a very sacred responsibility to fast.

J. G. Morrison has written, "We owe it to God to fast, and to do it sincerely, faithfully, and regularly. . . . God's people are responsible for all the divine power that He is able to release because we fast . . . for this responsibility and its dynamic possibilities we must some day give an account personally to Jesus our Lord."[3]

Let us add the words of John Wesley: "Can anyone willingly neglect it and be guiltless?" Wesley required all Methodists to fast Wednesdays and Fridays until about four in the afternoon.

"'Return to me with all your heart, with fasting and weeping and mourning.' . . . Blow the trumpet in Zion, declare a holy fast, call a sacred assembly. Gather the people, consecrate the assembly; bring together the elders, gather the children. . . . Let the priests, who minister before the LORD, weep between the temple porch and the altar. Let them say, 'Spare your people, O LORD. . . . Why should they say among the peoples, "Where is their God?"'" (Joel 2:12–17).

Let me urge you to discover for yourself the joy, the special blessing, and the special empowering in prayer from adding fasting to your prayer. Do it!

CHAPTER 29

Carrying a Prayer Burden

LEVEL FIVE: PRAYER BURDEN

WE HAVE DISCUSSED asking, seeking, knocking, and fasting. Now we consider the fifth level of prevailing prayer: interceding with a prayer burden. This level of intensity is marked by urgency, commitment to the priority of the need, and holy determination to pray until God answers. It is not only knocking at heaven's gate but prevailing in the Spirit.

You prevail with prayer burden only by the enablement of the Holy Spirit. He summons you to prayer for the need, guides you in your praying, and fills you with holy desire so intense that it becomes not only a deep concern but a consuming spiritual passion to prevail with God and over Satan.

Prayer burden begins as an inner impression that you should pray for a known or unknown need. It is a gracious work of the Holy Spirit applying spiritual pressure upon your heart. It is God's way to call you to intercession at a time when your prayer is needed by God who has ordained to work through the intercession of His children. It is needed and indeed demanded

194

by a situation that cries for God's answer. The burden is the Spirit's personal call to you to intercede.

Varieties of Prayer Burden

There are at least five varieties of prayer burden. All of them involve the Holy Spirit's calling you to prayer and your response as a priest of God (1 Peter 2:5, 9; Rev. 1:6) interceding on earth while your Lord intercedes on heaven's throne.

1. *Instant, emergency prayer burden.* This is a sudden, strong call of the Spirit, an unexpected, sudden compulsion in your heart. You feel an inner pressure to pray, a sense that your prayer is needed. It may be very specific. You may feel a certain person is in danger or at a crisis of decision, or you may suddenly be reminded of someone and feel constrained to pray. As soon as you begin to pray, the burden gets heavier, and you feel the Spirit's help in prayer.

It may begin with a sudden general sense of danger, urgency, or need, a feeling that something or someone needs prayer. As you pray, the burden will probably increase, and some person or situation may be brought to your mind.

You may not know clearly the reason for your SOS prayer burden until sometime later. You may never know. That is not important. It is important to go instantly to prayer. Of this you can be sure—God does not play games with you. When His Spirit prompts you to pray, perhaps by God's angel injecting the thought into your mind, your prayer is urgently needed. Emergency prayer burdens are usually for a brief urgent need. You pray at once, or you fail God and the situation.

If you do not know at first how to pray, you can always pray, "Lord, Your will be done. Whatever the need, may Your will be done. Defeat Satan. Help whoever is in need. Work in power. Work just now." You can plead in Jesus' name. You can plead the blood of Jesus. You can claim Christ's victory at Calvary. Prevail, prevail, and as you do, the Spirit may clarify more and more to your mind what you are praying for. Hold on till God lifts the prayer burden and gives you peace.

J. Oswald Sanders, respected leader of Overseas Missionary Fellowship, was traveling in central China in a robber-infested area. Later he received a letter from his wife asking if he had been in any danger at a specific date and time. She had been in bed at midnight when she received a great burden to pray for him. He later found that this midnight prayer burden was at the exact time when he was passing through the bandit-infested area.

During World War II, a British chaplain was on a ship crossing the English Channel. He was awakened in the night with a strong burden to pray for the welfare of all on the ship. He had been assured that there was no danger in the area, but he instantly called on God to spare them. He prevailed until peace came to his heart. Just about then, the ship's officer came up to him and stammered, "Chaplain, we just missed a floating mine by a few yards. It was seen just in time!" That same week, two troop ships went down in the same waters, and over fifteen hundred men were lost. God had given him instant burden in the time of need.

2. *Gradually deepening prayer burden.* Sometimes God attracts your interest to a person or situation that needs prayer. At first you may pray sporadically, when you happen to think of it, but as time goes by, you may find the need has a regular place in your prayer until it becomes a true prayer burden upon your heart. It may become one of the major items about which you pray. You begin to realize that God is holding you responsible to pray regularly and earnestly for the person or need until His answer comes.

In the early stages of this deepening prayer burden, you may not realize that the Spirit is specifically guiding your praying. But as you continue in prayer, you are increasingly sure that it is a true prayer assignment from God. Then it calls for disciplined intercession on your part. You can redeem spare moments by praying for this need. Your heartstrings become very closely bound with the need. Every believer should be carrying several such major prayer burdens on his or her personal prayer list.

While ministering in Perth, Australia, I felt led to set apart a day for prayer and fasting. I went alone on the beach, not knowing why God had led me. While in prayer, the burden deepened tremendously. Again I knew not why. That night a demon-oppressed woman was set free. The next morning her demon-possessed husband, for whom the deacons had been praying for six months, was saved, and several dozen others came into new spiritual blessing. One couple was called to the mission field and went within six months. I did not need to know the reason for the burden—I only needed to be faithful.

3. *Gradually deepening prayer concern leading to instant prayer burden.* At times God may place a person, situation, or special need upon your heart in a gradually deepening concern. You may be reminded of it repeatedly during your prayer time. Perhaps you feel led to place it on your prayer list. You may pray for the person off and on over a period of weeks or months. Then you realize that your concern has become a spiritual responsibility and that your love for the person being prayed for is deepening constantly.

It may even be for a period of hours or days you feel the prayer concern much intensified. God is calling you to a special prayer responsibility. Then one day you may feel the deep, deep instant prayer burden that I have just described.

I remember a deepening prayer concern that I carried over a period of months for a loved one. Then came a two-week period when I found this person often on my heart, and I used free moments again and again to pray. But one afternoon I was powerfully gripped by an instant prayer burden. I prevailed for several hours in deep prevailing intercession, and then God lifted the burden. I later found that at that exact time, several thousand miles away, God had answered that prayer. Thousands of God's children have had similar experiences.

Mrs. Les Wait, Taiwan missionary with Overseas Crusades, had a depressing burden heavily upon her for two days. She did not know why, but she felt that something was about to happen to someone they loved. On the third day the burden became very heavy. Mr. and Mrs. Wait went to special prayer for God to control the circumstances and defeat Satan. They later received a letter from their daughter, Debbie, in California. She reported that at the very hour they were prevailing in prayer, Debbie's car struck an unlighted road barrier, overturned, and was completely demolished, but the girls got out with only minor scratches and bruises.

Mrs. Hulda Andrus, the mother of Jacob DeShazer, who was shot down over Japan during the war, was repeatedly given prayer burdens for her son. She was awakened one night with a tremendous burden and cried out to God instantly. Suddenly the burden was gone, and she went back to sleep. Later she discovered it was the exact time when his plane was shot down and he was falling through space. She did not even know that her son was in that part of the world but later was informed by the government that he was a captive of the Japanese.

She, of course, continued to pray for him, and one noon she was starting to offer thanks for her lunch when suddenly a prayer burden gripped her. She walked the floor, crying out to the Lord for God to protect her son and save him. As she prevailed, she again received an assurance that God had heard her prayer.

But a little later a third heavy burden came upon her, this time very clearly for the salvation of Jacob. She was willing, if need be, to learn of his death if only his soul would be saved. Again she prayed to assurance that God had undertaken. God not only saved her son in the prison cell in Japan but called him to be a missionary. As far as could be checked, this work of God happened at the same time that she was praying for him. After the war, when DeShazer was set free, he trained for missionary service and returned to Japan as a missionary, where he was used to win many to Christ.

4. *Long-term prayer burden.* God may give a long-term prayer burden to His children. Undoubtedly all Christians should carry long-term prayer burdens that they should include in their daily prayers and especially in their longer times of prayer.

These long-term prayer burdens may be for such needs as an evangelistic campaign, with prayer beginning months in advance, or it may be for the granting of a missionary visa, a person's healing, or someone's salvation.

For as far back as I can remember, my mother had a prayer burden for China. Then when God called me as a child to India, Mother prayed for India and China every day. She not only prayed, she gave sacrificial gifts to support missionary work of OMS International in those two nations. I cannot remember a family prayer time when my mother did not pray for both nations by name and pray at some length with deep longing and earnestness. In fact, for the last twenty to thirty years of her life, I cannot remember hearing her pray one day in daily family prayer for these two nations without weeping because of the heavy burden she was carrying for their salvation. She was a very quiet person, not highly emotional, but she loved so deeply that she prayed with burdened tears day after day for these people. Think of the reward God will give to such prevailing, burden-bearing intercessors!

Miss Anna Nixon, Evangelical Friends missionary to India, tells the thrilling story of visiting Mrs. Ethol George, who for seventy years carried a prayer burden for missions, especially for India. She longed to be a missionary in India herself, but when her friend Carrie Wood went to India, she became her prayer partner. With tears she would tell how disappointed she was that she could not go herself. But the two ladies agreed that whenever Carrie Wood needed prayer, she would ask the Lord to tell Ethol George to pray.

After some years of such prayer partnership, Carrie wrote about the need to train four young men for Christian work. Ethol and her husband then took one of these, Stuti Prakash, and began supporting him. Day by day over the years she carried the prayer burden for Stuti. There on her dresser was the picture of Stuti Prakash, for whom she prayed, and the autographed picture of Anna's own cousin, President Nixon, for whom she also prayed. As Anna and Carrie knelt to pray, the presence of the Holy Spirit so surrounded them and filled them that Miss Nixon says never in her life has she felt such a

199

dimension of the Holy Spirit's praying through two people as they experienced that day.

You can take on your heart a prayer ministry for one or more people, carrying for them a long-term prayer concern that God can deepen into a real prayer burden. You can become that person's prayer partner, and you can enter into every phrase of the ministry of that person through your burden-bearing prayer.

Other possible long-term prayer burdens are for such things as the ministry of an evangelistic team (e.g., Billy Graham, Luis Palau, or others); mission harvest; the Muslim world; the Hindu world; unreached people; refugees; those imprisoned for their faith; crucial issues, such as crime, drugs, pornography, abused children; ethnic ministries; worldwide revival; revival in your own nation or in your own denomination; and the leaders of your nation. The list of possible long-term prayer burdens is almost endless. Every believer should be carrying prayer burdens constantly for several major concerns.

5. *Long-term prayer burdens that call for movements of prayer.* Many of the items in the previous list are so urgent that they call for whole movements of prayer. You can become a part of the movement of prayer for worldwide revival, for the Muslim world, for world harvest, or for unreached people. You may be able to receive prayer bulletins from several sources relating to such movements of prayer in which you desire to participate. Do all you can, not only to carry a prayer burden continuously, but also to enlist the prayer of as many other people or groups as possible. May God make us all prayer mobilizers.

Prayer Burden Described

A prayer burden is a spiritual concern on the heart of God that is imparted by the Holy Spirit to someone whose intercession the Holy Spirit desires to use. Jesus has been interceding for this need, and now the Spirit needs you to join with the intercession of Jesus. It is a specially sacred level of prayer intensity and prayer responsibility. It is always a special trust committed to you from the Lord, a special call of the Spirit for faithful intercession. It is an indication of the Spirit's priority for you.

1. *Prayer burden is a spiritual concern.* It is an unselfish concern for the Lord's will in a person or situation. It is a desire for God's mercy and help and for that which is highest and best. The concern weighs down upon the praying person, causing that one to pray as much as possible for the need. It shares with the praying person the same compassion and desire that God has.

2. *Prayer burden is God-given.* Its source is not natural sympathy, emotion, or predilection. It is not something worked up by long or loud praying. It is not the result of psychological manipulation or mass psychology. While it may spread from one person to another, it does so primarily among those deeply spiritual, deeply committed, and deeply involved in intercession. A burden that is primarily emotional will be superficial and will yield no lasting spiritual results. It is a burden born in the heart of God, which indicates it is a valid part of Christ's intercession, and it is conveyed to you by the Spirit's guidance and touch.

3. *Prayer burden is very personal.* Others may or may not share your vision, burden, or concern. But if it is something that God puts specially on you, you are the one responsible to intercede. It is a commitment between you and the Lord. You must bear the burden for the need on behalf of the Lord—or, more accurately, in intercessory partnership with the Lord.

It begins in a hidden way privately in your own heart. Prayer burden will be carried primarily before the Lord in the secret place. No one can fully know the depth of concern the Lord places upon your heart. The burden perhaps will rest so heavily on you that others will sense that something is resting heavily on you. Nehemiah carried such a burden (Neh. 2:2–3). It may be that others will sense it from the depth of your praying if you mention this particular need during your public prayer. It is not wrong if others begin to discern it, but you should not be sharing your concern widely unless you are specially led by the

Spirit to do so (Matt. 6:16–18). It is a sacred secret trust you have received from the Lord.

4. *Prayer burden may move you very deeply.* When the Lord places the burden upon you heavily, it literally weighs upon your heart. The more fully you identify with the need, the more deeply you will feel it. It may include an ever deeper God-given agape love for the ones involved in the need. It may involve a sense of foreboding danger or holy concern, lest God's will be missed or be unfulfilled.

You will notice that the more deeply the burden moves you, the more powerfully it involves your whole being. When you are almost totally absorbed and possessed by a burden that continues for a matter of hours or days, you may lose your desire for food and sleep. You may be moved to very sincere and expressive tears (Ps. 42:3), which can be a very powerful plea to God (56:8). God is moved by the depth of desire manifested in sincere tears (2 Kings 20:5; Ps. 126:5).

5. *Prayer burden makes you responsible.* A Spirit-given burden is a special mandate from the Lord. You may be the only one to whom the Spirit assigns this prayer burden. Or perhaps your earnest prayer is needed to be added in unity to the intercession being made by a number of others to whom God gives the same prayer burden. Christian biography and history record thousands of examples of how God worked, saved, blessed, protected, healed, sent revival, or gave other outstanding answers to prayer when someone was faithful to such prayer burden, such a call and mandate from the Lord. Often later evidence proves that the prayer was needed at the exact time when the Spirit called to this intercession by giving the prayer burden.

If God works so mightily at the exact time someone is faithful to a prayer burden given by God, what happens if the person fails to pray? Will we be shocked in eternity at the victories that were not won, the people who did not yield to God, or the great or potential answers to prayer that were never received because we or someone else were not faithful to the prayer burden God tried to give us?

CHAPTER 30

How to Carry
a Prayer Burden

1. *GIVE AS IMMEDIATE attention as possible to the burden.*
Sudden prayer burdens are God's SOS call for your help. If at
all possible, interrupt what you are doing and pray at once for
the need God places upon you.

2. *Concentrate primarily on this one burden.* If possible, get
alone where you will not be interrupted in your intercession. If
the prayer burden continues through mealtime, add fasting to
your prayer. If you are praying for a period of hours, have pen
and paper with you to write down any steps to which God
guides you to help answer your prayer or to recruit the
intercession of others.

Also write down any thoughts that come to your mind that
you do not want to lose or duties connected with your normal
life that you do not want to forget. Prolonged prayer times
often release our mind to very creative thought, but we do not
want to be diverted from the prayer burden God is giving us.
Because you free your mind from other things, you may
recollect important items. Jot them down so you can immediately get back to your primary intercession.

3. *Hold on in prayer until God lifts the burden.* If you cannot

give sufficient time to prayer at the time, pray as much as you can and then resume your prayer concerning it as soon as you can free yourself for concentrated intercession. If it is a prayer burden that God has been increasingly placing upon you for a period of time, seize every opportunity to pray additionally for this burden—whether for a matter of minutes or, if possible, a period of hours.

If the burden continues for a period of days or longer, there will be intervening periods of hours or days when God will let you rest from your burden and carry out your other duties. But then again at prayer times, free moments, or when you set apart specific time for this purpose, He will restore the burden to you and let you take advance prayer steps or amass additional prayer in His presence until God gives the breakthrough and the prayer is answered.

4. *In prolonged prayer burden, God may lead you to enlist the prayer of others.* Not all prayer burdens are of a nature that should be shared. Trust God to guide you in this matter. In the case of prayer burdens of a more general nature, such as revival in the church, healing of a nonconfidential illness, deliverance of someone from demon power, drugs, or similar entrenched need, it may please God for you to mobilize the prayers of spiritually perceptive intercessors that you know can stand heart and soul with you in this intercession. Many Christians may not be spiritually prepared for serious intercession and prayer battles. They may be marked more by lack of faith than by faith. Let God guide you in how widely you share the need.

HOW TO BE AVAILABLE FOR PRAYER BURDEN

1. *Maintain a disciplined prayer life.* It is usually to those who are already faithful in intercession that God gives an intercessory prayer burden or a sudden urgent SOS prayer burden. In some cases, however, God gives such prayer burdens to a very new Christian because He knows that person in his or her new love and zeal is instantly obedient, because God wants to show this new believer what He can do through prayer, or because

that person has a relationship with the person for whom prayer is needed. It is usually easier for God to alert us for prayer burdens for someone we already know or for whom we are already praying.

A woman in England knew my role in OMS International and had heard me speak, and thus it was probably easier for God to alert her when I had a need. When our youngest daughter lay bleeding to death in a yard in America, God spoke to the woman. He got her out of bed on her knees, and she prevailed for "Wesley Duewel's family." She did not know what the exact need was.

For some reason, God let me sleep blissfully in London, where I was speaking, yet alerted her to pray. She prevailed at the very time of need. Our daughter was found, and by a series of miracles her life was revived (though she had already ceased to bleed), and today she serves as a missionary in Indonesia. That dear woman was a faithful intercessor, so she was available to God.

2. *Live in the Spirit.* Prayer burdens are given to you by the Holy Spirit. The more fully your life is controlled by the Spirit, the more fully the Spirit can guide you and work through you. He is the Spirit of intercession, so He is eager to help you intercede. Unless you have been filled with the Spirit, He does not fully control you and is not able to use you completely. Be sure you have been filled with the Spirit. Be sure you are living in the fullness of the Spirit and that you are praying in the Spirit.

3. *Keep a listening ear.* You can learn to develop a spiritual alertness and availability to God, to be specially open to His guidance. See chapter 17, "The Secret of Listening," in my book *Let God Guide You Daily.* If you truly hunger for God to use you and, in particular, to use your prayer life, you can learn to sense His guiding touch or voice, and you will learn how eager God is to guide you in all the daily aspects of your living. Then you will discover that again and again God will guide you in your praying. As you are thus alert to God, you will be more open to the Spirit's giving you a prayer burden.

4. *Practice constant obedience.* Whenever God gives you a prayer assignment, be immediately and regularly faithful to it. Let nothing in your life grieve the gentle Holy Spirit. Be eager to walk in all the light God gives you. Let no tension develop between you and any other person. If it does, as much as lies in your power, humbly take the initiative to try to remove the tension. Put God's will, God's Word, and prayer in constant priority in your life.

5. *Expose yourself to vision and need.* Read writings and periodicals that will expose you to God's vision for your world and the hurting needs of people. Attend services where you can be exposed to need. Participate in activities where you will see prayer needs firsthand. Visit the sick. Cultivate the confidence of an unsaved person you seek to lead to the Lord. Write to a prisoner in your local or county jail; visit and show your Christian love. Get involved by prayer, finance, or personally in any other way possible in jail ministry, inner city ministry, or other missionary work.

6. *Use prayer lists.* Have a church prayer list, remembering your pastor or pastors, youth leader, lay leaders, new members, and membership prospects.

Ask God to guide you in which nations to put on your daily prayer list, and pray for one or more that especially need the gospel. Make at least a short list of unsaved people whom you long to see brought to Christ. Keep a temporary list of needs that are changing—people in the hospital, fighting a health battle, out of work, or discouraged—and special upcoming needs that you want to pray for. Use a short list of government leaders, including your president, vice president, one or more political leaders, Supreme Court justices, your senators, representatives, governor, and mayor. When you are interceding for God's cause and needs such as these, it is easy for God to put a special burden on your heart when these urgently need prayer.

Don't worry about when God is going to give you a sudden prayer burden. Just be faithful in daily disciplined intercession. Pray lovingly for the needs you know of. Schedule regular and adequate time alone with God. Plan special times alone with

God. Feed on His Word each time in prayer. Rejoice in the Lord. Love Him and others. And as you live in close partnership with the Lord, He will begin to deepen the concern for the needs He wants you to take special responsibility for. Then when you feel a special drawing to prayer for any person or situation, be quick to obey, and God will use you more and more in special intercession and burden bearing.

CHAPTER 31

Wrestling for Prayer Answers

LEVEL SIX: WRESTLING IN PRAYER

THE BIBLE TEACHES a sixth level of prevailing prayer—wrestling. Jesus wrestled in prayer in Gethsemane (Luke 22:44). Epaphras was "always wrestling in prayer" for the Colossian church (Col. 4:12). In both cases the Greek word used is related to the agonizing wrestling in the Greek Olympic-type games. From it we get our English word *agonize*.

Wrestling prayer is agonizing in prayer. It is prayer effort so strenuous that it becomes an agony. Agonizing prayer is always for a limited period of time. When Jesus agonized in the garden, it was for a period of about three hours. Epaphras agonized again and again as he prayed for his beloved Christians in Colosse (Col. 4:12–13).

Prayer burden may be experienced in varying degrees. But an agonizing prayer burden, a strenuous wrestling in prayer, is perhaps the highest level of prayer intensity of which man is capable. No one ever wrestled in prayer like Jesus, whose sweat became like great drops or clots (Greek) of blood. Ours will not be unto blood, but blessed are those of His followers who have followed their Lord into mighty prayer wrestlings. These efforts are often used by God to bring great victories.

There is an interrelation between prayer burden, wrestling in prayer, and prayer warfare. Prayer burden is a heaviness of concern but does not necessarily include agonizing in prayer. Wrestling in prayer is a very intense prayer burden, a spiritual form of all-out attack on the strongholds of Satan, or a costly agony of Spirit-given holy desire. Prayer warfare is a more long-term earnest prayer endeavor, which may include prayer burden and prayer wrestlings from time to time. It continues day after day until Satan is dislodged from lives or situations that he is determined to control. It will be described in a later section.

Bounds, writing about wrestling in prayer "until the fire falls and the blessing descends," added, "This wrestling in prayer may not be boisterous nor vehement, but quiet, tenacious, and urgent."[1]

Wrestling in prayer may be done silently, even in bed, with those around you unaware. Or it may involve strong crying and tears. The wrestling is done primarily in your spirit, though it may affect your body.

Let me emphasize that these three levels of intense intercession are not self-induced. They are Spirit-given. You do not work up your emotions but instead yield to the Spirit's mighty prevailings in you. All the Spirit's workings within you are dependent on your yielding yourself to His leading, to your deep life in the Spirit, so that He can impart to you His own holy longings and passion. You strive and toil, but you do so because within you is a heart-cry that reflects the heart cry of our Lord.

God knows your body and its limits. It would be too much for you physically and nervously to share a burden every moment, to agonize in wrestling prayer for long periods of time, and to be constantly involved in prayer warfare. God wants you to have times of joyous prayer communion, deep resting in God's faithfulness, and basking in His peace. The Holy Spirit exercises good stewardship of your body, for it is

His temple. You do not lose the spirit of prevailing prayer at such times. When you are living in the Spirit, praying in the Spirit, and guided by the Spirit, you are instantly available for the Spirit's assignments of intensified prevailing when He needs that level of prayer from you.

Wrestling Prayer Is Spiritual Labor

All intercession is real and serious communication with God. It is not casual, even when beautifully simple. It is sacred and important to God and to us. It is kingdom action, kingdom ministry. But prevailing prayer, especially in its more intense form, includes labor, effort, and perseverance.

Prayer—prevailing, wrestling prayer—can be the most difficult work you can do. It demands total sincerity, intense desire, full concentration, and whole-souled determination. It requires self-discipline to give full priority to your seeking God's answer. It does not make you a recluse but does cause you to choose between what is good and what is best. Its holy worth and potential can separate you from the trivial, the purely secular, and the transient and momentary.

Coleridge called prayer the "highest energy of which the human heart is capable."[2] Prayer can be the most intense form of Christian warfare. Prayer is so simple, so natural, that even a child can pray. But prevailing prayer can draw upon and avail itself of all one's spiritual experience and spiritual and physical energy, and all one's mental, emotional, and spiritual resources.

Probably one reason so few wrestle in prayer is that so few are prepared for its arduous demands. It can be very spiritually exhausting and physically demanding. You recognize that the success of an urgent endeavor, the life of a sick one, the eternal destiny of an unsaved one, the honor of the name of God, and the welfare of the kingdom of God may be at stake.

Wrestling in prayer enlists all the powers of your soul, marshals your deepest holy desire, and uses all the perseverance of your holy determination. You push through a host of difficulties. You push back the heavy threatening clouds of darkness. You reach beyond the visible to the very throne of God. With all your strength and tenacity you lay hold of God's grace and power. It becomes a passion of your soul. Samuel Chadwick wrote, "There is always the sweat of blood in prevailing intercession."[3]

Wrestling in prayer has a spiritual importunity that refuses to be denied. It has a humble, submissive, yet holy boldness that dares to remind God of His divine responsibilities, dares to quote to God His unbreakable promises, and ventures to hold God accountable to His Holy Word.

Was Jacob impertinent when he dared to continue wrestling with the supernatural being during his night of prayer (Gen. 32:22–31)? How dare he say to God, "I will not let you go unless you bless me" (v. 26)? Jacob had already wrestled all night, refusing to stop until he prevailed. God was doing a transforming work in his nature. He was being brought to the end of himself, but this position made him bold in faith. A new Jacob prevails with God because God has prevailed over him. No, Jacob was not impertinent. He was now on prevailing ground.

Writes E. M. Bounds, "The wrestling quality of importunate prayer does not spring from physical vehemence or fleshly energy. It is not an impulse of energy, not a mere earnestness of soul; it is an inwrought force, a faculty implanted and aroused by the Holy Spirit. Virtually, it is the intercession of the Spirit of God, in us."[4] You do not wrestle apart from the Holy Spirit. Only He can give you the holy boldness that is at the same time submissive to God yet bold to insist on God's promise, bold in the very face of God.

Jesus, as Son of Man, was filled with the Spirit at His baptism, returned from Jordan "full of the Holy Spirit," returned to Galilee "in the power of the Spirit," announced that the Spirit of the Lord was upon Him, and healed because "the power of the Lord was present for him to heal" (Luke 5:17). He spoke and people were healed, spoke and demons were cast out, spoke and water was turned to wine, spoke and wind and wave obeyed Him, spoke and the dead were raised to life. But when it came to prayer, He prayed for hours—at times all night. He wrestled, agonized, and cried out with loud cries and tears. It may take more of God's power to wrestle in prayer than to perform a miracle.

Samuel Chadwick bemoaned the lack of wrestling in prayer: "There is a marked absence of travail. There is much phrasing, but little pleading. Prayer has become a soliloquy instead of a passion. The powerlessness of the church needs no other explanation. . . . To be prayerless is to be both passionless and powerless."

Martin Luther was a man of constant prayer. He prayed morning and evening and often during the day—even during meals. He repeated memorized prayers again and again, especially the Lord's Prayer, and prayed the Psalms. But when he had a prayer burden, "his prayer became a storm, a wrestling with God, the power, the greatness, and holy simplicity of which it is difficult to compare with other human emotions," says Freytag, his biographer. He poured out his soul in holy emotion and bold complaint and even seriously exhorted God.

Such mighty prevailings in prayer have been described as "battering the gates of heaven with the storms of prayer." David Brainerd, under the date of July 21, 1744, wrote in his diary, "In prayer I was exceedingly enlarged and my soul was as much drawn out as ever I remember it to have been in my life or near. I was in such anguish and pleaded with so much earnestness and importunity that when I rose from my knees, I felt extremely weak and overcome—I could scarcely walk straight. My joints were loosed, the sweat ran down my face and body, and nature seemed as if it would dissolve . . . in my fervent supplications for the poor Indians. I knew they met together to worship demons and not God. This made me cry earnestly that God would now appear and help me. . . . My soul pleaded long."[5] The next day he awakened with the same burden on his heart. Day after day he wrestled in what became real prayer warfare.

When John Foster paced back and forth in the aisle of his

212

chapel, wrestling in prayer, he wore a track in the aisle from his feet. Canon Henry Liddon, a brilliant Oxford professor and also a powerful preacher, describes what prevailing prayer is: "Let those who have really prayed give the answer. They sometimes describe prayer with the patriarch Jacob as a wrestling together with an Unseen Power which may last, not infrequently in an earnest life, late into the night hours, or even to the break of day. . . . They have, when praying, their eyes fixed on the Great Intercessor in Gethsemane, upon the drops of blood which fell to the ground in the agony of resignation and sacrifice."[6]

In the Olympic-type games in ancient Greek, each wrestler sought to throw his antagonist on the ground and put his foot upon the neck of the other wrestler. It involved mighty unrelenting agonizing until victory. This is the term Paul used for this level of prevailing prayer, calling it both agonizing (Col. 4:12, Greek) and wrestling (Eph. 6:12). Paul reminds us of the reason—we are not just wrestling with stubborn or prejudiced human beings. Behind them are rulers, authorities, powers, and spiritual forces of darkness from the spirit world fulfilling Satan's deceptive strategies (Eph. 6:11–12).

It is an unrelenting conflict. Satan's dark forces are ever on the offensive against the church of Christ, ever seeking to deceive, dominate, destroy, and rout the forces of Christ. Comparatively few Christians know much in personal experience about wrestling against such forces and warring through prayer.

Why do we Wrestle?

Why has God planned for us to wrestle? The overarching purposes of God include developing us spiritually and making us partners and warriors now so we can share in the triumph and rewards of victory in eternity. It is of God's grace and love that He has ordained that His most faithful intercessors wrestle in prayer.

1. *To help us realize our dependence upon God.* The more

deeply we sense our own impotence and helplessness, the more fully we can cast ourselves upon God. Humility is always the first step to God's grace and power.

2. *To help us share Christ's heart.* Christ is the great Wrestler. He wrestled in prayer with the powers of darkness while on earth. The day of wrestling is not over until Satan is bound and cast out. Now Christ must wrestle through us, but He on the throne must share His heartbeat with us so we can see the world, the lost, and the opposing demonic forces from His perspective. Wrestling helps us share His vision, His hatred of sin, and His holy determination to oust Satan.

3. *To teach us spiritual alertness.* Paul recognized that Satan constantly tries to deceive and outwit us. We must beware of his schemes (2 Cor. 2:11). He tries to sift us like wheat (Luke 22:31). He masquerades as an angel of light (2 Cor. 11:14). He prowls around like a roaring lion (1 Peter 5:8–9). Wrestling in prayer teaches us to "be alert and always keep on praying" (Eph. 6:18). Just as a wrestler must be alert to every move his opponent makes, wrestling teaches us to keep awake and alert for God.

4. *To teach us spiritual passion and vehemence.* The more we wrestle in prayer, the more deeply the Holy Spirit is able to fire us with His passion and His holy but vehement opposition to Satan and all Satan's deceits, strategies, and forces.

5. *To teach us the secrets of triumphant overcoming.* We learn to triumph by the Spirit's helping us triumph. This is no textbook mock battle. We learn the deceits of Satan by confronting them. We learn the use and power of our spiritual weapons by using them. We learn spiritual warfare by confronting the powers of darkness in prayer. Victory requires skill as well as might. The Spirit teaches us spiritual skill as we wrestle.

6. *To strengthen our faith.* Faith is made purer and stronger by our overcoming the resistance we face in prayer and the obstacles to the answers of prayer. Faith is strengthened by exercise. We must feed on the Word and live in the Spirit, but only as we put faith in practice do we move from theoretical

faith to faith as God's means of victory. Faith seems mightiest in the simple trust of the new believer and in the mature, militant faith of the battle-tested warrior. Faith must become more than a confidence in Jesus. It must become a strong shield in battle and a mighty spiritual weapon of attack. Like a spiritual muscle, the more we use faith, the more it becomes tough and powerful.

7. *To enable us to amass prayer resources.* Intensive prayer and, in particular, prayer wrestling and prayer warfare can be amassed as if it were a bank reserve or a spiritual treasure.

Just as an army needs to amass weapons, munitions, and reserves before an all-out attack, so God prepares for spiritual breakthrough. We see this law of prayer at work even with the angels. Daniel prayed and Gabriel fought with the demons representing Satan for three weeks before God amassed the divine power of prayer and had Michael join Gabriel in the spiritual warfare (Dan. 10:2–3, 12–13). This whole incident is a mystery, but it is clearly revealed in the Word. The disciples failed because they had not been praying enough. They had not been amassing sufficient prayer (Mark 9:29).

CHAPTER 32

Holy Wrestlers

WRESTLING WITH WHOM?

WHILE OUR PRIMARY resistance in wrestling prayer comes from Satan, does God, as it were, wrestle with us? There are many men of God who believe that God does, though others strongly deny this. Does the wrestling of Jacob teach us that God can oppose us until we make some things in our life right with God and men? It probably does. But if there is nothing between us and God or between us and our neighbor, does God still at times, for His sovereign purpose, resist us for the time being, even though we are praying for what is in accord with His highest will?

James I. Packer writes, referring to Bishop J. C. Ryle, John Owen, and John Calvin, "These authors also showed me at the practical level what P. T. Forsyth later theologised for me . . . that God may actually resist us when we pray in order that we in turn may resist and overcome His resistance and so be led to deeper dependence on Him and greater enrichment from Him at the end of the day."[1]

Spurgeon, Stibbes, Finney, and Moody explain prevailing prayer as militant faith that "prevails over what seems to be

God's permissive will so that His ultimate will may be brought closer to fulfillment."[2]

In wrestling prayer there is a "taking hold of God," a seizing His mighty hand and refusing to let go. Just as in the Old Testament times the last refuge of one seeking mercy was to seize and cling to the horns on the four corners of the altar of the temple, so we in prayer go beyond the temple to lay hold of God Himself. The literal Hebrew of Isaiah 27:5 is, "Let them take hold of me." Isaiah laments in Isaiah 64:7, "No one calls on your name or strives to lay hold of you." These references refer to the laying hold of the horns of the altar, as it were, even laying hold of God Himself. This is what wrestling prayer does.

Our human language is so weak. How can we describe this holy intensity in prayer? To God it is not irreverent for us to come boldly to the throne of grace (Heb. 4:16). The Greek word means fearless, bold speaking to God. Holy boldness in prayer, heart hunger that produces vehemence of holy desire— such is precious in the sight of God.

God is in the truest sense wrestling with the powers of darkness through us. He is agonizing over man's sin. He has sent His Spirit to indwell us, fill us, and make us mighty in prayer—indeed, to pray through us His own holy groanings. God wants to set the captives free. Perhaps the only way He can do so is to teach us holy wrestlings until we are so strong we can wrestle with and defeat and rob Satan in holy prayer warfare.

WRESTLERS WITH GOD

Over the centuries men and women of God have known in their experience what it means to wrestle in prayer and obtain God's mighty answers. Some have wrestled and almost immediately gained outstanding, even miraculous, answers to their prayers. Others have had special times of wrestling before God and have seen their whole lives and ministry thereafter transformed. No doubt having learned the power and blessing from wrestling in prayer, they often thereafter wrestled before God as they prayed for the advance of Christ's kingdom.

Others have prevailed through mighty wrestlings in prayer and have left their imprint upon a nation, tribe, church, or organization. In their case it was not a wrestling for an immediate victory for a particular person or local place but a wrestling for the soul of a people or the future of a ministry.

The Reformation is undoubtedly the spiritual result of many holy wrestlers. Nicholas of Basle is one who helped prepare the way for the Reformation. He was known as a "friend of God," and he and others influenced by him wrestled in prayer for years. Nicholas, with two other "friends of God," died a martyr at the age of about ninety after years of wrestling for the sins of the church and of the world.

Thinking of the Reformation as extending roughly from the mid-1400s to the mid-1600s, we can quickly recognize that the Reformation and related awakenings in the church were prayed to pass by mighty prevailing of bold men and women of God. Many were known for their wrestling in prayer: Savonarola—the revivalist of Italy; Martin Luther—the father of the Reformation; John Knox—who moved Scotland for God; George Fox—who founded the Quakers. Among the holy wrestlers have been mothers in Israel like Monica, the prevailing mother of Augustine; Madam Guyon, the French woman revivalist of the 1600s; and Catherine Booth, the mother of the Salvation Army.

John Flavell, pastor in Dartmouth, England, in the late 1600s wrestled mightily with God just before a major sea battle between the British and French. He knew many of the seamen belonged to his parish and would be in great danger. He called his people together for fasting and prayer, and as he led them in prayer, he himself wrestled in tremendous prayer agony. Not one sailor from Dartmouth lost his life in that sea battle.[3]

Henry Martyn, fearless missionary to India around 1800, spent much time in fasting, self-humiliation, and prayer. He wrote, "My whole soul wrestled with God. I knew not how to

218

leave off crying to Him to fulfill His promises, chiefly pleading His own glorious power."[4]

Charles G. Finney often experienced periods of great prayer wrestlings throughout the years of his ministry. His whole life and continued ministry were transformed by a tremendous day of wrestling in prayer on shipboard in 1834 as he returned from the Mediterranean. He was praying for revival in America.

> My soul was in utter agony. I spent almost the entire day in prayer in my stateroom, or walking the deck in intense agony, in view of the state of things. In fact, I felt crushed with the burden that was on my soul. There was no one on board to whom I could open my mind or say a word.
>
> It was the spirit of prayer that was upon me; that which I have often before experienced in kind but perhaps never before to such a degree, for so long a time. I besought the Lord to go on with His work, and to provide himself with such instrumentalities as were necessary. It was a long summer day, in the early part of July. After a day of unspeakable wrestling and agony in my soul, just at night, the subject cleared up to my mind. The Spirit led me to believe that all would come out all right, and that God had yet a work for me to do; that I might be at rest; that the Lord would go forward with His work, and give me the strength to take any part in it that He desired.[5]

Shortly thereafter Finney began a series of lectures on revival, which was then published as *Lectures on Revival of Religion,* a volume that was circulated around the world and reprinted in Welsh, French, and German. There were several English-language editions, with one publisher in Britain publishing over eighty thousand in a short period of time, a phenomenal distribution in those days.

These writings prepared the way for revival in Wales, England, Canada, the island world, and all across America. Supported by his continuing prayer ministry of wrestling before God, they laid the foundation for the great revival of the United Prayer Meetings that swept across America in the 1850s and undoubtedly helped prepare the way for the great revival in Wales in 1904–5. The records of eternity will probably show that directly and indirectly several million people were won to Christ as a result of that day of wrestling prayer.

Finney was restored to health and continued a revival ministry the rest of his life. He himself summarizes:

> Let the reader remember that long day of agony and prayer at sea that God would do something to forward the work of revivals, and enable me, if He desired to do it, to take such a course as to help forward the work. I felt certain that my prayers would be answered, and I have regarded all that I have since been able to accomplish as, in a very important sense, an answer to the prayers of that day.
>
> The spirit of prayer came upon me as a sovereign grace bestowed on me, without the least merit. He pressed my soul in prayer until I was enabled to prevail, and through infinite riches in grace in Christ Jesus I have been many years witnessing the wonderful results of that day of wrestling with God. In answer to that day's agony He has continued to give me the spirit of prayer.[6]

CHAPTER 33

Prayer Groans and Prayer Agony

PRAYER GROANING IS SPIRIT-BORN

THE HOLY SPIRIT in His mighty prevailing for us prays with unutterable groanings. The word for "groan" in Romans 8:26 is *stenagmos*. It is an inward groaning, and it is in the plural. *Alalētos* is the word meaning "inexpressible." The heart-cry of the Spirit is too deep for human words. It therefore becomes groanings within our hearts that manifest a prayer desire so infinite that it is incapable of being totally expressed.

God the Father understands the Spirit's meaning as He groans within us (Rom. 8:27). Our weakness (v. 26) is that our human words cannot adequately and fully articulate the depth of divine longing, just as our personality cannot experience the fullness and depth of the Spirit's longing. We can express it truly but not totally. We are finite; He is infinite.

Nor do we know what is best in every circumstance. Our knowledge is limited, so we do not know what is best to pray for in each situation. The Spirit's very definite and infinitely deep desire must be expressed in groanings rather than in our words, since our words are inadequate. Spirit-born groaning is always in accord with God's will. The Spirit could desire

221

nothing other. But God can translate these groanings into His fullest understanding and do "immeasurably more than all we ask or imagine, according to his power that is at work within us" (Eph. 3:20).

What infinite condescension that God should choose for the Holy Spirit to indwell us and so fill us that He prays through us, even when our capacity is so limited that His deepest longings can only be partially expressed by us and so inadequately expressed. Yet He chooses to involve us in His intercession. He has chosen to prevail through our intense prevailing. Luther wrote, "Nor is prayer ever heard more abundantly than in such agony and groanings of struggling faith."[1]

In a truly blessed sense the Holy Spirit gives birth to His petitions within us, and He kindles faith within us. As a result, our prevailing prayer of faith "has the almightiness of God linked to it. It reaches round the world. It can touch the highest heaven or shake the lowest hell. Prayer is a Jacob's ladder, with God's angels ascending and descending, taking up the petitions and bringing down the answers." Payne adds, "He has mastered but little of prayer who knows little of the Spirit-groaning which cannot be uttered."[2]

Praying Payson of Portland, Oregon, was one who prevailed mightily in prayer. After his death he was found to have calloused knees. By the side of his bed, where he wrestled in prayer day after day, were two grooves worn into the hard boards as he moved back and forth on his knees in prayer. Payson used to say that he pitied the Christian who could not experience the meaning of the words "groanings which cannot be uttered" (Rom. 8:26).[3] Of Redfield it is said that in his prayer wrestling he at times groaned as if he were dying, but such mighty groanings were then followed by tremendous spiritual transformations in lives as people repented and confessed their sins.[4]

Holy prayer groanings are probably more often in the silent depths of our soul than sounding from our lips, and they are often expressed in deep sighs of burden or longing. I have known the silent groanings of the Spirit more often than the loud cries of groaning. Words do not need to be spoken orally or groans be expressed vocally for God to hear, understand, and answer the deep inner groaning.

PRAYER AGONY IS GODLIKE

Do you begin to realize why Spirit-born prayer agony is so precious to God, so powerful before God, and so dreaded by all the demon forces of hell? The Philistines of Beth Shemesh cried in terror, "Who can stand in the presence of the LORD, this holy God?" (1 Sam. 6:20). Even so, the demons in hell must cry or shriek to one another, "Who can withstand such prevailing before God?"

No prayer is more godlike than agonizing prayer because no one ever agonized in prayer as the Son of God did in Gethsemane. Christ did not spare Himself. Dr. Luke tells us that in Gethsemane, "being in anguish, he prayed more earnestly, and his sweat was like drops of blood" (Luke 22:44; or, "clots of blood," NEB, Weymouth). Angels must have been astonished as they watched Jesus agonize in the garden. Indeed, one angel went to Him to strengthen Him physically so He could survive until the cross and thus complete God's plan (v. 43). Only then (v. 44) was He physically able to survive the sweat of blood.

Alexander Whyte, the great Scottish preacher who died in 1921, describes the astonishment that gripped the Roman soldiers sent to arrest Jesus. "They had never before found such a prisoner as that. There is no sword stroke that they can see upon Him; and yet His hands and His head and His beard are all full of blood. What a coat was that for which the soldiers cast their lots!"[5] And how could Judas have had such a calloused soul to betray Christ with a kiss when Christ's agony was so apparent?

F. W. Farrar, dean of Canterbury, envisioned the scene as follows: "The disciples saw Him, sometimes on His knees, sometimes outstretched in prostrate supplication upon the damp earth. . . . They saw Him before whom demons had fled in terror, lying upon His face upon the ground. They heard that voice wailing in murmurs of broken agony which had commanded the wind and the sea, and they obeyed Him. The great drops of anguish which fell from Him in the dreadful struggle looked to them like heavy gouts of blood."[6]

But oh, Jesus saw infinitely more than the disciples saw. He saw the sin and anguish of the whole human race. He saw the tears of the orphans and widows, the blood of the victims of murder and crime, the slaughter on all earth's battlefields. He heard the cries of the wounded, the screams of the tortured, the thunder of all earth's wars. He saw earth's billions fettered by sin, degraded by Satan, hastening on by the millions to eternal hell. He saw it all.

The agony of Christ's soul, the torture of man's hatred, and the agony of Gethsemane and Calvary altered the very appearance of Christ, as prophesied by Isaiah. "There were many who were appalled at him—his appearance was so disfigured beyond that of any man and his form marred beyond human likeness—so will he sprinkle [by his blood] many nations" (Isa. 52:14–15). Isaiah then questions, "Who has believed" such a message? as he goes on to describe even further Christ's agony and suffering as He redeemed us with His blood. "The LORD has laid on him the iniquity of us all" (Isa. 53:6).

"He poured out his life unto death . . . and made intercession for the transgressors" (Isa. 53:12). Christ deliberately chose earth's mightiest travailing in prayer. Jesus could have refused it, but He chose Gethsemane. Yes, He took up His cross (John 10:18). He took up and drank fully the cup.

Our experience in no way compares with the depth of Christ's experience. But as we purposefully commit ourselves to take up our cup and give ourselves to prayer wrestling, as we take up deliberately our cross, the cross of prayer travail, we become most like Jesus, our mighty Intercessor. "If anyone would come after me, he must deny himself and take up his cross daily and follow me" (Luke 9:23).

Giving oneself daily to costly prevailing prayer for the unsaved, the church, earth's harvest, and man's countless needs is not the only way deliberately to take up one's cross. Such prayer and fasting, though, are probably the ways most universally available to every Christian. It is constantly available to you and to me.

Such mighty prayer travail is not forced upon us. We must choose to take it up, disciplining our life so as to provide daily time for intensive prayer. Jesus says your cross is something that you yourself take up, denying yourself in order to follow Him. How better can you follow Him than through prevailing prayer and fasting?

Jesus' prayer burden and agony is described by Mark: "He began to be deeply distressed and troubled. 'My soul is overwhelmed with sorrow to the point of death,' he said to them" (Mark 14:33–34). The Greek for "deeply distressed" here is *ekthambeomai,* an intensive form of *thambeomai,* which means be amazed, astonished, to the point of almost immobility. Jesus describes the agony as overwhelming. Martin Luther called these words the most astonishing words in the Bible.

Gethsemane was undoubtedly the most intense period of Christ's prayer travail. But this was far from being the only time of our Savior's prayer agony. He faced it in His forty days in the desert. He faced it, no doubt, on many a night of prayer. Hebrews tells us that He prayed in this manner "during the days" of His life on earth (Heb. 5:7).

Says F. F. Bruce of the writer of Hebrews, "He probably knew of a number of incidents in the life of Jesus when he 'offered up prayers and supplications with strong crying and tears unto him that was able to save him from death.' "[7]

WE ARE MOST GODLIKE WHEN WE SHARE GOD'S TRAVAIL

Our prayer travail, prayer groaning, and prayer agony can never compare with that of our Savior, but we have not followed Christ very closely or very far if we do not know in our own prayer experience times of deep prayer burden, prayer wrestling, and even perhaps prayer agony. Said Martin Luther, "I question if any believer can have the burden of souls upon him—a passion for souls—and not agonize in prayer."[8]

Charles Finney states, "Doubtless one great reason why God requires the exercise of this agonizing prayer is that it forms such a bond of union between Christ and the church. It creates such a sympathy between them. It is as if Christ comes and pours the overflowings of His own benevolent heart into His people, and leads them to sympathize and cooperate with Him as they never do in any other way."[9]

Yes, perhaps you are never more Christlike than when you are prevailing in prayer wrestling and prayer agony. Perhaps nothing endears you more to His heart than when you thus share His love, compassion, and burden for the world He longs so infinitely to save.

Prayer groaning and prayer agony also make you unusually one with the Holy Spirit. It makes you more like Him also. The Spirit is equally as infinite in His longing and burden as the Son of God is in interceding on heaven's throne. "How burdened these intercessions of the Holy Spirit! How profoundly He feels the world's sin, the world's woe, and the world's loss, and how deeply He sympathizes with the dire conditions, are seen in His groanings which are . . . too sacred to be voiced by Him."[10]

The Spirit's role is to share with you and impart as deeply as possible to you the deep, deep love and passion of all three persons of the Trinity—God the Father, God the Son, and God the Holy Spirit. The price of redemption for our lost world was completely paid at Calvary. That infinite cost was paid not only by God the Son but by God the Father, too, as He saw the suffering of His beloved Son. It was also of infinite cost to God the Spirit, who for that dark hour had to leave alone God the Son.

They paid redemption's price. Now they long infinitely for that redemption to be made available to and to be appropriated by more of the lost and sin-bound people of our tragic world.

The more you share that burden with them, the more you enter into the continuing intercession of God the Son and the continuing groaning of God the Spirit, the more holy thrill you bring to their hearts. O my friends, what a sacred privilege to ones so unworthy as you and I are!

The phrases "wrestling in prayer," "agonizing in prayer," and "working hard in prayer" were common in the vocabulary of the early church. Paul told the Colossians, "Since the day we heard about you, we have not stopped praying for you" (Col. 1:9). He added, "I want you to know how much I am struggling for you" (2:1; lit., "how great an agony I have on behalf of you"). He told them that Epaphras "is always wrestling in prayer [or, agonizing] for you," adding, "I vouch for him that he is working hard for you." Epaphras was with Paul in Rome, agonizing and working hard by prayer (4:12–13). His praying is a model for all pastors.

Today our prayer life is so weak and our passion for Christ and souls is so lacking that we have lost words such as these from our conversation and even from our sermons. They sound like foreign concepts to us and almost sound like fanaticism! What a commentary on the low level of our prayer lives!

The Holy Spirit does not tap you on the shoulder each morning, lift you out of bed, and place you on your knees. He does not rearrange your schedule so you have time for adequate prayer. You will have to discipline yourself. You will have to choose to have a life of prayer, a disciplined habit of prayer. If you cannot even do that much, don't talk about taking up your cross and following Jesus. Perhaps you are following Him at a distance, like Peter before he denied his Lord (Matt. 26:58).

There is no more sacred or practical way to follow Jesus, daily taking up your cross, than in daily wrestling intercession. You will have to deny yourself of some other things in order to have time for such prayer. Take your choice. Will you follow Jesus closely in intercession till the Spirit teaches you the secrets of prevailing prayer, or will you disappoint your Lord?

Jesus is even now interceding at the right hand of the Father. He is waiting for you to join Him as His intercessor-priest.

Because God has ordained to work through your united prayer—the intercession of Jesus plus your intercession—God's cause will suffer unless you fulfill your role in this holy partnership. How closely will you follow Jesus? How willing are you to learn to prevail? The choice is yours.

"Blow the trumpet in Zion, declare a holy fast, call a sacred assembly. Gather the people, consecrate the assembly; bring together the elders, gather the children, those nursing at the breast. Let the bridegroom leave his room and the bride her chamber. Let the priests, who minister before the LORD, weep between the temple porch and the altar. Let them say, 'Spare your people, O LORD. Do not make your inheritance an object of scorn, a byword among the nations. Why should they say among the peoples, "Where is their God?"'" (Joel 2:15–17).

CHAPTER 34

Prayer Warfare Defeats Satan

LEVEL SEVEN: PRAYER WARFARE

PRAYER WARFARE IS the seventh and highest level of prevailing prayer. It is the prolonged, intensified form of prevailing prayer focused on defeating and routing Satan so that Christ's will may be done and His kingdom advanced. Prayer warfare is militant, prevailing intercession. It involves and includes from time to time all other forms of prevailing prayer. Prayer warfare is fought individually and collectively. It requires constant alertness and readiness and is coordinated by God the Holy Spirit.

The Role of Satan

Prayer warfare is necessary because Satan deceived man and introduced sin and rebellion against God into our world. He is the tyrant, the usurper of all he can dominate. He is constantly and inveterately antagonistic to God, God's plan, God's people, and God's activity. He is anti-Christ, antichurch, and antihumankind. He will deceive, falsely accuse, and destroy in any way he can.

229

While Satan is eager to destroy all families, all nations, and indeed all people, he most hates and opposes those who follow Jesus. He plotted to destroy Adam and Eve and then all civilization before the Flood. When God chose Abraham to found a race through whom Messiah could come, Satan specially concentrated the venom of his hatred against the Jews to try to prevent Christ from being born. He still hates them because of God's plan for them after Christ returns.

Whoever or whatever is chosen by God is specially hated by Satan. He tried to destroy Christ, beginning at His birth. He and his demon followers have conspired to destroy the church from its inception. He is always antichurch, but most of all, antievangelism, antimissions, and antiprayer. As Christ's return nears, we can expect his malignant warfare to intensify just as it was intensified at the time of the Exodus and at the first coming of Christ.

In order to destroy a person, family, or group, Satan tries to deceive, falsely accuse, divide, and divert from what is best. He deceives by masquerading as an angel of light where that disguise is most likely to accomplish his deceptive purpose (2 Cor. 11:14), and roars like a lion where fear is most likely to succeed (1 Peter 5:8).

If he cannot stop you from becoming a Christian, he will focus on defeating you, slowing your spiritual growth, discouraging you, and trying to make you passive and inactive. If that tactic does not work, he will try to get you so busy in daily activities or even Christian activities that you have no time to pray down the power to make your activity successful.

Satan, the destroyer, will destroy you in any way he can. If he cannot destroy you spiritually, he will seek to destroy your fellowship with other Christians and the unity and effectiveness of your church. He knows disunity, disagreement, and doubt can tragically destroy any Christian's effectiveness and therefore delights to accuse one Christian to another (Rev. 12:10). The amazing thing is that he tricks Christians to do his work by inciting them to repeat and circulate his accusations in the form of rumors, criticism, and divisive statements. He even gives morbid enjoyment in telling the latest accusation, rumor, or scandal.

If Satan cannot destroy you spiritually, he will try to destroy you physically. Christian biography and history are full of accounts of God's children being delivered from unusual accidents, diseases, and dangers. He may tempt you to drive your car at excessive speeds or otherwise carelessly. Many greatly used by God in their later lives had miraculous deliverances or healings in childhood or youth.

If Satan cannot destroy you by accident, he may try fear, worry, pressure, or wrong eating habits. Many who have convictions against using alcohol, tobacco, or other substances that destroy the body are nevertheless a slave of their own appetite and enjoy eating so much that they shorten their lives by obesity and the diseases that often result from being overweight. If Satan cannot tempt you with sin, he will gladly tempt you with food to shorten your life and stop your prayer.

Prayer is the greatest means of spiritual power and spiritual victory to you as a Christian. So Satan fears it more than all else you can do. Apart from God Himself and His heavenly beings, prayer is the greatest danger to Satan's purposes, plans, and activities.

The Limitations of Satan

Do not be ignorant of Satan or his ways (2 Cor. 2:11). You need to understand Satan's limitations. Many Christians have a morbid fear of the Devil. Remember, he is a created being who is already under the wrath of God, defeated at Calvary by Christ, and whose doom is already announced in the Bible. As a created being, he is limited in power (only God is all-powerful), limited in knowledge (only God has all knowledge), and limited in presence (only God is everywhere present).

1. *Satan is limited in authority.* Only God is sovereign. Satan can act only within the limits God has imposed on him by the way God originally created him and by God's command. Satan could not touch Job (Job 1 and 2) or Peter (Luke 22:31), and he

cannot touch you without God's permission. God tells him, "Thus far and no further." God will not let him touch you unless it would open the possibility of spiritual growth, blessing, and eternal reward for you.

2. *Satan is limited in knowledge.* Only God is infinite in knowledge. Satan often knows more of the future than you do, but often he does not know enough to decide wisely. He frequently does not know what people will say or do. He makes repeated mistakes. He has to depend on his demons to relay him information, and he has taught them to deceive. Undoubtedly, they often deceive him. Satan cannot feed his false prophets correct information that he does not have, so they often make false prophecies. All fortune-tellers, astrology experts, and followers of the occult are repeatedly deceived.

3. *Satan is limited in power.* Only God has all power. Satan has great power, but all God needs to do is to assign more angels to handle him (Dan. 10:13). "The one who is in you is greater than the one who is in the world" (1 John 4:4). Those who are with us (the angels) are more than the demons who are against us (2 Kings 6:16). Satan does not have enough power or authority to make a promise. God is the God of promise. There is no power in Satan's name. We have divine power in Jesus' name.

4. *Satan is limited in presence.* Like all other created beings, Satan is never in more than one place at a time. Only God is everywhere present. Since Satan cannot be present with you often, if ever, he has to depend constantly on his demons. They have less power than he does. Each demon also can only be in one place at a time.

Perhaps you will go through a whole lifetime with Satan personally never being near you (his demons will, but you are not important enough for Satan himself to spend his time by you or watching you). At worst, he will be by you only occasionally. But God is always with you. God's angels far outnumber the demons. So you always have angels available to help or protect you.

Satan's doom is certain. Every day it is nearer. Satan is well aware of this fact, which makes him and his demons all the more frantic and desperate. But we have adequate resources to defeat Satan.

Prayer the Nemesis of Satan

There is nothing on earth that Satan so fears as prayer. He does not know how to cope with prayer, so he concentrates on keeping you from prayer or getting you to give up before you get prayer's answer. He can often manipulate persons and circumstances so as to delay prayer's answers, but he cannot stop the angels from bringing God's answers. Prayer is his nemesis. He cannot triumph over prevailing prayer.

Satan is more afraid of your praying than of your pure life or zealous witness. One's life may be a beautiful witness that cannot be silenced, but prayer is a militant force that has the potential of defeating Satan, destroying his works, and driving him out of places and lives he claims for his own.

So how does Satan react? He tries to deceive and hinder by bluff or bluster. He refuses to acknowledge his defeat by Christ. He stubbornly holds on to all he claims till he is forced to surrender his dominance. He yields only when he is compelled to. You must repeatedly call his bluff, reaffirm and insist on Calvary's victory, and force his vacating all he has so arrogantly usurped.

Keep up your prayer offensive. Mobilize all your prayer resources. Fasting prayer is heavy artillery in your arsenal. Prayer burden is powerful bombardment of Satan's territory. Wrestling prayer sends mighty guided prayer missiles to destroy Satan's works. Satan is always vulnerable to the prevailing prayer of God's intercessors. He cannot stop prayer or escape your prayer. Press on. God's power is available and unlimited. It is released with devastating effect on Satan's forces as you militantly prevail.

OUR HOLY PRAYER WARFARE

We Are at War

In the mystery of God's wisdom, the victory Christ won once for all at Calvary is not enforced by his iron scepter with which He will one day put down all evil (Rev. 2:27; 12:5; 19:15). The throne of Christ today and until the end of the age is an intercessory throne. Christ is ruling by intercession. He is defeating Satan, driving him back, ousting him, making him flee from where he has been illegally squatting and refusing to vacate. He is doing so primarily by His own nonstop intercession, in partnership with the prayers of His people and backed by His own heavenly angels.

The New Testament not only applies to prayer the intense terminology of the great Greek games (wrestling, agonizing, contending), it also uses military terminology (army, armor, armed, fight, warfare, weapons). The whole Christian life and service is seen as warfare. It is "the good fight of the faith" (1 Tim. 6:12). You are to "put on the full armor," "take your stand against the devil's schemes," "stand your ground," have your armor in place, and "take up the shield of faith" and "the sword of the Spirit" (Eph. 6:11–17).

The final and climactic verse of this passage describes the actual fighting: "Pray in the Spirit on all occasions with all kinds of prayers and requests. With this in mind, be alert and always keep on praying.... Pray ... Pray" (Eph. 6:18–20).

We are the church militant, the church alive on earth's battlefield and at war. This situation will continue till Christ returns. The heart of the whole Christian warfare, the strategy for all Christian victory, and the battleground for all Christian advance is prayer. The early church advanced through prayer. They drove back Satan, battle by battle, through prayer.

"Their prayers and their faith carried all before them. They were like an army of invincible warriors. Nothing could stand before them.... The church, says one, is resistless for the purpose of her great mission when armed with the power of prayer. The whole power of imperial Rome, the mistress of the world, proved unable to resist the power and influence of their intensified prayers."[1]

They prayed, and the place where they were meeting was visibly shaken. They prayed, and the earthquake rocked the prison walls. What a divine amen to their prayers! Prayer was their weapon in every situation. They were using it not primarily for defense but as an offensive attack on Satan and his strongholds.

Our Strategic Role

The prayer warrior stands between the authority and power of heaven and the darkness and power of hell, between the Lamb on the throne and Satan, the great dragon. Christ has delegated to the prayer warrior His authority, the right to use His name and plead His blood. And He has armed the warrior for spiritual conquest. The prayer warrior is to enforce the victory of Calvary on the battlefield of earth.

The best way to fight against sin and Satan is by prayer warfare. The prayer battlefield is the arena of world conquest for the church. O. Hallesby wrote, "The secret prayer chamber is a bloody battleground. Here violent and decisive battles are fought out. Here the fate for souls for time and eternity is determined, in quietude and solitude."[2]

Through the prayer warfare of the interceding believer, Christ takes His stand on earth's spiritual battlefields. The church on its knees, the church wrestling and agonizing in prayer, the church with the shield of faith and the sword of the Spirit, the Word of God, praying always with all forms and levels of prayer under the generalship of the Holy Spirit—this is the militant host of God on earth.

In the invisible realm of the heavens, the mighty angels of God join us by battling the forces of darkness unseen by our eyes, but fighting in awesome reality. It is holy, all-out, victorious war for Christ, but all through prayer.

Christ's messengers are covered by God's canopy of protection, and unseen but real dangers intended by Satan are warded off by prayer. Satan's weapons are blunted, vaporized, and evaporated by the divine laser beams of prayer. Demonic schemings of people and Satan are confronted and frustrated as God's warrior-saints prevail on and on in prayer. Outer defenses of the bastions of Satan are breached, fortresses are pulverized and leveled, and captives of sin and Satan are set free by the power of Jesus as the warrior-saints pray on.

Hatreds are calmed, angers and determined evil and violence are brought under control, and the captives of Satan's forces are forcibly freed by the invincible power of the love of Calvary. Satan's demons are made either to surrender to the Lord, against whom they have fought so long and hard, or else to retreat. They are made captives by the power of Calvary and the powers of the Spirit as the warrior-saints prevail on.

Forward on Your Knees

Do you want to see the tide of battle turned and Christ proved victor in battle after battle on earth today? Get the church to prevailing. Enlist and train the believers in prayer warfare. It is never too late for God. No battle is too nearly lost for God to win. No combination of opposing forces is too strong or too numerous for God. Forward on your knees!

Stand in the victory of Calvary. Glory in the defeat of Satan at Calvary. Insist on enforcing the victory of Calvary. Enter into mighty prayer warfare, with the name of Jesus, the infallible Word of God, and the blood of Calvary your confidence and your invincible weapons. Challenge the forces of darkness. Confront the invading legions of hell. Move into attack on the frontiers of Satan. It is always God's hour to prevail through your holy prayer warfare. Raise your banners high. Raise your hand to heaven's throne, as Moses did. Claim victory for Jesus.

Our battles are fought in the heavenlies, but our praying is down here on earth's prayer battlefields. Our voices may be silent, our lips may not move, but our eye is on our Captain. Our hand is touching His throne. Our faith is raising the banner of the cross. Our soul is shouting the name of Jesus. Not only when we are on our knees but as we go about our daily work we can maintain the spirit of militant prayer, lifting high, as it were, the shield of faith, shouting our battle cry—the name of Jesus—and prevailing in prayer.

"Pray," says Paul, "with all kinds of prayers and requests." All are legitimate in this holy war. We will be surprised when we get to heaven to discover how extensively all kinds of prayer contributed to Christ's victories. We will be amazed to realize how worldwide has been this prayer warfare, how strategic the prayers of God's hidden saints, the mighty prayer warriors known primarily to God. We will be astonished to realize the scope and intensity of the prayer battles all across the church as it faced the world and its need.

We must war with the right weapons and the most powerful weapons—the forms and levels of prevailing prayer. Heaven fights with us as we prevail in prayer. We are prevailing with God and for God.

Who are we, unworthy and so weak in ourselves, that God should entrust such mighty weapons to us? Who are we that God should count on our prayer to turn the tide of battle into resounding victory? Who are we to stand in a strategic gap in the battlelines and hold off, seemingly almost single-handedly, Satan's onslaughts?

We feel so ill equipped. Ah, no! There are no mightier weapons than the weapons of our spiritual warfare. Satan has nothing that can match or withstand them. We feel so inadequately trained. Ah, no! The skills of war we learn while fighting. The strategies of our warfare will be given to us by the Holy Spirit as we advance on our knees.

Listen to Coleridge: "Believe me, to pray with all your heart and strength, with the reason and the will, to believe vividly that God will listen to your voice through Christ, and, verily, to do the things He pleases thereupon—this is the last, the greatest achievement of the Christian's warfare on earth."[3]

CHAPTER 35

Strategies in Prayer Warfare, Part 1

AS PRAYER WARRIORS, we need to know well the weapons and methods of victory in our warfare. We must not only be aware of Satan, his schemes, and his methods (2 Cor. 2:11), we must be wise and skilled in our God-provided means of defeating and routing him. God has available all the strategies we need for prevailing.

1. *Put on the armor God provides.* "Put on the full armor of God" (Eph. 6:11). Paul repeats these words because they are so urgent. We need to be fully armed before the battle, and the only armor that will be adequate is that which God provides. We are wholly dependent on Him. In the Ephesian passage, Paul lists six elements:

a. *The belt of truth.* The truth about God—His sovereignty, almighty power, immediate presence with us, unchangeableness, infinite knowledge and wisdom, total opposition to Satan, and prophesied judgment of Satan—all that the Bible tells us of God is absolute truth. We can stake our lives upon it. It girds your waist so that you are ready to do instant battle, but you yourself must be permeated by truth.

b. *The breastplate of righteousness.* The breastplate protected

238

the vital organs extending from the neck to the thighs. It was sometimes called the heart protector. Righteousness, the transformed character only God can give, provides the absolutely essential protection in spiritual warfare. There is no prayer power unless there is full appropriation of Christ's righteousness. We will leave no unguarded vulnerability if we are possessed of the character of Christ.

Only someone who is pure in heart and hates evil can move freely and unmolested into enemy territory. We must have not only a pure life but a pure heart—pure motives and desires. We must have total integrity. Pride can destroy all our power for warfare. Jealousy, negative criticalness, carnal anger, ill will—none of these can be tolerated in our heart if we are to engage in spiritual warfare.

c. *The army boots.* In Paul's days, soldiers wore strong leather boots with the soles thickly studded with nails, says Josephus. Such boots gave the feet firm grip in fighting and durable protection on long marches. The warrior could spring instantly into action. Wars have been won or lost because of footwear. The gospel of peace—peace with God and peace with all men—gives a firm foundation that will not slip or slide. Again this piece of the armor emphasizes that successful fighting depends on character.

d. *The shield of faith.* Saving faith is absolutely essential, but this element goes beyond salvation to faith used in spiritual conquest and warfare. It is faith for action, for attacking the fortresses of Satan, for taking the prayer offensive to drive Satan back. This faith God desires in us and gladly supplies to us. It is faith that seizes the promise and wields it like a weapon.

It is faith that quenches every flaming arrow of Satan. He is the false accuser of God and of our Christian brethren, and he even tries to accuse us. He wants to disable us by doubt. Satan accuses us of weakness; we agree—our strength is in the Lord not in ourselves. He charges us with ignorance; we agree—the Lord is our wisdom. The Spirit is our guide and counselor. Satan charges us with not knowing how to pray; we agree—

for that reason the Spirit prays within us and is Lord of our praying. Our shield of faith is big. It is adequate. It can quench every flaming arrow Satan shoots at us.

e. *The helmet of salvation.* Our mind is guarded by the salvation of the Lord. He is our assurance of salvation. It is a present-tense deliverance from sin because Jesus saves us from our sins. Our head, so vital in the warfare, is totally protected. We see needs as God sees them. We see sin as God sees it. We have God's understanding, God's concerns, and God's attitudes. Salvation equips us to fight and pray wisely, courageously, and effectively.

f. *The sword of the Spirit—the Word of God.* This Word is our mighty weapon in both defensive and offensive warfare, allowing us to ward off the attacks of Satan and to leap to attack all the powers of hell. What tremendously effective and universally applicable power is in the Word! Let me cite a few militant phrases to use at the appropriate point in your prayer: "thus says the Lord"; "in the name of Jesus"; "Your will be done"; "get behind me, Satan"; and "by the blood of the Lamb."

Each one of these can be a piercing, slashing, sword thrust in your prayer warfare. Use Scripture in your praying. Use Scripture militantly. Use Scripture in the command of faith.

Scripture is called the sword of the Spirit because it is inspired by the Spirit. It is His sword because He is the one who hands it to you and because it is the great weapon He uses through you. The literal Greek is "receive it," because the Holy Spirit must place it in your hands.

The use of Scripture in prayer warfare is a work of the Holy Spirit. He brings it to your memory as you pray. He gives it piercing and sharp-slashing power as you wield it against Satan. Satan cannot stand against the Word of God when it is used in the power of the Spirit. Jesus silenced Satan with the Word, and so can you when you wield it by the Spirit.

All these are the armor and weapons of your warfare, but prayer is the actual warfare. Therefore, Paul closes this description of the armor and weapons with the exhortation that when you have been fully armed, you should use it all by prayer in battling Satan in Christ's name (v. 18).

2. *Accept and adopt the warrior spirit.* Victory depends on the warrior spirit. The Goliaths of our day are commissioned by Satan to challenge us as followers of Christ. Become like David, a man after God's own heart (Acts 13:22). God loved and honored David's warrior spirit. Like David, challenge your Goliaths. David could hardly wait for the battle with Goliath. He had learned the warrior spirit from encounters that God had permitted with the lion and the bear. He could not be God's man as king of God's people unless he had the warrior spirit. You cannot be God's person with anything less than a militant spirit of prayer.

God is expecting you to be so militant that you attack Satan's territory, demolish his arguments, confront any opposition, and destroy it by spiritual weapons. Prayer can give to you a spirit of militancy. Prayer puts aggressiveness in your inmost nature. You burn with the fire of holy desire to expose the falsehoods of Satan, thrust aside the mountains Satan has thrown up against God's will and progress, and free all Satan's captives.

As a prayer warrior you breathe the righteous indignation of God. You are aflame with holy determination and the Spirit's power to overthrow all opposing powers and clear the way for the conquering Christ. You are not foolishly rash or presumptive. You are militant.

God's honor is at stake. God's will is being thwarted. Jesus' name is being questioned and dishonored. Like David, be willing to lay your life on the line for God. Like Paul, challenge the power of darkness in the name of Jesus. God needs victories. God's victories are won by prayer battles. The Holy Spirit wants to give you the warrior spirit and make you part of His holy prayer "Marine Corps."

Do you hate sin like God hates sin?

Do you feel the scandal of God's name being dishonored and God's will hindered?

Do you see humankind enslaved and abused by Satan and his followers?

Do you burn with zeal for God's will and God's glory?

Are you unwilling for spiritual détente and relaxation of tension with Satan? Are you unwilling for peace through spiritual coexistence?

Don't be afraid of spiritual warfare, of prayer warfare! Don't fear the price of victory!

Give yourself to the Holy Spirit, and ask Him to instill His holy militance in you. Ask Him to saturate you with His holy warrior spirit. With Isaac Watts sing:

> *Am I a soldier of the cross?*
> *Are there no foes for me to face,*
> *Must I not stem the flood?*
> *Sure I must fight if I would reign;*
> *Increase my courage, Lord!*

3. *Stand against Satan.* The New English Bible translates James 4:7, "Stand up to the devil and he will turn and run." Barclay translates the verb, "Take a stand against." The Greek literally says "oppose." This is a command. You do not defeat Satan by passively "looking to the Lord."

In certain situations when Satan wants to harm you, the Lord shields and protects you. He has promised to do so, and His angels are always available to help you. But God also requires you to take a stand against Satan, to stand on the battlefield and fight.

The command to take a stand against Satan, to resist and oppose him, is as much a command as the command to witness or to preach the gospel. Our world is a battleground. We are to be warriors for Christ. Calvary was planned by God not only to deliver us from our sins but to empower us so that we can defeat Satan. God the Son defeated Satan at Calvary and depends on us now to enforce His victory by prayer warfare.

You are to stand up against Satan, to take your stand by prayer. Satan is the intruder. He had no authority, and compared to God, he has few resources. He loves to roar like a lion, but in many respects he is chained. He cannot go beyond the limits God sets. Paul says you are to stand "without being frightened in any way" (Phil. 1:28). Stand on the character of God, on His power and faithfulness. Stand on God's inherent right as Creator and Owner of the universe. Stand on His right as victor over Satan at Calvary.

You have no alternative to battle! You have no acceptable alternative to victory in Jesus' name! You are committed to oppose Satan and triumph in Christ. Nothing less is worthy of God. No compromise on this point is safe. The starting point to prayer battle is to stand. "Take your stand. . . . Put on the full armor of God, so that . . . you may be able to stand your ground. Stand firm then" (Eph. 6:11–14).

4. *Plan and take the offensive.* The battle order of Churchill to Lord Mountbatten in World War II was, "You are to plan for the offensive. In your headquarters you will never think defensively."[1] You are born again for battle and victory. Christ's orders to you are to press for victory.

Prayer is not a child's toy. It is not a weapon for recreational hunting, not even merely for self-defense. Prayer, *prevailing* prayer, is a mighty weapon for all our spiritual warfare against Satan. It is heavy artillery for offensive action against Satan. It is God's provision for conquest.

Arthur Mathews has written, "In any situation where Satan dominates and threatens, God looks for a man through whom He may declare war on the enemy. He purposes that through that man Satan be served notice to back up, pack up, and clear out."[2] God is waiting for prayer warriors both to stand in the gap against Satan's onslaughts and, even more, to target Satan's strongholds and attack them.

Scripture clearly expects us to have a militant spirit and attack strongholds of Satan. "The weapons we fight with . . . have divine power to demolish strongholds. We demolish arguments and every pretension that sets itself up against the knowledge of God, and we take captive every thought to make it obedient to Christ" (2 Cor. 10:4–5).

Take the shield of faith. Take the sword of the Spirit. Pray militantly. Demonstrate your being armed for war and your plan for victory. Stop bemoaning Satan's attacks! Stop all futile consideration of alternatives to conquest! A church fails God if it does not arm its believers with the attitude of faith and the skills of prayer warfare. We must plan for victory, arm for victory, train for victory, and launch an offensive for victory.

5. *Take the initiative of faith.* Not only be on the offensive for God, be alert to take the initiative of faith. God has planned the initiative to be in our hands. He has made full provision for prayer-won victory, but we must do the prevailing. He has provided promises adequate for anything in accordance with His will, but we must claim the promise and exercise the faith.

On the battlefield the greatest enemy to overcome is fear. God has armed us for spiritual war, but unused weapons win no wars. We must be alert for every opportunity to take the initiative for God. Faith is not passive, and prayer is not neutral. Faith and prayer are God's super weapons for His children. The sword of the Spirit is to be used on every possible occasion. God calls for the action of faith.

Prayer initiative—faith initiative exercised in prevailing prayer—can win any battle that is for Christ's glory and in accord with God's will. Satan occupies many strategic positions by our default. Not to use the mighty weapons of prayer and faith when Satan is so illegitimately staking his claims, so vulnerable to our attack, and so certain of ultimate defeat would be serious dereliction of our spiritual responsibility and duty.

Victory comes only as we will to use the weapons God has provided. There is nothing automatic in spiritual victory, but "when God sees a weapon being used in His name and faith daring to attempt the impossible, He musters heaven's cohorts and moves in to confound and rout the enemy."[3] Gospel advance is constantly impeded through prayerlessness and lack of spiritual militancy on the part of God's children. "Forward on your knees" should be the watch-cry of all believers.

CHAPTER 36

Strategies in Prayer Warfare, Part 2

6. *BATTLE FROM THE position of victory.* On the cross Jesus defeated Satan in a total and final victory. "And having disarmed the powers and authorities [terms for Satan's hierarchy of evil], he made a public spectacle of them, triumphing over them by the cross" (Col. 2:15). Christ's victory was not only a victory in depth, it was a victory with eternal consequences. Satan and his forces are defeated rebels, usurpers who have been stripped of all power. They have already been led like prisoners in disgrace by Christ in His triumphal procession. They have become "Christ's prize of war."

God in the mystery of His sovereign will is permitting them for a time to continue ranging about, within limits He has set. While awaiting their final expulsion and being cast into the lake of fire, they try to deceive humankind by bluffing as if they had not been defeated. But their doom is already settled.

God permits them to show their fury and hatred within the limits He has set for this brief moment of eternity that we call time. At the cross Christ won an eternal cosmic victory over Satan. It was decisive and final and needs never be repeated. It can never be reversed. Satan's doom is already decided and announced. He and his demon princes of darkness are like wild beasts captured and chained. They can roar and thrash around, but they are to some extent chained.

Even before Calvary the demons shouted, "What do you want with us, Son of God? . . . Have you come here to torture us before the appointed time?" (Matt. 8:29). Now, as an accomplished fact, they have been disarmed (Col. 2:15). At the cross they have been paraded, defeated for all the spirit world to see.

They could not keep Christ from the throne, where He is now seated. God the Father has said to Him, "Sit at my right hand until I put your enemies under your feet" (Matt. 22:44). "Yet at present we do not see everything subject to him" (Heb. 2:8). In the mystery of God's purpose, God is permitting Satan to fight back, to bluff his way, to hinder us for the time being.

God left some of Israel's enemies to occupy their lands temporarily and oppose Israel. "He did this only to teach warfare to the descendants of the Israelites who had not had previous battle experience" (Judg. 3:2). God seems to have a similar plan for the church today. He is teaching His choicest saints prayer warfare. Satan has been totally and forever defeated by Christ, but God has planned for you and me to enforce that victory by prayer warfare. He is teaching us priceless spiritual experiences for which we will be eternally grateful as well as eternally honored and rewarded.

You are already in a very real sense enthroned with Christ. You are already in spiritual fact a king and a priest, a royal priest (Rev. 1:6; 1 Peter 2:9). "God raised us up with Christ and seated us with him in the heavenly realms in Christ Jesus" (Eph. 2:6). So while you battle Satan by prayer here, you are in spiritual reality also sitting with Christ on His throne.

In perspective, you battle Satan from the throne. You see Satan already defeated. You look down upon the battlefield from the vantage point of Christ's throne. But in the meantime God has assigned you to battle Satan and occupy for Christ all the territory that Satan is presently holding. The promise to Joshua is, in effect, your promise: "I will give you every place where you set your foot. . . . No one will be able to stand up against you all the days of your life" (Josh. 1:3, 5). Stuart Holden has said, "We go into battle not from the perspective of our circumstance here on earth, but from our position above in Christ."[1] This is the position of faith.

Your assignment is to wrest from Satan's control the territory he has no right to occupy. Your assignment is to rescue the souls and lives that Satan is holding in his bondage. You battle forward, routing Satan from one stronghold after another. You point Satan back to the blood he shed—the blood that sealed his doom. He was eternity's fool to lay his hand on Jesus. He suffered eternity's greatest defeat, and it will prove to be his eternal defeat.

You would think Satan would give up. He knows he has been defeated. He knows his position is hopeless. He knows he is involving in his own eternal punishment all the people he deceives. He knows he is going to continue to be defeated again and again. Every battle he fights increases his eternal punishment. But in his stubborn and inveterate hatred of God and humankind, he fights on. In the triumph of Christ you and I are to dislodge him, rout him, and drive him back in battle after battle.

Understand your position in Christ. Understand your sacred role. Here you war in His name in holy prayer warfare. You will be rewarded eternally with Him in His eternal reign. Understand and use all the authority Christ has delegated to you. Earn your eternal honors in the prayer battles of time.

7. *Win the invisible war first.* Behind every visible hindrance, opposition, and roadblock that Satan throws up against you is the invisible reality of his demonic opposition. Although you are most aware of the visible, the greater reality is the invisible. The visible is but the expression of the invisible. "Our struggle is not against flesh and blood, but against the rulers, against the authorities, against the powers of this dark world and against the spiritual forces of evil in the heavenly realms" (Eph. 6:12).

The all-important standing against Satan is in the invisible. The shield of faith is in the invisible. The skillful wielding of the sword of the Spirit is in the invisible. You may be led to quote Scripture a lot to Satan, but it echoes through the realm of the Spirit far more loudly than in the place where you raise your audible voice.

You must overthrow the invisible forces of Satan if you would see things and lives changed visibly before you. The mountains must be moved in the invisible before their being forced aside is evident in the visible. You must bind Satan and his demons before you see his helpless captives freed. Jesus must put Satan under your feet invisibly before things are under Jesus' feet visibly.

This is not romantic Christian fiction but awesome and glorious spiritual reality. Prayer warfare is real. It is costly. It is waged on earth, but it is also in an even greater sense waged in the heavenlies. In truest reality, you fight not *for* victory but *from the position of* victory.[2] And yet the war continues. Christ routs Satan invisibly by your prayer warfare, in the face of the visible hostility and opposition that Satan motivates.

F. J. Huegel, battle-trained missionary veteran, writes, "Praise God, it is all real, real because God who cannot lie says it is so, real though ten thousand circumstances and feelings thunder and say it is not."[3] When you have won the victory in the invisible and taken your seat with Christ invisibly on His throne, when by your invisible victory Christ has placed Satan under your feet (Rom. 16:20), then you can reign already with Christ and watch God bring the invisible victory into visible reality.

Arthur Mathews, veteran missionary, told of God's placing a burden on his heart for two specific areas in Southeast Asia. Strong opposition to the progress of the gospel was being faced there. The prayer burden continued as Mathews prayed on. "So asserting my position with Christ in the heavenlies on the basis of God's Word and strengthened by His might, I took unto me the whole armor of God in order to stand against the wiles of the devil and to withstand his opposition to the gospel." As Mathews held on, news from both places began to change.

"The resisting powers in both cases were weakened, making possible victories for the Lord."[4]

Do you know the joy of having the Spirit give you the invisible victory in prayer that puts things under your feet? What a new perspective! What new liberty of spirit! Mountains that overwhelmed you before now seem as small as molehills. You sense the power of the Spirit upon you and in you. Throne life has begun. Nothing so terrifies and enrages Satan. This form of resistance truly makes Satan run.

8. *Pray in the Spirit.* "Pray in the Holy Spirit," says Jude (Jude 20). Paul adds, "Pray in the Spirit on all occasions with all kinds of prayers and requests" (Eph. 6:18). If praying in the Spirit is important in all prayer, it is specially urgent in prayer warfare. Only those who are consciously filled with the Spirit can know the continuous empowering of the Spirit for prayer. Arthur Mathews writes concerning confrontation with the Devil, "Nor is it to be entered into under conditions in which the individual is not filled with the Spirit." S. D. Gordon adds, "We are never really men of prayer in the best sense, until we are filled with the Holy Spirit."[5]

We need the Holy Spirit in order to love with the love that makes prayer truly prevail. "The love of Christ . . . that surpasses knowledge" (Eph. 3:18–19) is the result of "power through his Spirit in your inner being" (v. 16). God's ability to do through our prayer "immeasurably more than all we ask or imagine" is "according to his power" working in us (v. 20).

Prayer weaknesses can hinder effective prayer, but the Spirit's purpose is so to infill you that He can help you in your prayer weakness (Rom. 8:26). Only in total reliance on the Spirit can you prevail in prayer. Therefore receiving the fullness of the Spirit, living in the fullness, and praying in the fullness are absolutely essential in all prayer warfare. This subject has been treated more fully in chapters 14 and 15.

9. *Concentrate on prayer targets one after another.* Prayer warfare is being so militant in Jesus' name that you seize from the enemy all that rightfully belongs to Christ. Christ is the victor, and prayer warfare takes from Satan the victor's spoils.

Not only are you to pray for blessing, you are to pray against Satan, against every ramification of his work and his kingdom of darkness. You must so breathe the spirit of Christ that you have the battlefield spirit—the determination to free Satan's captives, to take possession away from Satan, and to give it rightfully to Christ.

Jesus went about challenging and defeating Satan, setting free those who were physically sick, troubled by demons, and enslaved to sin. In many respects you are to do the same. The early church understood this mission. The revival in Samaria was an invasion of Satan's territory. Every time Paul began a campaign in another city, he was invading Satan's territory. Wherever he went, demon-possessed people or demon-led opposition confronted him. He had a vision of occupying the Roman Empire for Jesus. He planted Christian churches in centers of political and commercial life like Jesus-forts behind Satan's lines. Then he counted on the Christians reaching out by prayer and witness, conquering for Christ in the surrounding areas.

The early church sought to take the name of Jesus and plant churches of Jesus Christ in every stronghold of Satan. They wanted to rid the earth of all vestiges of Satan's power. They even built church buildings on spots where pagan shrines had been located. They did not want pagan and demonic rites ever to be performed there again. They were "occupying" for King Jesus.

Missionary pioneers planned and prayed in the same terms. When Jonathan Goforth planned to launch new work in North Honan Province in China, Hudson Taylor wrote to him, "Brother, if you are to win that province you must go forward on your knees."[6] Every fortress of spiritual darkness must be conquered on your knees.

It was Hudson Taylor's personal habit to cover with militant prayer each of their mission centers, every missionary, and every urgent circumstance that he knew about.[7] It was deliberate, specific, aggressive prayer warfare, persisting until the spiritual victories were won.

Prayer warriors are called to be Christ's spiritual assault troops. Satan has assaulted us long enough. Let's turn the battle against him. Jesus wants to overthrow Satan's strongholds one by one through us. Satan yields ground only when we compel him to. We must advance step by step, stronghold by stronghold, from victory to victory. Begin claiming one person after another for Jesus. Set the captives free. Begin claiming one place after another for Jesus. As the early European empires claimed territory in the New World of the Americas in the name of their sovereign, so we must claim places, situations, and people for Jesus. Keep the aggressive, militant spirit; keep taking new prayer-warfare initiatives for Jesus.

10. *Continue to cover past victories with prayer.* Satan does not give up his lost territory readily. Often even after the victory has been won in the heavenlies, in the invisible, he continues to resist your prayer warfare and to fight on. He knows it is hopeless, but he is so stubborn in his hatred of Christ that he holds on till the last minute, trying to do as much injury and damage as possible.

Even after you feel sure the battle is won, he will attempt another attack upon you and your position of faith. Do you remember the battle of Rephidim (Exod. 17:8–16)? Moses, Aaron, and Hur are on the hill lifting holy hands in prayer to God. As they do, Joshua routs Amalek. So with the enemy fleeing and his hands weary, Moses lets his hands down. Immediately Amalek rallies their forces and attacks again. So again Moses lifts his hands in prayer, and again Joshua routs Amalek. But as soon as Moses lets his hands relax, Amalek again returns and attacks. The spiritual lessons are obvious. First, visible victories depend on the spiritual battle. Second, the victories won must be followed up with continual, relentless attack until Satan is finally defeated. Finally, Satan refuses to accept defeat. Therefore, victories won must be covered with "occupying prayer" in order to maintain the victory. S. D. Gordon writes, "Prayer must be persisted in after we have full assurance of the result, and even after some immediate results have come, or, after the general results have commenced coming."[8]

So Moses summarizes for us, "Hands were lifted up to the throne of the LORD. The LORD will be at war against the Amalekites from generation to generation" (Exod. 17:16). In the words of the hymn writer George Heath:

> *O watch and fight, and pray.*
>   *The battle ne'er give o'er.*
> *Renew it boldly every day,*
>   *And help divine implore.*
> *Ne'er think the victory won,*
>   *Nor lay thine armor down;*
> *The work of faith will not be done,*
>   *Till thou obtain thy crown.*
> *Fight on, my soul. . . .*

CHAPTER 37

Dangers in Prayer Warfare

SATAN TAKES YOUR prayer warfare very seriously. He does not leave lives, situations, or places unless he is driven out. He opposes your advance with every weapon at his disposal. He attacks you on every level that he dares— physically, emotionally, mentally, and spiritually. There is safety and refuge in the Lord. His angels join you in your prayer warfare, assuring you of ultimate victory. But you must ever be alert and aware of Satan's efforts and methods.

Any individual or group that enters into prayer warfare as a ministry, as a call from the Lord, will be opposed by Satan. He is terrified of those who give themselves to prayer. Do you remember how, in the days of the prophet Zechariah, the high priest Joshua could not begin his priestly ministry of intercession until Satan had been rebuked? God showed Zechariah in a vision that Satan was standing at the right side of the high priest trying to hinder. It was also important for Joshua to be spiritually clean and obedient if he was to have the assistance of the heavenly hosts (Zech. 3:1–7).

Attacks by Satan in a particular location or attacks on people are proof of the very real war in the heavenlies. If prevailing prayer were not so mighty, Satan would not fear it so greatly or oppose it so violently. A storm of onslaughts, a fury of battle in a specific situation, does not prove we are losing the battle. If anything, it proves the effectiveness of our prayer warfare. Satan does everything he can in a last-ditch effort to frighten us or stop us. He is sometimes permitted to hinder or delay our victory for a time, but we are on victory's side because we are on the Victor's side. Satan's most violent opposition is often in the last moments before he is forcefully ejected by God's power.

The storm on the Sea of Galilee did not prove that Jesus or the disciples were in danger. It proved Satan was angry. But one command of Jesus was all it took to rout him. For every attack of Satan, Christ has vision for victory.

But we must by faith appropriate and claim the protection that God has available for us. Claim protection for your body against accident, weakness, and disease. Claim protection for your mind against carelessness, forgetfulness, and all Satan's lies and deceptions. Claim protection of your spirit against passivity, indifference, battle weariness, and temptation. Claim protection for your work against the onslaughts of Satan and his demons through hostile people or circumstances. Claim protection through God's Word, through the blood of the cross, through the name of Jesus. Claim God's wisdom, guidance, and power. Claim the assistance in the invisible of the angel forces of God.

1. *The danger of being engrossed in your work.* We are in constant danger of being so preoccupied with our work, so absorbed in the demands of our daily life and the pressures of our Christian ministry, that we have no time for real prayer warfare. The restlessness of our age gets into our souls until it is hard to take time for quiet alone with God and for several hours for a personal prayer retreat that we set apart to engage in spiritual battle. We work when we ought to pray. We have become such workaholics that we feel more comfortable working than praying.

It is so easy to become spiritually shallow and comparatively powerless because we have spent so little quality time with the

Lord. We have become victims of the tyranny of our work. We lack the discipline and sense of true priority to put prayer first. Prayer time must be planned, reserved, and seized for God.

I am not speaking merely of time in personal prayer communion and fellowship, time for feeding your own soul. We must go further and budget time for prevailing prayer for the needs of others and for Christ's cause. Prayer warfare deserves time and demands time. No Christian is meeting the New Testament standard who does not give time both to prayer communion and fellowship and to prevailing prayer, joining the Son of God and the Holy Spirit in prayer warfare.

Prayerlessness, neglect of intercession, and absence from the field of prayer battle must be confessed to God and repented of and His forgiveness obtained. Then we must set our soul to give priority to prayer in a definite yet reasonable way. We must ask the Spirit to put the hunger for God's presence and God's mighty answers back into our soul again. We have failed our interceding King too long. By God's grace do something about it today.

2. *The danger of fear.* We, as Christ's ambassadors, should not fear Satan's opposition. He is a defeated foe. Satan wants to immobilize us by fear so that we will go on the defensive instead of on the attack for God. All the wonderful "fear not" Scriptures are ours to claim (Isa. 35:4; 41:10, 13; 43:1, 5; 44:8; 54:4). When we are fighting God's battles, God takes the responsibility for our protection. His angels are our guard.

Andrew Bonar reported that he never entered into a season of pure prayer without a fierce battle at the beginning. Satan so fears prevailing prayer that he exerts every effort to try to back us away from our prayer commitment, to try to frighten us. His one concern is to keep us from praying. He does not fear prayerless study, prayerless preaching, prayerless work, or prayerless Christianity. He laughs at our prayerless busyness but trembles when we take prayer warfare seriously. Therefore, he tries to frighten us away from this holy ministry.

We should not be foolhardy. We should not recklessly spite Satan. But when we are fighting the Lord's battles, sharing His prayer burden, wrestling in the power of the Spirit, we can claim the protection of the name of Jesus and the blood of Jesus. In cases where demons must be cast out, if at all possible take a Spirit-filled prayer partner with you. There may be times when you cannot do so. Do not fear. Use the name of Jesus. But do not attempt such battles if you are in spiritual defeat or out of God's will.

Jesus prayed for you and me, "Holy Father, protect them by the power of your name" (John 17:11). The protection of His name is the protection of His presence, of His promise, and of His angels. "The name of the LORD is a strong tower; the righteous run to it and are safe" (Prov. 18:10). So once again we can sing with Martin Luther:

> And though this world, with devils filled,
> Should threaten to undo us,
> We will not fear, for God has willed
> His truth to triumph through us:
> The Prince of Darkness grim,
> We tremble not for him;
> His rage we can endure,
> For lo! his doom is sure;
> One little word shall fell him.

3. *The danger of unfocused prayer.* Indefinite, generalized prayer never brings definite answers. Faith and prayer must be specific to be effective. There is a legitimate role of holy desire in certain general areas of prayer need, such as hunger for revival, for harvest, for a new day for God, for a spirit of prayer among God's people, for funds for God's cause, and for laborers in the harvest. Your soul can and should cry out to God for such needs as these again and again.

Such generalized petitions are all right as you begin your prayer time with God or when you snatch brief moments during the day while you are doing work that requires a certain minimum of mental concentration. But praying that is effective prayer warfare must, wherever possible, become highly specific and personalized. The more detailed your prayer can become, the more comprehensive your prayer burden can become. The more personally you pray, the deeper grows your holy love for the person prayed for and the more powerfully the Spirit can empower you in praying for that one.

Beware of praying so generally that you do not remember what you have prayed. Beware of being so unspecific that you would not be able to recognize it if your prayer were answered. All needs are specific needs. The situations of life are wonderfully and tragically detailed. You will never know all about a particular need, but the more you know, the more effectively you can prevail. Prayer opportunities are specific opportunities. Prayer needs are highly specific and detailed.

It takes the amassed prayer of many people to prepare the way of the Lord for nationwide revival. But you or a few people can prevail for revival and see God work in power in a specific life, family, church, or perhaps even in a whole community. It is good to long for nationwide revival. But the more your prayer for revival is focused on a specific situation, the sooner you will probably see the answer to your prayers. Pray for both.

Mighty prayer burdens are usually for specific situations. Holy prevailing, wrestling in prayer, is usually guided and empowered by the Spirit for urgent specific needs. Our longings can include the whole world, but to be answerable they must become concrete, detailed, and specific. Effective faith is faith for a particular need that you can name before the Lord, describe in detail in your prayer, and so be specific enough that you can know when the answer comes. Paul prayed for his people by name. Name the people and needs for which you pray, and be as concrete and specific as you can.

In business, in banking, in travel, and in life in general, you have to be specific in asking to get what you need. Spurgeon called specific prayers "business prayers." Take a definite need and a specific promise, ask God clearly for exactly what you need, and trust for the concrete answer. Finney points out that your mind cannot intensely desire many things at one time. You must focus on one at a time. So it must be in prevailing prayer.[1] God does not expect you to prevail for every need in the world. He wants to give you specific prayer assignments that become your personal responsibility and burden before the Lord.

4. *The danger of unguided prayer.* Two elements should be before us in all intercession and particularly in prayer warfare: the human need and the divine plan. To pray with effective prevailing you must get in harmony with the intercessions of Christ on His throne and of the Spirit praying within you. S. D. Gordon writes that prayer is "finding out God's purpose ... and insisting that that shall be done here. The great thing then is to find out and insist upon God's will."[2] God's will is always best. What we desire may be good, but it may not be the best.

God is far more eager to answer prayer than you are to receive the answer. He alone knows what is best. Your yearnings are the faint echo of God's infinite yearnings. Your love is imperfect; His is always perfect. The plans of His love are not only the best—they are perfect. How foolish you would be to pray for anything but His will.

How could the Spirit anoint and empower you to pray for that which is not God's perfect will? How could He assist faith for what is not God's holy desire? Calvin said, "Never will man pray as he ought unless the Master will guide both his mouth and his heart."[3] It is a waste of breath and time to ask for something outside God's will.

Successful prevailing prayer and prayer warfare thus depend as much on your listening as on your repeated asking. Habakkuk was praying, but he realized he needed to hear from God. "I will stand at my watch.... I will look to see what he will say to me" (Hab. 2:1). You need the Spirit to convey to you God's perspective, overview, and plan from the standpoint of eternity. Only He knows what will be most to His eternal glory and for your greatest eternal good.

"He guides the humble in what is right and teaches them his way" (Ps. 25:9). As you humble yourself before God, confessing your total need of His wisdom and guidance and being eager only for His will, you will learn to develop a listening ear for

His voice and a repeated consciousness of His touch. Andrew Murray has said, "The Christian learns that the soft, gentle touch of the Spirit is very sensitive. No liberties can be taken, or the sense of the abiding presence is withdrawn."[4] Paul was sensitive to the Spirit's gentle voice and touch as he prayed about ministry in Acts 16:6–7.

When you confine your intercession to your own understanding, you not only may miss God's intent but may hinder His plan. Wait on God until He confirms His will to you. Do not force your will upon Him, but when you understand His heart and will, then add all the force of your praying to His mighty prevailings. When the prayer burden seems to change, wait in God's presence for the Spirit's next guidance concerning your request.

You do not know the strategic moments in prayer warfare. You cannot manufacture a prayer burden. But when you as a prayer warrior are maintaining a continuing prayer warfare or carrying a continuing prayer burden, the Holy Spirit at the crucial moment may burden you with intense prayer wrestling. Or a group may be continuing in several hours of earnest prayer for a need when suddenly intense prayer burden comes upon one after another. Such united prayer warfare has great power to bring God's victory. God's timing of such intensive prayer warfare has often been miraculously exact. But why should this surprise us, when the Holy Spirit is our divine Strategist?

In 1909 at the close of wonderful meetings in Tungchow, near Peking, China, Jonathan Goforth left for the United States. En route he stopped in London. While there he was told of an invalid lady who was a real prayer warrior. He was eager to meet her. During their conversation she told him that she had heard of his proposed meetings in China and had felt a great burden laid upon her to pray for him. Then she asked him to look at her notebook. She had recorded three dates when a special prayer burden came upon her. Goforth was overawed when he discovered that those dates were the very times when he realized the greatest power and mighty moving of the Holy Spirit in his ministry in Manchuria.[5]

Mrs. Ed Spahr was awakened at midnight one night with a prayer burden for Rev. and Mrs. Jerry Rose in Irian Jaya, who worked among a Stone Age-culture people. Her prayer warfare was so clear and specific that the next moring she wrote a letter to them, telling them about it. In time the Roses received similar letters from five prayer partners in five different continents, each of whom had been led by the Spirit to prevail in prayer on that specific occasion. At the very time and date that all five were prevailing, Mr. Rose was standing with his arms tied behind his back, and a savage stood before him ready to pin him to the ground with his spear. Just then another man from the tribe stepped up to him and spoke to him, and he walked away, leaving Mr. Rose unharmed.[6]

Isobel Kuhn and her husband were experiencing great opposition in the South China village where they were laboring. It seemed impossible for people to leave their sinful customs and turn to Christ. At one point, however, without any explanation that they could find, a sudden, amazing change took place. Three quarreling clans made up their differences, and there were outstanding cases of conversion. Then in time they received a letter from a prayer warrior who told that at the exact time when the change came in China she was so gripped with a prayer burden for the Kuhns and their work that she went to the telephone and called another praying lady. She immediately said she had been feeling the same prayer burden and suggested that they call a third lady. They did so, and each of the three ladies went to prayer in prevailing intercession in her own kitchen. As they prevailed, Satan was defeated and lives were set free.[7]

5. *The danger of wrong motives.* Since all spiritual warfare depends on the power of the Spirit, you need to be sure not only that you are filled with the Spirit but also that you keep your prayer motives spiritual. The only weapons that prevail against Satan are spiritual weapons. Self-generated zeal can cause you unconsciously to pray for what you desire rather than

for what the Spirit desires, or can cause you to misunderstand God's timing.

It is very easy for the glory of God to be a secondary motive and for some self-related motive to be primary. That reversal can block your answers to prayer. You can be very subtly motivated for success more because you do not want to be a failure than because you hunger for the glory of God. You can pray zealously because it is "your" children, "your" church, or "your" nation.

It is not sinful to have personal interests, but beware lest self become a main motivation. Jesus warned His disciples against glorying in the fact that demons had to submit to them when they used the authority of Christ's name. Glory in Christ rather than in your authority in Christ. Jesus rejoiced in the Spirit (Luke 10:21); they were rejoicing in success (v. 17). Paul thus gives two cautions in relation to prayer: "Devote yourselves to prayer, being watchful and thankful" (Col. 4:2). Prayer warfare requires constant watchfulness—of Satan's attacks, of your prayer priorities, and of your motivation in prayer.

Your love for people must be for God's sake and their sake, not just to add another statistic to your membership or for benefits you may incidentally receive. Your prayer warfare must be for God's sake and their sake, not just to stop the problems that are causing you such difficulty. Your boldest prayer, your most faith-filled prayer, your most mightily empowered prayer can be only for those needs in which self does not motivate you in any primary way.

6. *The danger of giving up too soon.* "Jesus told his disciples a parable to show them that they should always pray and not give up" (Luke 18:1). Then after telling about the unjust judge who finally answered the persistent widow's pleas, Jesus summarized, "Listen. . . . Will not God bring about justice for his chosen ones, who cry out to him day and night? Will he keep putting them off? I tell you, he will see that they get justice, and quickly" (vv. 6–8).

We have already discussed the dynamic of persistence. Yet lack of persistence is a great danger in prayer warfare also. You begin to prevail in prayer for a need. God starts the combined ministry of His providence, His angels, and His Spirit. But what if before all the details can be related to one another, perhaps just before the miracle answer comes, you give up? Paul assures us that "at the proper time we will reap a harvest if we do not give up" (Gal. 6:9).

Thousands upon thousands of prayers have been granted by God, but often before the answers can be received, the intercessor gives up. Many prayer answers require the wills of certain people to submit to God's plan. God does not shuffle people around like checkers on a board. He persuades by many influences and pressures that He brings upon people. Give God time to work out the details. God always has reasons for seeming delays. God often has a better time and a better way.

The danger is that your desire is not deep enough, that your persistence is not strong enough. Don't stop your prayer bombardment just before Satan raises up the flag of surrender and clears out. Battles are always finally won in the last hour. Don't give up too soon. Some answers to prayer will come only if you hold on in prayer. The only way some people will reach heaven is if you refuse to give up.

Rev. Lars Olsen Skrefsrud, Norwegian minister mightily used of God, was won through prevailing prayer warfare. An ordinary country girl, Bolette Hinderli, was praying once when she was given a vision of a prisoner in a prison cell. She could see his face and body in the vision. The voice seemed to say to her, "This man will share the same fate as other criminals if no one takes up the work of praying for him. Pray for him and I will send him out to proclaim my praises among the heathen."

Bolette began to prevail in prayer. Day after day she held on for the salvation of this unknown prisoner. She waited and prayed and believed to hear some day of a convict who had become converted and called into missionary work. After a considerable time, she was visiting in Stavanger, Norway, when she heard that a converted former convict was to preach that evening in one of the churches. She went, and as soon as Skrefsrud stepped into the pulpit, she recognized him as the very person she had seen in her vision and for whom she had prevailed.[8]

CHAPTER 38

How to Bind Satan, Part 1

SATAN CAN BE BOUND. Is that not glorious news? One day God's angels will bind "the powers in the heavens above" (Isa. 24:21). The context in this chapter shows that this promise is related to our Lord's second coming. Obviously, these are the principalities and powers in the heavenlies against which we wrestle in prayer in our prayer warfare (Eph. 6:10–18). In Revelation 22, one angel will be sent from heaven and will bind Satan, and he will remain bound for a thousand years. It will take only one angel to do it!

Evidently Jesus intends for us to share in some way in binding Satan. While on earth Jesus to some extent had bound Satan's influence. In explaining His casting out demons in His ministry, Jesus said that what He did was by the power of the Spirit (Matt. 12:28). We will have to bind Satan in exactly the same manner. He explained further, "How can anyone enter a strong man's house and carry off his possessions unless he first ties up the strong man?" (v. 29). Jesus was saying, in other words, "I have bound the strong man." We know these are figurative words, but they are very significant for us in prayer warfare.

When the seventy-two returned, telling how even the demons were compelled to submit to their authoritative use of Jesus' name, Jesus replied, "I saw Satan fall like lightning from heaven" (Luke 10:18). Again, these are figurative words, but Jesus is saying Satan is being defeated, Satan's plans are being frustrated, Satan's forces are being stopped, and their captives are being set free. Satan's sham authority is being exposed and broken. Satan's pseudopower is being shown how limited it is.

Then Jesus continued, "I have given you authority to trample on snakes and scorpions and to overcome all the power of the enemy" (Luke 10:19). What does Jesus mean by "snakes and scorpions?" Probably He is referring to Satan's demons. But Jesus' last summary statement in the whole discussion is no longer figurative. Jesus says plainly, "I have given you authority . . . to overcome all the power of the enemy."

Satan is the enemy. His "power" includes all his strategies, all his superhuman might, and all his forces. Jesus wants us to confront and defeat all that Satan tries to marshal against us. Let Satan do his worst. Let him throw against the church or against you and me his full might. Through Christ, through the Holy Spirit, and through the authority of the name of Jesus, we can trample his forces down like snakes. We can overcome.

But can we bind him? In what sense can we bind him? Let's answer these one at a time. Many, many godly expositors and writers have used Matthew 16:19 and 18:18 to explain that we can bind Satan. Is that a legitimate interpretation of this passage? Be patient while we study the Bible together for a moment.

When the Jewish rabbis announced certain rules of conduct to be required or not required by God, they referred to this situation as "binding" and "loosing." Does the verse "whatever you bind on earth will be bound in heaven, and whatever you loose on earth will be loosed in heaven" refer only to rules of conduct required for the church? Was Jesus only appointing the apostles to be successors of the rabbis? Obviously not.

In the very same verse, reference is made to the keys of the kingdom, which Jesus announced He was giving. This phrase obviously referred to the gospel door being opened for people. We are well aware that Peter used the keys (plural) on more than one occasion—for the Jews at Pentecost and for the Romans at the house of Cornelius. Please note that the "you" in the Greek in Matthew 16:19 is in the plural. Jesus did not give the keys to Peter alone, but to all the disciple group that were traveling with him, which included women as well as men. In other words, it is for all Christians.

Before we can finally answer the question, we need to read the similar statement of Jesus in a different part of the country and on a different occasion. This truth of binding and loosing was so important to Jesus that He taught it on more than one occasion. In Matthew 18:18 it is part of a three-verse statement. This time Jesus spoke in a most emphatic way. In the Greek it is "Amen, I say to you." He wanted them to be sure to understand and remember. Hence, He used the "Amen" first. The verb is in the plural; He speaks to all His disciples.

Verse 18 is the repeated statement about binding and loosing, just as in chapter 16. But this time it is part of a statement on prayer. "I tell you that if two of you on earth agree about anything you ask for, it will be done for you by my Father in heaven" (v. 19). The binding and loosing includes what we do by agreeing together in prayer—any two of Christ's disciples. But wait, verse 20 adds, "For where two or three come together in my name, there am I with them."

So the power of binding and loosing, the power of the keys of the kingdom, and the power of agreeing in prayer are all interrelated and are guaranteed because Jesus Himself joins in this agreement in prayer and in binding and loosing. He is present with them as they agree. Can we agree in prayer against Satan? We certainly can! Does this include binding in some way the power of Satan? Indeed it does! God's people have done so again and again.

But in what way do we bind Satan? "Bind" is the normal Greek verb *deō*. Satan bound and kept bound for eighteen years a woman who was bent over. That was a literal binding. Jesus said that a spirit did this (Luke 13:11–13). When she was loosed, she was set free from the Devil's power, and she could stand erect immediately. Furthermore, Paul was "bound" in Spirit, that is, compelled by the Spirit (Acts 20:22), to go to Jerusalem.

So the binding can be literal or figurative. It is a restraint or compulsion. To bind Satan is to restrain Satan, to compel him to do or not to do something. It is to restrain, hold back, or prevent his power from being used and his evil work accomplished.

Has Jesus enough authority to do this? He certainly has. He chose while on earth to meet Satan again and again. In the beginning of His ministry during the forty days in the desert to the last final confrontation in Gethsemane, He chose to meet Satan on the same level that we do. He resisted him as we must resist him—in prayer. He rebuked him to his face. He defeated him in the power of the Spirit. Now He has delegated to us the authority to act on His behalf, to use the authority of His name.

Today, by mighty prevailing prayer, by using the authority Jesus has given us—the authority of His name, His cross, and His resurrection—we can restrain Satan's activities in many significant ways. We can bind and restrain his demon cohorts, back them off from the places they claim for Satan, and help the Spirit set Satan's captives free. How shall we do this?

1. *Recognize Satan's activity.* Satan's evil spirits are very numerous and highly organized. They probably all fell into sin in some past rebellion against God, so they are all angry, full of hate, certain of their doom, and organized under Satan's dominance. They are malignant, vile, deceitful spirits. We need the Spirit's help to enable us to recognize when they work through people and circumstances. We need to recognize Satan's strategems.

The most numerous of Satan's helpers are the demons. Their chief purpose today seems to be to help Satan deceive and destroy humankind and thus to strike back at God because God loves man so infinitely and has provided redemption for man. Wherever people are found, the demons seem to be present. We can assume that they follow all sinners around constantly—

in their home, at their work, as they travel—trying to entice to sin or trying to influence wrong decisions. We know also they are often where Christians are, watching for an opportunity to accuse falsely or to discourage, divide, tempt, or hinder. Since Satan is only one and can be at only one place at one time, he must depend on the multitude of demons to do his work. Charles Wesley wrote:

> Angels our march oppose and still in strength excel,
> Our secret sworn eternal foes, countless, invisible;
> From thrones of glory driven, by flaming vengeance hurled,
> They throng the air and darken heaven, and rule this lower
>   world.

Until the day when Christ finally binds Satan and his followers and casts them all into the lake of fire (Rev. 20:10; 21:8), these are the forces that oppose us. Since Christ is no longer on earth, Satan directs his venom against mankind in general, and especially against the church. He is unusually incensed at all the evangelism of the church and especially manifests his opposition and power on the mission field. The Bible tells us that wherever people worship other gods, behind the façade of the religion, rituals, images, and so forth are the demons deceiving the worshipers (1 Cor. 10:20; Deut. 32:17; Ps. 106:36–37; Rev. 9:20). The demons are the main spirits confronting us.

The Bible uses a different Greek word for the fallen angels. These are not roaming about the earth but are imprisoned in Tartarus (Greek), or in gloomy dungeons, and held for the judgment day (2 Peter 2:4). Jude adds that they are in darkness, bound with everlasting chains (Jude 6). So they do not interfere with us today.

There is a hierarchy of fallen spirit leaders referred to in Ephesians 6:12 as rulers, authorities, powers, and spiritual forces of evil. We need not know the details of these spirit beings—we merely need to be alert to their role and purpose so that we can be wise in resisting them.

Paul wants us to recognize that behind the people who seem

to oppose, endanger, and hinder us are the unseen evil spirits, who are using and manipulating the people who are their unsuspecting slaves and dupes. Our spiritual warfare is not against the people we see but against the unseen spirits behind them seeking to manipulate them and work through them. The primary emphasis of Paul is that they are against us (repeated five times in Eph. 6:11–12). Adam and Eve failed to recognize Satan behind the snake. Jesus recognized Satan behind Peter's suggestion (Matt. 16:23) and behind Judas's betrayal (Luke 22:53). We need to recognize when to bind Satan's forces and who they are that we are binding. They are powerful and knowledgeable (sometimes seeming to know more than we do), but already defeated by Christ.

2. *Recognize the superiority of Christ's hosts.* Christ's forces are greater in number than Satan's. Only one-third of the angels fell (Rev. 12:4), so there are twice as many unfallen angels. Undoubtedly the Lord has His angels well organized. They are unified in mutual love and perfect, loving obedience to Christ. Since they have access to God, they are far wiser, far better informed, and undoubtedly far more interrelated and unified than are Satan's forces.

There are suggestions that every child, probably every human being, has a guardian, helping angel (Ps. 34:7; 91:11; Heb. 1:14). Jesus Himself confirms this truth (Matt. 18:10). They are available according to the will of God for whatever worthy help we need. We know from Scripture that they protect us and carry messages (often probably by mental suggestions and reminders to us) and are undoubtedly used by the Holy Spirit to guide and to restrain us. They are instantly available to you to reinforce your prayer warfare by blocking and opposing Satan's dark forces.

Satan influences and at times indwells his followers. But Christ, who is in us, is far greater than Satan (1 John 4:4). The angel forces surrounding us are greater in number and power than all who can combine against us, whether visible or invisible (2 Kings 6:16; 2 Chron. 32:7–8). They will help us bind Satan.

3. *Take the initiative to bind Satan and his representatives.* You do not necessarily ask the Lord to bind Satan or the angels to bind Satan. The binding is done by you—"Whatever you bind." You must neutralize your enemy before you can set his prisoners free. First, tie up the strong man, says Jesus (Matt. 12:29). We, the church, must take the initiative against Satan's kingdom.

The strong man (i.e., the demon), says Jesus, is fully armed (Luke 11:21). He tries to guard his territory and his captives against our prayer attack. His possessions in his captives probably include the love of sin (John 3:19), the love of the world, the lust of the eyes, and the boastful pride of life (1 John 2:16), the cravings of the sinful nature (Eph. 2:3), and hostility to God (Rom. 8:7). Satan tries to guard his followers so as to keep them enslaved to these attitudes and desires.

Satan is vulnerable to your assault in prayer warfare and your using the authority of Christ and the command and rebuke of faith. His head was crushed at Calvary (Gen. 3:15). Now when you take the initiative, heaven endorses and enforces Christ's victory through your praying.

CHAPTER 39

How to Bind Satan, Part 2

4. *WIN THE BATTLE in the invisible realm.* Prayer warfare is largely a battle, directly or indirectly, against the spirit world. We must confront and defeat the powers of darkness in their own realm of the invisible before our victories for Christ are visible on earth. Our weapons are not visible weapons, but they are divinely real. Ours is a battle of faith and prayer. We are to conquer in the heavenly realms (Eph. 3:10; 6:12), but the results will become visible here on earth.

We attack the cause, not the effect, just as Jesus did. Our binding is an invisible binding. The Spirit can enable us to recognize the invisible fetters binding people, the invisible power corrupting them, the unseen spirit whispering in their heart and motivating them.

Often the results of our victory in the invisible are immediately recognizable in the visible. At other times we cannot see for a time whether our prayer has been answered. But our warfare is a faith warfare. Just because we cannot instantly measure the results does not prove that God has not acted and that Satan has not begun to leave. The unseen battle sometimes takes time. We, having done all, must stand, stand,

stand. This is Scripture's exhortation concerning the battle in the heavenly realms (Eph. 6:10–14).

A Christian foreman in the maintenance department of a garage was burdened about the constant swearing and filthy speech of the men working there. He came to realize that it was Satan's demons, influencing the minds and conversation of these people. He immediately began to bind the powers of Satan. He arranged to arrive each morning before his fellow workmen. Then in the name and authority of Jesus Christ, he commanded the evil spirits to leave the place and forbade them to come again and influence the men. He said to them, "I hold God's most holy curse on you." He maintained his prayer warfare, binding Satan day after day for several months. The whole atmosphere of the place cleaned up, and the men seemed to forget their foul vocabulary and impure discussions.

The Kneeling Christian tells of a Chinese Christian boy of twelve years of age, named Ma-Na-Si, who left boarding school and came home for a vacation time. As he stood on the doorstep of his father's home, he heard a horseman galloping up to him. The man, a non-Christian, was greatly agitated and wanted to see the Jesus man—the pastor, the boy's father—immediately. Ma-Na-Si explained that his father was away from home. The visitor became very distressed. He said he had been sent to get the Jesus man to cast a demon out of a young woman in his village. She was torn by demons, raving, reviling, pulling out her hair, clawing her face, tearing her clothes, smashing up furniture, and dashing down food dishes. He described her blasphemy, her raging outbursts, and her foaming at the mouth until she was exhausted physically and mentally.

The boy kept explaining, "But my father is not here. My father is not here." Finally the frenzied man fell on his knees and said, "You, too, are a Jesus man. Will you come?"

The boy was surprised for a moment. Then he made himself available to Jesus. Like little Samuel, he was willing to obey God in everything. He agreed to go with the stranger, who then jumped on his horse and put the boy behind him.

As they galloped away, Ma-Na-Si began to pray. He had accepted an invitation to cast out a demon in the name of Jesus, but was he worthy to be used by God? He searched his heart, prayed for guidance, what to say and how to act. He tried to remember how Jesus had dealt with the demons. Then he simply trusted God's power and mercy and asked for Jesus to be glorified.

When they arrived at the house, several family members were by force holding the tortured woman upon the bed. She had not been told that someone had gone for the pastor. But when she heard footsteps outside, she called out, "All of you get out of my way quickly, so that I can escape. I must flee! A Jesus man is coming. I cannot endure him. His name is Ma-Na-Si." Ma-Na-Si entered the room. He sang a Christian song, praising the Lord Jesus, and in the name of Jesus Christ, the risen Lord, glorified, and omnipotent, he commanded the demon to come out of the woman. Instantly she was calm. From that day on, she was perfectly well. She was amazed when they told her that she had announced the name of the Christian boy who was coming. Even a twelve-year-old by Christ's authority can bind Satan's demon and cast him out.[1]

5. *Use your mighty spiritual weapons.* The weapons Jesus provides you are mighty to restrain Satan and his demons. Jesus came to destroy the Devil's work (1 John 3:8). The Greek verb here means to annul, do away with, deprive of authority; hence, to destroy. In other words, Jesus came to destroy Satan's power, deprive him of all authority, and neutralize his influence. As His representative, you are to enforce this defeat by using the supernatural weapons He has provided. The nearer our Lord's return, the more you can expect the Devil to rage and try to hinder Christ's work. But Christ has delegated to you the authority to use these weapons on His behalf.

We are to continue Christ's restraining, neutralizing, and destroying of Satan's works for Jesus' sake and by His appointment. These weapons are indeed mighty through God. Paul assures us, "The weapons we fight with are not the weapons of the world. On the contrary, they have divine power to demolish strongholds" (2 Cor. 10:4). The Greek word translated "demolish" means to cast down, take down, pull down.

Our God-given weapons are divinely powerful and designed for our prayer warfare; they exactly serve God's purpose and our need. They are divinely effective to defeat Satan, to drive back his forces, to nullify his efforts, and thus to win God's objectives. Skill in using these weapons will make your prayer warfare feared in hell.

a. *The name of Jesus.* There is no more effective spiritual weapon than the name of Jesus. It announces His presence, reminds of His victory on the cross, and gives you authority as His representative. So important is the use of the name of Jesus in spiritual warfare that we discuss it separately in chapter 32.

b. *The blood of Jesus.* The unbeliever does not understand the seriousness of sin, the infinite worth of each human being, the absolute necessity of the sacrificial redemptive death of Jesus Christ upon the cross as our only hope, our only Mediator between God and ourselves. To such unbelieving and uninformed people, mentioning the blood of Christ may sound offensive. But to anyone who understands spiritual truth and who knows the Scripture references to Christ's blood, the cross, and His atoning death, nothing is more precious than the blood of Christ.

However, we so often neglect to use Christ's blood as our symbol and powerful weapon in our spiritual warfare with Satan. The blood of Jesus represents the death of Jesus. The death of Jesus finally and eternally defeated Satan and sealed his doom. The blood of Jesus stains Satan's hands and disgraces his name. The blood of Jesus reminds the universe of the awful evil of Satan's nature, the cruel hatred of his heart, and the tragic cost of his rebellious efforts.

The very mention of the blood of Jesus is torment to the ears of Satan and torture to his memory. Throughout eternity he will wish he could blot out that sight from his eyes, but he will never forget that memory. That sight will torment him for ever and ever in hell.

The blood of Jesus, so precious to us, is a terrifying weapon against Satan. It shouts "defeat" in his ears. It shouts "doom" to his mind. It proves him the ultimate villain of the whole universe. It causes him to be despised by both heaven and hell. It has covered him with eternal shame. It has made him the most contemptible of all beings in history, the vilest of the vile. Plead the blood of Jesus. It is agony to Satan. He will want to flee from the sound of your prayer.

But the blood of Jesus speaks more than that. It is the guarantee of Christ's victory. It is the measure of the infinite commitment of Christ to the elimination and the destruction of Satan and all his works. The Passover blood in the Old Testament was total protection against the death angel. The blood of Jesus, our Passover (1 Cor. 5:7), is our total protection in time and eternity. We are covered by His blood, sheltered by His blood, and made infinitely precious to God by Christ's blood. We are saved, purified, and made victorious by His blood—by His death on Calvary. His blood, His death, His cross are our glory, our guarantee of victory.

Satan cannot stand before the blood. Satan cannot fight the blood of Jesus and must flee from its reminder. It is your battle cry; it is your spiritual weapon. Use it to defeat Satan. Plead and praise the blood of Jesus, and drive Satan from the battlefield.

c. *The Word of God.* Scripture tells us to take "the sword of the Spirit, which is the word of God" (Eph. 6:17). When you take the name of Jesus, when you militantly praise the name of Jesus as you launch your attack, and as you flash the sword of the Word in the power of the Spirit, Satan knows that heavy fighting has begun. At any time he may decide to run, to abandon his fighting position, to fall back still further in retreat.

The Word is full of battle instructions. It is your manual of war. The Word is full of battle resources, for it records God's holy war and promises power for your total and final victory. It is full of God's ammunition for you. Take it and use it. This topic also is so important that we devote chapter 31 to the militant use of God's Word.

d. *The prayer and command of faith.* Above I have written of the dynamic of faith. Here I will emphasize only the militant use of faith in restraining Satan. The prayer of faith, the command of faith, and the song of faith are God's weapons for you to restrain and bind and defeat Satan.

Restraining and binding Satan has to be a work of faith. By faith we insist that Satan advance no further. By faith we shield from his attack. And then by faith we launch an attack upon his strongholds. The faith that binds Satan is the faith that takes the offensive: it immobilizes Satan's forces and disarms his weapons (doubt, discouragement, fear, temptation). The prayer of faith maintains the flow of heaven's power to us and on us. The prayer of faith applies the victory of Calvary. It exercises the authority of the name of Jesus.

Hebrews reminds us of the militant use of faith by God's Old Testament heroes, as it mentions those "who through faith conquered kingdoms ... gained what was promised; ... escaped the edge of the sword; whose weakness was turned to strength; and who became powerful in battle and routed foreign armies" (11:33–34). Faith is always the battle weapon of God's conquerors. Use faith to bind Satan.

The command of faith is the verbalization of your faith and authority. You may want to review what I said about it in chapter 13 above. See also chapter 15 in my book *Touch the World Through Prayer,* which is devoted to the command of faith. Just as God wants you to speak to the mountains blocking your way and remove them from your path (Matt. 17:20; 21:21), so in Christ's name you have the authority to restrain and bind Satan by your command of faith.

God's children have commanded Satan to be silent when he has tried to bring thoughts to their mind or when he spoke through the mouth of a demon, interrupting a service or objecting to being cast out. They have commanded Satan to get behind them, even as Jesus did when Satan misled Peter until he spoke suggestions that Satan whispered in his mind (Matt. 16:23). In militant, believing prayer Satan has been commanded to take his hands off a family, a home, or a church situation.

The command of faith can at times carry the effect of a holy rebuke. Saints of God have boldly rebuked Satan to his face. This is not contrary to 2 Peter 2:11 and Jude 9. The relevant Greek words in the two verses are related to the verb *blasphēmeō,* from which we get our word *blaspheme.* It means rail at (abusive, scorning language) or revile (even stronger implication of abusiveness and obscene language). We are not to abuse but to command calmly in the name of Jesus.

Jesus did not shout abusively when He cleansed the temple, nor should we shout a tirade at Satan. But through the blood of the cross and in the authority of the name of Jesus, we can firmly command Satan. The rebuking aspect of the command of faith is seen in Jesus also. Not only did He rebuke Satan in person, but He rebuked the wind and the waves, and they were instantly calm (Luke 8:24). He knew Satan was stirring up the elements to try to harm Him and His disciples. So by rebuking the wind and waves, He was rebuking Satan, who was manipulating them. Similarly, He rebuked fever (4:39). Thus, sometimes in your command of faith the Holy Spirit may lead you to include an element of rebuke to Satan.

e. *The word of praise.* Praise and singing can also be used militantly in faith as a weapon against Satan. God can make your faith a hymn, a militant song of triumph. Faith is the victory that overcomes the world (1 John 5:4–5). You must pray from your position in the heavenlies to defeat Satan, and when are you more in the heavenlies than when you praise God? Luther, that mighty prayer warrior, often assaulted Satan and his demons by singing. He spoke of doing despite to Satan by singing. Even on the last evening of his life, having just preached four times and feeling ill, he came downstairs, saying, "There is no pleasure in being alone. Nothing frightens the Devil so much as when two or three Christians get together and sing, and are happy in the Lord."[2] After the singing, he retired and awoke in the chill of death and went triumphantly to his Lord.

Praise lifts your faith and your perspective far above the battle. Praise powerfully resists and repels Satan. Not only does he hate praise, but somehow praise seems to bring God's angels rushing to assist you in your battle. The angels are always with you during your prayer warfare. You need them to help bind Satan. But they seem specially near when you assault Satan with praise. Praise becomes a mighty phalanx to drive Satan back and paralyze his power.

6. *Make a united attack.* Binding and resisting Satan often calls for our united attack on Satan's strongholds. Binding Satan's power in a given situation so God can work in mighty power often takes time and united efforts. Remember that Matthew 18:18 (binding on earth so that heaven endorses and enforces it) immediately precedes verse 19 (if two of you on earth shall agree). Both verses are speaking of our actions on earth being ratified and helped from heaven. God the Father does this by working through the Holy Spirit, through the multitude of His angels, and by His miracle answers to prayer. He gives this help when we unite in prayer initiative to bind Satan and all his forces.

Mrs. Jessie Penn-Lewis reports how in a large market square in the north of England crowds of people would gather to be harangued by Communists and atheists. These speakers opposed and attacked the Christian workers of the town and their ministry. One of the local ministers called his Christian people together one Sunday afternoon and showed them from the Bible how Satan was behind these efforts and that he needed to be bound.

About one hundred Christians took Christ at His word and, with united hearts and voices, repeated aloud, "In the name of Jesus Christ, we bind the strong man from stirring up these people and from attacking God's work." They sang a hymn of victory. They committed themselves to a faith position of absolute reliance upon God to fulfill His Word.

The very next day a division arose among the atheists. Their leader disappeared from town. A week later he was brought to court and sentenced because of other aspects of his life. Then the town authorities intervened, cleared the market square, and stopped all the activities there. Satan's attack was completely bound.[3]

CHAPTER 40

The Militant Use of Jesus' Name

ALL FORMS OF Christian prayer—adoration, commun- ion, thanksgiving, praise, petition, and intercession—should be in the name of Jesus. There is great spiritual significance in the more general use of Jesus' name. But there is also a significant militant use of the name of Jesus in prayer warfare. The general use of the name of Jesus is the basis upon which you build the militant use of the name of Jesus.

THE MEANING AND USE OF "NAME"

Technically, it is not always necessary to include the actual words "in Jesus' name" in every prayer you pray. Many brief prayers ascend from your heart without a formal beginning or ending. You just tell Jesus you love Him, usually using His name as you address Him at the beginning. Many brief praise notes mention Jesus but do not use the words "in Jesus' name." Similarly, there are many brief telegraphic requests to the Lord that do not begin with "Jesus" and that do not close with a formal "in Jesus' name" or a formal "amen."

However, in all more structured praying, you should mention at the beginning whom you are addressing: Lord

Jesus, Lord, Father, Holy Spirit, O Lord, and so on. And in all more structured praying it is good to close "in Jesus' name," "in Your name," "in Your holy name," or in some such way. Jesus wants you to do so. Probably most prayer that closes with an amen should be prayed "in Jesus' name," "in Jesus' mighty name," or some similar ending. Certainly all public prayer should include such an ending. Since public prayer is not only prayer but also a witness to your faith, "in Jesus' name" is really appropriate as your prayer-testimony.

But you need to pray your whole prayer in the name of Jesus and not just conclude your prayer with a recognition of His name. Since we are told, "Whatever you do, whether in word or deed, do it all in the name of the Lord Jesus" (Col. 3:17), you should certainly pray in the name of Jesus. Nothing is more sacred than prayer, and nothing should be more precious to you than the name of Jesus. Since He is your Lord, since you love Him above all others, His name should be often on your lips and especially so in your prayer. When you pray with true sincerity and deep love and a deep sense of need, your repeated use of His name does not cause you to lose either the sense of its preciousness or the wonder that you are privileged to pray in His name.

The name always represents the person. The better you know the person, the more meaning His name holds for you. The closer you walk with Jesus and the better you know Him, the more precious His name becomes to you. The name of a person represents that one's personality, character, ideals, lifestyle, activities and work, life history, reputation, and distinguishing characteristics. Once you know a person, that one's name distinguishes that person from all others when you recall it. You know who you are talking about.

Have you ever thought how important your name is to you and to others? Have you ever noted how many times God speaks of "My name"? That phrase is found 65 times. "Your name" is used of God 101 times; "name of the Lord," 95 times; and "name," in reference to God or Jesus, 85 more times. So "name" is used in connection with God or Christ in some way at least 346 times in the Bible.

When Jesus prayed to the Father, "I have revealed your name" (John 17:6, margin), He meant He had told His disciples and shown His disciples so much of the Father that they now knew Him—not exhaustively, but very truly. To believe in the name of Jesus is to believe in all the Bible teaches about Him in His deity; His loving, sinless life; His death, resurrection, and ascension; and His sovereign kingship today. To believe in Jesus is to believe in all He is, all He taught, and all He does for you as far as you know it.

USE OF THE NAME DEPENDS ON YOUR LIFE

To pray in Jesus' name is to pray in harmony with His character. It is to pray in the fullest oneness and identity with Him. For the sinner to pray in His name is to pray to Him, accepting Him as Savior and God. For the mature Christian to pray in His name is to pray in unity with His holiness, His love, His purposes and desires, and His total lordship.

The Bible says you can have the mind of Christ (1 Cor. 2:16). You are to let His mind, His attitude, be in you (Phil. 2:5). To pray in Jesus' name is to pray with His mind, perspective, motive, and attitude. To pray rightly in Jesus' name, we must testify with Paul, "I have been crucified with Christ and I no longer live, but Christ lives in me" (Gal. 2:20).

To pray in Jesus' name is to pray in His victory and in the fullness of His Spirit. Only a life filled with the Spirit knows moment-to-moment victory with nothing to hinder the empowered use of the name of Jesus. The promises associated with Christ's name, like all other promises, cannot be claimed with unshaken faith if there is a spiritual defeat on the conscience. A life with on-again-off-again victory cripples faith and makes a prayer life feeble.

A half-and-half Christian is of little use to God or man. He or she cannot prevail when necessary and cannot use the name of Jesus with any sense of spiritual authority. Total commitment, total obedience, and a life filled and refilled with the Holy Spirit are the only basis for empowered, authoritative use of the name of Jesus. To pray in the name of Jesus is to pray out of a life that is Christlike.

THE ROLE OF THE NAME

1. *The name of Jesus gives instant access to God's throne.* The authority of the name unlocks heaven's door. Its fragrance identifies and gives acceptance to God. You have no right of access except through the name of Jesus. You are unworthy, a forgiven rebel, but the name identifies you now as a child of God with full access to God. Six times Jesus referred to our asking in His name.

2. *The name identifies you with who Jesus is.* There are said to be 143 names and titles given to Jesus in the Bible.[1] Each is another ray of God's light illuminating who Jesus is and what He does. Using the name of Jesus identifies you with all that the Scripture reveals of our Lord. But central to all is the glorious reality that He is the Son of God who became the Son of Man to make atonement for your sin and who defeated Satan forever. Praying in His name identifies you as having been redeemed by Christ. Your prayer is grounded on the finished work of Christ at Calvary.

You have no priority claim upon Christ. But Jesus died for you and for the whole world. His name empowers your plea with His shed blood. It identifies you with His resurrected lordship. It unites your prayer with His prevailing mediation and intercession at the right hand of the Father. He, as it were, places one of His holy hands upon the Father's throne, and with the other He grips your hand uplifted in prayer. In turn, you grip, as it were, the sacred hand of your Co-Intercessor with your one hand, and with your other hand you touch the world.

Who are you that you should have such a sacred authoritative role? Who are you that you should be Jesus' channel of mediating salvation, victory, and blessing to others? You are nothing in yourself. But in Christ you are chosen to touch the world through prayer. With Christ you transmit God's blessings through prayer. With Christ you lift up holy hands in prayer warfare just as Moses did at Rephidim (Exod. 17:10–16).

Because Jesus bridged the gap between God and man, you can now be empowered by all He is, though you are less than nothing in yourself. No human illustration can begin to portray the sacred reality, but let me try. A wire attached to a mighty generator is as nothing, but attached to that dynamo of power it is the only hope of power, light, heat, and all the benefits of electricity being available to many people. Even so, you are nothing, but in Christ, in the name of Jesus, you are God's chosen means to bless the world.

A. B. Simpson illustrates Jesus' role thus: Two brothers were enlisted in an army. One brother was very unreliable and several times had been court-martialed, but each time the pleadings of his brave brother had won commutation of the sentence and eventual freedom for the unworthy brother. Once more the reckless soldier was derelict in his duty and was court-martialed, and the general was about to give the death sentence when he saw the loyal brother in the background silently weeping.

The general kindly asked the brother if he had anything to say. Silently he held up his stump of an amputated arm that had been lost in battle, while the tears ran down his cheeks. Other soldiers nearby saw what was happening and began to weep as they saw the upraised stump of that arm. That was his only plea. The general was deeply moved. "Sit down, my brave fellow, you shall have your brother's life. He is unworthy of it, but you have purchased it by your blood."

Samuel Chadwick wrote, "Prayer reaches its highest level when offered in the Name which is above every name, for it lifts the petitioner into unity and identity with himself."[2] The name of Jesus identifies you with Christ's death and resurrection. You have no other plea. You need no other plea. Jesus died for you and gives you the right and authority of His name.

3. *The name of Jesus sanctifies your prayer.* You can pray no

unworthy prayer in His name. Any prayer that is selfish, vindictive, or with wrong motive dies on your lips when you take His name. Prayer does not fail because of the inadequacy of your words in expressing your requests. Prayer fails when it is silenced by His name. His holy name is a flaming fire that consumes all that is unworthy in His sight and contrary to His will. His name judges your motive, cleanses your desire, and demands your total integrity.

Unworthy prayer cannot penetrate to Christ's intercessory throne. Jesus will never "amen" such a prayer. He will never commend it to the Father. It dies on your lips the moment you pray in His name. Only when your heart-cry is in holy harmony with His holy desires can you be authorized to use His name. Augustine, around A.D. 400, prayed, "O Lord, grant that I may do Thy will as if it were my will, so that Thou mayest do my will as if it were Thy will."[3]

4. *The name unites with His will.* You cannot ask in Jesus' name what is contrary to His will, what Jesus would not ask if He were praying. The perimeter of your prayer becomes, "Your will be done." Simpson says, "Within this large and ample space there is room for every reasonable petition for spirit, soul and body, family and friends, temporal circumstances, spiritual services, and utmost possibilities of human desire, hope, or blessing."[4]

"This is the confidence we have in approaching God: that if we ask anything according to his will, he hears us. And if we know that he hears us—whatever we ask—we know that we have what we asked of him" (1 John 5:14–15). But how do you know what God wills for you to ask? By God's Word, the Spirit's guidance, and the mind of Christ. In a secondary sense, by providence, conscience, your common sense, and the counsel of God's people. (For a fuller discussion of this topic, see chapters 18–35 in my book *Let God Guide You Daily*). As you keep open to God's will as He guides you, as you maintain a prayerful listening ear, and as you live in God's Word, He will make it comparatively easy to know that many things are or are not His will.

For those things that are not clear in the above way, many prayer warriors have found it is wisest and best to pray until they felt sure of God's will before they sought to maintain prayer warfare about any deep concern.

5. *The name gives you His authority.* When you ask in His name, you come as His representative, you come for His sake—not for your own sake. You have no right to insist on a prayer answer just because you want it. But when His name has sanctified your request and united it in His will, then you have the full authority of His name as you intercede. You are heard because you represent Jesus. You are heard for His sake.

Heaven's authority backs any prayer that you truly pray in Jesus' name—not because you use those words but because you and the prayer are truly in His name. Your prayer is not prevailing prayer without the Spirit of God or without its being in His name. In fact, you cannot pray in the Spirit for anything not truly in Jesus' name. But when prayed in the Spirit, in Jesus' name, your prayer is clothed with "the omnipotence of God's grace," in the words of Andrew Murray. The living Christ knows the potency of His name and makes it a power in you as you use it in prevailing intercession.

When Jesus tells you to pray in His name, it is as if He said, "Pray as if I were praying, and then I will pray through you. I will make your prayer Mine. I will present it before God as the joint prayer of you and Me." Such praying is not child's play. It is dynamic, and it is prevailing in moving heaven and changing earth.

God recognizes your authority as you truly pray in Jesus' name. The angels recognize it, and Satan and his demons recognize it. They also recognize a prayer "in Jesus' name" that is spurious. The book of Acts records how some demons trounced the seven sons of Sceva when they tried to use Jesus' name as if it were some magic phrase (Acts 19:14–16).

To pray a prevailing prayer in Jesus' name makes tremendous demands upon you as a prayer warrior, but it yields results and victories that only God can provide. The more completely you experience the fullness of living and praying in

Jesus' name, the more freely you will be able to wield the authority of His name.

6. *The name gives Jesus' endorsement.* Jesus is the amen of all prayer prayed in the Spirit. Through Him we say the amen to the promises of God, because in Him God's "Yes" is said (2 Cor. 1:20). So Jesus says the primary amen, and we say the secondary amen. In fact, Jesus is called "the Amen" (Rev. 3:14). In the words of Samuel Chadwick, "Prayer is endorsed by the Name, when it is in harmony with the character, mind, desire, and purpose of the Name."[5]

Jesus wants you to live a life of holy harmony with His character, holy agreement with His purpose and heartbeat, and holy fellowship in His prevailing intercession so that again and again you have the inner witness that you are truly praying in His name. All such prevailing He endorses with His unwavering almighty amen.

THE MILITANT USE OF THE NAME

There are many militant uses of the name of Jesus. This list is only suggestive. You will no doubt recall other important ways that the Holy Spirit has led you to use it to win victories for Christ. In the light of the role of the name, use the name again and again to the glory of God and to the advancement of His kingdom.

1. *Use the name to clear the spiritual atmosphere.* There are times when a spiritual oppressiveness clouds your horizon, darkens your outlook, and attempts to cripple your faith. There are times and places in the world that Satan so claims for his own that some spiritually sensitive Christians actually feel Satan's power there. Satan uses such spiritual oppression at times to try to take advantage of any weakened physical condition you may have. But it may be totally unrelated to anything for which you can account. Sometimes in the midst of prayer battles, the heavens almost seem to close in upon you. You know Satan is trying to block your prayer and fight against your prevailing.

285

Use the name of Jesus to clear the spiritual atmosphere and to push back the spiritual darkness. Use it to break through to God's sunlight. Cleanse away the demonic influence, pressure, and oppression by using the name of Jesus in praise, in song, and in militant faith. Sometimes just the word *Jesus* repeated over and over in spiritual insistence will clear the heavens for you. You may repeat it silently. You may be led to repeat it audibly. The name of Jesus can be torture to the ears of demons. They hear it whether you say it audibly or not, but in some situations it seems to be better to repeat it aloud. Take your stand—drive the darkness away by using the name of Jesus.

2. *Use the name to claim protection.* Whether you need to claim spiritual or physical protection, use the name of Jesus. I have seen a humble woman call "Jesus" and receive instant intervention by the Lord.

Dr. Laws, missionary to Livingstonia, Africa, told of two African preachers walking to a village to preach one Sunday morning. They suddenly felt they were being followed. When they turned around, they saw a large lion stalking them. There were no trees to climb, and they were terrified. As they turned, one of them prayed, "O God, protect us as You did Daniel in the den of lions." Coming to a path that led to one side, they stopped. So did the lion. "In the name of Jesus, we command you to go that way!" one called. The lion growled angrily and pawed the ground while they hurried on. Looking back, they saw the lion going down the other path.

3. *Use the name to express your longing.* There may be times in your prayer warfare when your longing or your burden becomes so great that you do not know how to pray. You can call the name of Jesus, and the Holy Spirit, who knows your deepest heart-cry, will interpret it aright.

4. *Use the name to enforce the honor of Christ.* You may be in a group that is blaspheming the name of Jesus, and because of your work you may not be able to avoid hearing them. Use the name of Jesus in silent prayer to silence the vile language of the others. You may be in an angry, shouting mob—use the name

of Jesus in silent prayer to calm the enraged emotions. Whatever the emergency, use the name of Jesus as your weapon in silent or in vocal prayer.

5. *Use the name of Jesus in militant faith.* You may be sitting beside a sick one's bed, one too ill to disturb. Pray all that you feel led to pray. But you can rebuke Satan just by repeating the name of Jesus or pleading over and over, "In the name of Jesus."

A Haitian pastor, of small stature but a real giant in faith, served God in a lonely, remote mountain post. He told me how one night voodooists gathered nearby, determined to drive him from the community because they wanted to destroy the Christian witness in the area. They began beating their voodoo drums, performing their voodoo rites, threatening dire consequences. But the little pastor stood in his door in the dark with his hands raised to heaven, pleading, "Jesus, Jesus, Jesus."

Suddenly, although no sign of rain had been evident, a storm burst in a tremendous downpour of rain. The thunder reverberated, the lightning flashed, and the voodooists with their witch doctors ran to escape the storm. The name of Jesus, in faith, had won the battle in the spirit world, and God enforced that victory in the world of nature.

King Asa expressed his militant faith thus: "LORD, there is no one like you to help the powerless against the mighty. Help us, O LORD our God, for we rely on you, and in your name we have come against this vast army" (2 Chron. 14:11).

I have found that even when I am too sick to think or pray clearly, if I just repeat the name of Jesus in militant faith, God can answer and touch. Whatever the need, pray as God leads you, but be sure to pray in faith, using militantly the name of Jesus.

6. *Use the name in holy determination.* Militant faith and militant determination are often closely associated. In your prayer assault on Satan's strongholds that are thus far refusing to yield—whether prayer for the salvation of someone, for the restraint of evil, for the healing of a sick person, or for the casting out of a demon—you can take your stand in the name

287

of Jesus and pleading the blood of Jesus. You can press ahead; you can express your holy determination to see Christ's will be done. The psalmist expressed his militant determination thus: "Through you we push back our enemies; through your name we trample our foes" (Ps. 44:5).

7. *Use the name in the command of faith.* When commanding your mountains to move, when commanding Satan to stop agitating division among Christians, when resisting Satan's onslaughts, when commanding a demon to be silent or to leave, or when commanding Satan to release a captive, use the almighty name of Jesus—the Jesus who defeated him at Calvary, the Jesus who will one day be his Judge.

Peter commanded the cripple, "In the name of Jesus Christ of Nazareth, walk" (Acts 3:6). Paul commanded the demon, "In the name of Jesus Christ I command you to come out of her" (16:18).

CHAPTER 41

The Militant Use of the Word

GOD'S WORD HAS an essential role in all aspects of your prayer life. Your communion with God will be based on and include much communion through the Word. Your praise must of necessity make much use of Scripture as you praise the Lord. Whatever time you spend on your devotional life, surely about half will be spent reading and feeding on God's Word.

Devotional books are good, as long as they do not take the place of God's Word. If you spend most of the reading portion of your daily devotional period reading from a devotional book rather than from God's Word, yours will be a very superficial spiritual life. Most devotional writings are skim milk as compared with the milk of the Word (1 Peter 2:2). A major reason for weak prayer lives is a neglect of God's Word.

1. *God's Word is basic to a militant life of prayer.* The God who hears prayer is the God of the Bible. Prayer and the Word are interrelated. Praying people love God's Word, and those who love God's Word long to pray and love to pray. When you feed on God's Word, you will repeatedly find that your reading becomes prayer. You will be so blessed by the Word that as you read you begin to love the Lord, to thank and praise Him, to

289

ask the Lord to apply the Word to your heart and fulfill it in your life, or to ask Him to fulfill a particular promise for you. The Word flows into prayer again and again almost before you realize it.

The more constantly you feed on the Word, the richer and deeper your life of prayer becomes. The Word of God is the food that makes you strong to pray. Jesus, quoting from Deuteronomy 8:3, defeated Satan by pointing to the essential role of the Word. "Man does not live on bread alone, but on every word that comes from the mouth of God" (Matt. 4:4).

God's Word nourishes your prayer, strengthens your prayer, and warms your heart and fires your spirit as you pray. You cannot have a strong spiritual life apart from constant feeding upon and assimilating God's Word. Spiritual growth depends upon daily spiritual food. Earnest, even forceful praying, if not nourished on God's Word, may be weak and flabby.

Andrew Murray taught, "Little of the Word with little prayer is death to the spiritual life. Much of the Word with little prayer gives a sickly life. Much prayer with little of the Word gives more life, but without steadfastness. A full measure of the Word and prayer each day gives a healthy and powerful life."[1]

Power in the use of the Word depends on the prayer life. Power in prayer depends on the use of the Word. The Holy Spirit is the Spirit of the Word and the Spirit of prayer. Both prayer and the Word thus are centered in God. God reveals His heart in the Word. You reveal your heart to Him in prayer. He gives Himself to you in His Word. You give yourself to Him in prayer. In the Word He comes to your side and lives with you. In prayer you ascend to His throne and sit with Christ.

Prayer depends on the Word of God. It is built upon the message, truth, and power of the whole of Scripture. Prayer absorbs the power of the Word and incorporates all its vision, urgency, and force into its prevailing. Jesus promised, "If you remain in me and my words remain in you, ask whatever you wish, and it will be given you. This is to my Father's glory, that

290

you bear much fruit, showing yourselves to be my disciples" (John 15:7–8).

Four truths are very evident from this passage: (1) prayer answers are closely related to "remaining," that is, really living in the Word; (2) this abiding in the Word is the secret of having much fruit for God; (3) this prayer fruit is what really brings glory to God; and (4) prayer fruit is what proves your genuine discipleship.

While this teaching applies to all prayer, it is specially true for militant prayer warfare. Spiritual power for prayer warfare is inseparable from constant feeding on the Word, on massive incorporation of the Word into your spiritual life. Samuel Chadwick wrote, "I never take any book but the Bible into the secret place. It is my prayer book." J. Oswald Sanders testifies how his Christian life and prayer were transformed. "A change came when I learned to use the Scriptures as a prayer book, and to turn what I read, especially in the Psalms, into prayer."[2]

Jonathan Goforth, so mightily used in missionary revival and in his prayer life, constantly saturated his soul with God's Word. He stated, "It is appalling how God and souls are defrauded because we know so little of His saving Word." Every morning Goforth, within a half hour of rising, began intensive Bible study with pencil and notebook. Whether preaching or doing personal evangelism, Goforth always had an open Bible in his hand. At one point in his life he had read the entire Bible thirty-five times in Chinese alone. He had read his Chinese New Testament sixty times, and by the time of his death he had read the entire Bible consecutively seventy-three times. He said, "I am ever wishing I could spend several hundred years at the Bible."[3]

2. *God's Word initiates prayer time.* It is normally best to begin regular prayer time with reading God's Word, especially so when entering into a time of militant praying. There are emergencies when we must resort instantly to prayer. But when at all possible, begin with the Word.

a. *Devotional reading of Scripture brings a sense of God's nearness.* The more you are aware of God's presence, the more joyfully, believingly, and powerfully you can pray. The Bible can set your heart aflame.

b. *Devotional reading of Scripture helps you shut out distractions.* Jesus taught the necessity of closing the door on the thoughts, worries, and concerns that tend to throng into your mind when you quiet your soul for prayer. "Go into your room, close the door and pray," Jesus instructed (Matt. 6:6). You may not be able to go into a literal room and shut the door, but somehow you must really get alone with God. Reading the Word—perhaps for a longer period of time—is one of the most effective ways to close out the world and its distractions.

c. *Devotional reading prepares your heart attitude for prayer.* In the Word you sense God calling you to prayer, drawing you near, and then your heart can respond to God's voice and initiative (Ps. 27:8). Sometimes you may feel spiritually dry and comparatively lifeless. The Word reinvigorates you, fires your soul, and makes you ready to meet the Lord. This preparation is very important when prayer warfare is needed. The Word can help fuel and renew the spirit of spiritual militancy so essential in prayer warfare. George Mueller testified that often he could not pray as he desired until he focused his heart on a Scripture verse or passage.[4]

3. *God's Word will guide your militant prayer.* God's Word not only feeds your prayer and arms you for militant prayer, it guides your prayer. The Word tells you the kind of God He is, and thus it guides you in what to pray for and what to pray against. Militant prayer is the means to advance God's kingdom and to oppose Satan's deceits, obstructions, plans, and strategies. God's Word guides you in all the basics of God's holy and sovereign purposes.

God's Word exposes many of Satan's timeworn methods. It guides you concerning the areas where you should seek to bind his power and his demons.

God's Word guides you in many ways in which the Holy Spirit has led God's people to victory over the centuries. The Bible is God's Word to you for many great purposes, but among them are His purposes for your spiritual warfare. It contains highly specific exhortations and commands concerning prayer strategies. It has been called your manual of prayer warfare.

4. *God's Word arms with faith for prayer warfare.* Faith is your shield in spiritual warfare (Eph. 6:16). But it is also a weapon of offensive warfare. Faith feeds upon God's Word and especially upon God's promises until you are strengthened and full of zeal to advance for God. Faith is the essential and inseparable spirit and power of prevailing prayer. We have discussed the dynamic of faith in chapter 13.

a. *Faith arms militant prayer by grasping hold of the purpose of God.* God's purpose and your praying are interdependent. He depends on your militant praying to achieve His holy purpose. In militant prayer you arm your intercession with the power of His sovereign purpose. All God's purposes are divinely possible. Faith "amens" the purpose of God.

b. *Faith arms militant prayer by focusing on God's power.* Faith refuses to be depressed by your past weakness, inefficiency, and unfruitfulness. Faith believes God in spite of the past because it is focused on God's almighty power. Faith knows God is able to defeat any combination of forces that Satan can gather to block your way, fortify his strongholds, or make assault upon you. Faith glories that God "is able to do immeasurably more than all we ask or imagine, according to his power that is at work within us" (Eph. 3:20).

c. *Faith arms militant prayer with specific promises of God.* Whatever your need or urgent request, God has a promise in His Word that is exactly appropriate to your use in prayer. It may be a specific promise or a general one that covers many needs, including the one for which you are praying. It may be the general trend of Scripture, or how the Bible reveals God has worked in the past. Now the Spirit applies it specifically to your heart.

Every promise of God in His unchangeable Word was written for you. Go to God, quoting His Word to Him, asking Him to do exactly what He has said. God will not deceive you. He will not violate His promise to you. His whole character is bound in His promise. His power makes possible everything needed to advance His cause. His love assures everything needed. His wisdom knows how to supply everything needed to defeat Satan and accomplish His divine purpose. His unchangeableness assures that He will carry out His plan.

5. *God's Word is your powerful prayer weapon.* In the Spirit-inspired description of spiritual armor in Ephesians 6, the Word of God is the one offensive weapon. It is the Sword of the Spirit. He uses it directly in convicting people of sin. He may guide and empower you to use it in militant prevailing. It is, of course, a strong weapon in defense, but the Spirit intends us to use it often in attack.

What does it mean to use Scripture militantly? It means to use it in holy boldness, whether with God in praying or with Satan in rebuking him. Using Scripture militantly means taking the spiritual initiative, daring to claim promises for spiritual conquest and for setting free the souls and lives of those in bondage to Satan. Using it militantly means to quote it and use it with determined insistence and with believing perseverance.

Such use includes quoting or reading Scripture praises to drive back doubts, fears, and spiritual darkness. It includes standing on God's Word when every visible indication seems to prove that Satan is succeeding and that your prayer warfare is hopeless. It means to say with Paul when he stood on the deck of a storm-tossed sailing ship as death seemed ready to engulf all on board, "I have faith in God that it will happen just as he told me" (Acts 27:25).

Alas, so much Christian use of the Word is merely for spiritual food, for light and comfort, and for defense. When will we learn to use it continually in militant attack? When will we make major use of it in driving Satan from his strongholds? When will we use it mightily in setting Satan's captives free?

a. *Use the Word to remind God.* It is not irreverent to hold God to His Word. When Israel had sinned so grievously that God was ready to strike them down, Moses quoted God's own Word back to Him in a mighty plea for forgiveness for the people (Num. 14:19). The Lord did not rebuke Moses. He honored and loved him all the more. He answered Moses, "I have forgiven them, as you asked" (v. 20).

Alexander Maclaren wrote: "Our prayers are to remind God.

The truest prayer is that which bases itself on God's uttered Word. The prayer that prevails is a reflected promise."[5] Humbly, reverently, but boldly hold God to His promise.

b. *Use the Word to silence Satan.* Sometimes Jesus commanded interfering demons to be silent. Remind Satan that he was defeated at Calvary. Quote to him Philippians 2:9–11, and then in the name of Jesus command him to be silent or to leave a demon-oppressed person alone or to take his hands off the life you are claiming for God. Remind him, "You shed the blood of Jesus Christ, the Son of God. You are guilty of sinning against the body and blood of the Lord. Your authority is broken. Your doom is sure."

c. *Quote Scripture phrases to strengthen your prayer.* I know no mightier brief militant prayer than Jesus' words given to us for our use when praying—"Your will be done" (Matt. 6:10). Repeat this over and over as you stand on the promises of God. Fill your prayers with phrases and verses of Scripture. Also fill your words to Satan with Scripture when you are rebuking him. Verses of hymns and choruses that paraphrase Scripture statements are very useful to intersperse between your prayer time, such as: "There's nothing too hard for you, dear Lord"; "Faith is the victory"; "In the name of Jesus, we have the victory"; and "There is power in the blood."

6. *God's Word will refresh and renew during battle.* There come times of weariness during prayer warfare. Militant praying can be physically and emotionally exhausting. As you persevere in the face of Satan's opposition, you do not always feel like shouting, "Hallelujah!" Paul tells us that in the evil day we should stand our ground. "After you have done everything," keep on standing (Eph. 6:13). It is only human to become battle weary. You are not spiritually defeated when you are battle fatigued. You just need rest and refreshment. Oh, how great is the strength we find in God's Word in such times! Take a longer time to saturate your soul in the Word. Sing or read Scripture-saturated hymns. You will find renewed refreshment, courage, and zeal.

CHAPTER 42

Holy Pleadings and Argument Before God

THERE IS A SENSE in which prevailing with God can take the form of holy reasoning—yes, even presenting holy arguments before God. The Bible at times uses court terms for our face-to-face meeting with God. "'Come now, let us reason together,' says the LORD" (Isa. 1:18). This is an invitation to a court-type hearing, a court appeal at the throne of God. God asked Israel to debate its case with Him.

Spurgeon preached a great sermon entitled "Pleading." Said he, "It is the habit of faith, when she is praying, to use pleas. Mere prayer sayers, who do not pray at all, forget to argue with God; but those who would prevail bring forth their reasons and their strong arguments. . . . Faith's act of wrestling is to plead with God, and say with holy boldness, 'Let it be thus and thus, for these reasons.'" He preached, "The man who has his mouth full of arguments in prayer shall soon have his mouth full of benedictions in answer to prayer."[1]

Job lamented, "If only I knew where to find him; if only I could go to his dwelling! I would state my case before him and fill my mouth with arguments. I would find out what he would answer me" (Job 23:3–5). Moffatt translates Job as saying, "Oh that I knew . . . how to reach his very throne, and there lay my case before him, arguing it out to the full."

This holy argumentation with God is not done in a negative, complaining spirit. It is the expression not of a critical heart but of a heart burning with love for God, for His name, and for His glory. This holy debate with God is a passionate presentation to God of the many reasons why it will be in harmony with His nature, His righteous government, and the history of His holy interventions on behalf of His people.

George Mueller urged us to use "holy argument in prayer." Sibbes urged strong arguments because "they are of use and force to prevail with God." This is exactly what Moses did. It is what Luther and other men of importunate power have done.

You do not plead like a negative, legal adversary in the presence of God the holy Judge. Rather, you plead in the form of a well-prepared brief, prepared by a legal advocate on behalf of a need and for the welfare of the kingdom. At times you are, as it were, petitioning God's court for an injunction against Satan to stop his harrassment. The Holy Spirit guides you in the preparation and wording of your prayer argument.

When you walk closely with God and are His constant companion in communion and constant partner in prayer, you have a Spirit-given freedom in prayer that enables you to place your pleas and arguments before the Lord without fear or strain. Your heart is so committed to the Lord in total devotion and in selfless intercession for God's glory and for all that advances Christ's kingdom that pleading with God is almost as natural to you as expressing your love to the Lord.

After all, your holy argument with God and your Bible-based reasonings as you plead are largely for God's sake and are all accompanied with total submission to God's will. While there may be some personal interest at times because of natural ties, your plea is primarily for Christ's sake.

Your holy arguments and pleas with God should be only for those things that on the basis of God's Word you believe to be God's will. You have become convinced that these prayer answers are willed by God because of the sense of God's nearness and blessing as you pray for them. You can pray "Your will be done," not as a trite catchall or sanctifying sentence or as a plaintive concession of pious submissiveness. You pray "Your will be done" militantly as you reason with God with all the holy and God-glorifying reasons you can command. You plead and argue for what you know is God's ultimate desire and for His ultimate glory.

Does God resent your bold presenting the grounds of your pleas before Him in the form of holy arguments? Is it irreverent or impertinent to present, humbly but firmly, the need for which you prevail point by point? No, never, if it is done in a biblical way.

Please remember that God's holy pleaders in Bible times pressed their case before God point by point. Holy importunity before God need not hesitate to outline before Him all the reasons why He should grant the request. There are Bible reasons you can plead before Him and Bible examples of those who have done so. You have every spiritual right to present your case thoughtfully and methodically, even as lawyers in court would plead the case of their client.

Watch Abraham plead for Lot and Sodom (Gen. 18:22–33). "Abraham remained standing before the LORD" (v. 22). When God announced His investigation and intended judgment on Sodom, Abraham detained God, standing longer before Him to plead for mercy. He was audaciously bold, although he humbly acknowledged that he was "nothing but dust and ashes" (v. 27).

Abraham approached still closer to God to plead personally with Him (v. 23):

1. *He pleaded and humbly argued the justice of God.* How could God punish the righteous with the wicked?

2. *He pleaded for the wicked to be spared for the sake of the righteous and again pleaded for God's justice for the righteous* (Gen. 18:24). Abraham was sure God's heart was like his own. He had risked his own life to rescue Lot and in doing so had rescued the same people of Sodom for whom he was now pleading (Gen. 14). The people of Sodom were not worthy then, nor were they worthy now, but Abraham had shown

298

mercy. Would God not be as merciful as he had been? He appealed to God's mercy.

3. *Abraham argued from the righteous character of God.* "Far be it from you to do such a thing—to kill the righteous with the wicked, treating the righteous and the wicked alike. Far be it from you! Will not the Judge of all the earth do right?" (Gen. 18:25). He humbly recognized that God was the Sovereign of the universe. As the righteous and final Judge, how could He do anything but the right?

Abraham got God's promise to spare the whole city if His investigation found fifty righteous people (Gen. 18:28). Then Abraham began to bargain with God—but not for any selfish purpose. He was bargaining for God's mercy to be extended even more generously to the undeserving. What if there were only five short of the fifty? "Will you destroy the whole city because of five people?" (v. 28). Boldly, point by point, Abraham pressed God for more mercy, from forty-five to forty, to thirty, to twenty, to ten.

Repeatedly Abraham pleaded, "Don't be angry with me, but let me plead one more time." Did God become angry? Absolutely not. He loved and honored Abraham all the more for his longing for God's righteous mercy, for longing for the doomed sinners. Abraham had a heart like God's. God always longs to be merciful whenever He can. Abraham proved himself the friend of God (James 2:23) by his holy pleading and bargaining for mercy.

Moses too, with whom also God spoke "face to face, as a man speaks with his friend" (Exod. 33:11), engaged in reverent, humble but bold prayer argument with God (32:9–14). We have only the brief summary in Exodus of what may have been several hours of pleading argument by Moses. God says to him, "Now leave me alone so that my anger may burn against them" (v. 10). It is apparent that Moses was already interceding for God to forgive Israel, which had just made the golden calf.

Perhaps God's "leave me alone" was a test of Moses' character, of Moses' commitment to Israel and the total unselfishness of his loyalty to God, for God had just offered to build a new and greater nation through Moses. Moses did not let God alone. He began the holy arguments with God that prevailed and permitted God to act in mercy.

1. *Moses argued from the history of God's redeeming acts for Israel.* He told God that it would be out of character with His great acts of mercy if He destroyed Israel now.

2. *Moses argued from the glory of God's name.* Why should God permit the Egyptians to think Jehovah was like their Egyptian gods, who had evil motives and vile and evil tempers and who had to be pacified by bribes in the form of sacrifice? "Why should the Egyptians say, 'It was with evil intent that he brought them out, to kill them in the mountains and to wipe them off the face of the earth'?" (Exod. 32:12).

3. *Moses argued from God's faithfulness to His loyal servants Abraham, Isaac, and Israel, and from the promises He had given them.* He boldly quoted back to God the promise He had made and held God to His own word (Exod. 32:13). Then God accepted Moses' holy and impassioned plea. Was God angry with Moses for having interfered? Did God charge him with disrespect or irreverence? No, far from it! Immediately after this account we are told how God spoke face-to-face with Moses as with a very close friend. Also immediately afterward, Moses spent another forty days fasting and alone with God on Mount Sinai, till the glory of God filled him and radiated from his face (34:29–35).

These are two of the wonderful Bible examples of how prayer warriors who walk with God can argue their pleas before His throne and receive great and God-glorifying answers to prayer.

CHAPTER 43

How to Plead Before God

HERE ARE SOME of the holy pleas that can be powerfully used in bold prayer before God's throne. Be sure your own heart is pure before God and that there is no controversy between God and your own soul. Be sure that you are arguing for that which glorifies God, for the extension of God's kingdom and in accordance with God's will. This last point is very important. The Holy Spirit can confirm to your heart that what you desire is indeed the will of God. When you are confirmed in this assurance, then you can make bold your pleadings and arguments before the Lord.

You do not need to pray to inform God about the need that burdens you, for God knows the whole situation better than you do. (However, it pleases the Lord for you to describe it fully to Him.) You need to pray because God has ordained to work through your prayer, added to the intercession of Jesus at the Father's right hand. In a different context God, through Isaiah, revealed His heart: "'Present your case,' says the LORD. 'Set forth your arguments'" (Isa. 41:21). Presenting your case and detailing your arguments not only pleases God, it helps you understand the need more completely, moves your compassion,

301

strengthens your determination, and arms you with greater holy hunger.

1. *Plead the honor and glory of God's name.* The honor of God's name is involved in many ways in the answer of prayer needs. The answer to prayer usually brings glory to God. If God does not act in some situations, it can dishonor His name. Many situations bring dishonor to God if they are allowed to continue. So God's name is at stake in most needs.

God saved Israel at the Red Sea "for his name's sake" (Ps. 106:8). Joshua pleaded with God to help Israel, asking, "What then will you do for your own great name?" (Josh. 7:9). Samuel prayed for the sake of God's name (2 Sam. 7:26). David, knowing the God-given responsibility of kingship placed upon him, prayed for guidance (Ps. 23:3; 31:3) and help (109:21; 143:11) for God's name's sake. Asaph prayed for God to help Israel "for the glory of your name" (79:9).

When God's honor, glory, name, and reputation are at stake, you can prepare a very strong plea. Jeremiah pleaded with God, "O LORD, do something for the sake of your name" (Jer. 14:7); and again, "Do not dishonor your glorious throne" (v. 21).

The glory of God should be the prime motive in all you do. But above all else, it should be the prime motive when you intercede. You plead with God and present holy arguments with God, but not because of self-interest. That would be fatal to your prevailing. You plead God's honor and God's glory.

Present your strong arguments for what will most glorify God, and God's heart will open wide to your prayer. The Lord in His model prayer for us taught us that our first concern in prayer is to hallow God's name (Matt. 6:9). To hallow is to make it holy, to help it truly reflect God's glory, to set it apart from all that is common.

There is no name like God's name. At the name of Jesus every knee will bow and every tongue confess that Jesus Christ is Lord, all to the glory of God the Father (Phil. 2:10–11).

Present and plead your case to God. Show how the petition that you are pressing is for the purpose of exalting the name of Jesus, extending the lordship of Jesus, and so fulfilling God's highest will and highest glory. Thus your pleas are mighty before God.

2. *Plead God's relationships to you.*

a. God is your Creator, and you are the work of His hands (Job 10:3, 8–9; 14:15). The psalmist reminded God that we are the work of His hands (Ps. 119:73). For the sake of God's creation, the work of His hands that brings Him glory, you have the right to plead.

b. God is your Helper (Ps. 33:20; 40:17; 63:7), your ever-present Help (46:1). Plead the fact that He has been your Helper (27:9).

c. God is your Redeemer (Ps. 19:14). He calls Himself your Redeemer (Isa. 41:14; 54:5). He has promised that because He is your Redeemer, He will teach you what is best (48:17). He will prove to the world that He is your Redeemer (49:26). Plead this fact that He is your Redeemer. He will have compassion on you because He is your Redeemer (54:8). He dare not neglect His role and His name of Redeemer. Isaiah made this plea in his mighty intercession (63:16). You belong to Him by redemption. He is responsible for you.

d. God is your Father. Plead that fact. Isaiah pleaded God's role as both Creator and Father. "Yet, O LORD, you are our Father. We are the clay, you are the potter; we are all the work of your hand" (Isa. 64:8). Because He is your Father, you can plead the compassion of His Father-heart (Ps. 103:13; Mal. 3:17). Jesus repeatedly pleaded the fatherhood of God in His prayer. So did Paul. "Abba, Father" is a powerful plea (Mark 14:36; Rom. 8:15; Gal. 4:6).

As your Creator, Helper, Redeemer, and Father, will He not remember you, protect you, and provide for you and for all that He has created and redeemed? What powerful pleas you can make on the basis of God's relationships to you!

3. *Plead God's attributes.* Spurgeon said, "It is well in prayer to plead with Jehovah his attributes."[1] Abraham, as he interceded for Lot and Sodom, pleaded the justice of God. "Far be it from you to do such a thing. . . . Will not the Judge of all the earth do right?" (Gen. 18:25). Nehemiah, leading his people

303

in intercession, did the same (Neh. 9:33). The Old Testament saints frequently pleaded the righteousness of God.

It pleases God to do things for His righteousness' sake (Isa. 42:21). He intervenes for the sake of the righteous (59:16–17). Righteousness prepares His steps (Ps. 85:13). God clothes (Isa. 11:5) and arms Himself with righteousness (Isa. 59:17). Righteousness and justice are the foundation of His throne (Ps. 97:2). So He who is perfectly righteous in Himself and in all He does can be moved to act in righteousness now (Ps. 96:13). Christ speeds the cause of righteousness (Isa. 16:5). So do not hesitate to plead like David and Isaiah for the sake of God's righteousness. It is a powerful plea.

Bible characters also pleaded God's faithfulness in their intercession. In Psalm 89 Ethan six times makes God's faithfulness the basis for His plea. David pleaded God's faithfulness (Ps. 143:1). Moses affirmed, "He is the faithful God" (Deut. 7:9). By reminding God of His faithfulness, you can make it the basis of powerful pleas.

No attributes of God are used more frequently and constantly in prayer pleas than the mercy and love of God. Moses pleaded His great mercy (Deut. 9:18). Oh, how David depended on the mercy of God in his praying! He pleaded God's mercy (Ps. 4:1; 27:7; 30:10; 86:6, 15–16) and His "great mercy" (25:6). Asaph pleaded God's mercy (Ps. 79:8). Daniel and his three Hebrew prayer partners pleaded God's mercy (Dan. 2:18). From Jacob to Zechariah, God's prevailers have pleaded His mercy. Surely you have also done this time and again.

Similarly, you, like David and the psalmist, can plead the love of God, the loving kindness of God, the tender mercies of God. The psalmist combined the love and faithfulness of God into a mighty plea or argument before God. "To your name be the glory, because of your love and faithfulness. Why do the nations say, 'Where is their God?'" (Ps. 115:1–2). Spurgeon preached, "We shall find every attribute of God Most High to be, as it were, a great battering-ram, with which we may open the gates of heaven."[2]

4. *Plead the sorrows and needs of the people.* Holy people of God have always identified with people, especially the people of God in their sufferings. God has a tender heart. He feels all the suffering of the whole universe. It is all directly or indirectly a result of sin. God suffers intensely each additional day He permits earth's sinful, tragic civilization to continue. He feels far more deeply than any human being can ever do. This truth is a tremendously powerful plea.

David was one who took on himself the sufferings of his people. He even wept for the suffering of his enemies (Ps. 16:9). Nehemiah, and especially Daniel, used this plea greatly as they vicariously identified themselves with the sufferings of the people.

Jeremiah, perhaps more powerfully than all others, used this form of plea as he prevailed for his people. He pleads for God to look and see the sufferings (Lam. 2:20), to remember, look, and see (5:1). In great detail he lists for God all the sufferings of the people. He does not try to justify his people, for he knows how deserving they are of all God's judgments. Yet he pleads on the basis of their sufferings. Nothing is more eloquent to God than the tears, heart-cries, and groaning of God's children as they vicariously identify with the sufferings of the world and plead for God's mercy.

5. *Plead the past answers to prayer.* It is always good to praise the Lord for all that He has already done. Remind God of how heavily He has already invested His mercy, His faithfulness, and His power. Remind Him of how the task is incomplete. You are where you are today (or God's cause is where it is today or your nation is where it is today) because of God's repeated patience, mercy, goodness, protection, help, and guidance.

This is the way Moses pleaded. On Mount Sinai Moses began his intercession by recounting how much God had already invested in Israel (Exod. 32:11–12). David, too, reminded God of His past mercy: "You have been my helper" (Ps. 27:9). "Since my youth, O God, you have taught me. . . . Even when I am old and gray, do not forsake me, O God" (71:17–18). A number of the Psalms remind God and the people in detail of His past mercies (78; 85:1–7; 105–6; 136).

Present your pleading arguments for new mercies on the basis of the history of all He has already done. But the task is unfinished. God has invested too much to stop now. Plead for God's mercy and power to be renewed and to bring final victory.

6. *Plead the Word and the promises of God.* Follow the example of God's prevailing Bible saints and quote to God His holy promises. In the night when Jacob wrestled with God, he held God to His word and promise. "O God of my father Abraham, God of my father Isaac, O LORD, who said to me . . . " (Gen. 32:9). He added, "You have said . . . ," and he quoted more of God's promise back to Him (v. 12). From that praying ground Jacob could not retreat, no matter what it cost him, and he prevailed.

That was also the holy insistence of Moses. "Moses said to the LORD, 'You have been telling me. . . . You have said . . . '" (Exod. 33:12). Moses pressed his point: if what You said is true, then "teach me your ways so I may know you and continue to find favor with you. Remember that this nation is your people" (v. 13). That was bold reminding of God of His sacred duty.

God replied, "I will do the very thing you have asked, because I am pleased with you and I know you by name" (Exod. 33:17). Was Moses content? No! He still pressed for more of God's answer and blessing. Then Moses said, "Now show me your glory" (v. 18). "And the LORD said, 'I will . . . I will . . . I will . . . I will . . . I will . . . I will'" (vv. 19–22). Moses got his full heart-cry, his full answer, because he pressed his case with holy pleas and holy arguments.

Do you dare to pray like that? Do you know how to quote God's Word reverently back to Him, to keep presenting your full needs, insisting that God's full will be realized? That is mighty prevailing. Such prayer endears you to the Father, Son, and Holy Spirit.

David held God to His word. Reverently, humbly, lovingly, but with holy insistence, David pressed for the fulfillment of

God's promise. "Do as you promised . . . that your name will be great forever. . . . So your servant has found courage to pray to you. O LORD, You are God! You have promised these good things to your servant" (1 Chron. 17:23–26).

Solomon prayed the same way. He held God to the promises He had made to David, his father. "O LORD, God of Israel, there is no God like you in heaven or on earth—you who keep your covenant of love. . . . You have kept your promise to your servant David my father. . . . Now LORD . . . keep for your servant David my father the promises you made to him when you said. . . . And now, O LORD, God of Israel, let your word that you promised your servant David come true" (2 Chron. 6:14–17). This was no mincing of words. God had spoken. Now Solomon insisted that God fulfill His word.

All of God's Word is for you—all His promises and all His truth. Use the Word in your praying; lovingly, humbly, but boldly hold God to His Word. The Word does not say beautiful, meaningless words. You honor God when you take Him at His word. God is in earnest. The Holy Spirit is in earnest. You must be in earnest and go all out for God's answers.

Spurgeon pleaded, "Oh, brethren, let us learn thus to plead the precepts, the promises, and whatever else may serve our turn; but let us always have something to plead. Do not reckon you have prayed until you have pleaded."[3]

7. *Plead the blood of Jesus.* Perhaps the greatest, most powerful, most unanswerable plea of all is the blood of Jesus. There is no more prevailing argument we can bring before God than the sufferings, blood, and death of His Son. We have no merit of our own. We do not prevail by prayer techniques or past experience. There is no prayer "know-how" that prevails. It is only through the blood of Jesus.

Do you really understand that Jesus, the Son of God, shed His blood for you, me, and for our sinful world? Do you really understand how totally Satan was defeated once for all at the cross? Do you really understand the power of the plea of the blood of Jesus before God the Father?

Just as there is no higher name in heaven or earth than the name of Jesus (Phil. 2:9–10), so there is no greater plea in heaven or earth than the blood of Jesus. It is the supreme evidence of the supreme love of the universe. It is the supreme seal of the supreme vicarious sacrifice of the universe. It is unspeakable, irresistible, all-conquering, and ever-efficacious.

Plead the blood. Pray till you have the assurance of God's will. Pray till you have been given by the Spirit a vision of what God longs to do, needs to do, waits to do. Pray till you are gripped by the authority of the name of Jesus. Then plead the blood of Jesus. The name of Jesus and the blood of Jesus— glory in them, stake your all on them, and use them to the glory of God and the routing of Satan.

Bring before the Father the wounds of Jesus; remind the Father of the agony in Gethsemane; recall to the Father the strong cries of the Son of God as He prevailed for our world and for our salvation. Remind the Father of earth's darkest hour on Calvary, as the Son triumphed alone for you and me. Shout to heaven again Christ's triumphant call, "It is finished!" Plead the cross. Plead the blood. Plead them over and over again.

Said Spurgeon, "That unlocks the treasury of heaven. Many keys fit many locks, but the master key is the blood and the name of Him that died and rose again, and ever lives in heaven to save unto the uttermost."[4]

Satan is too terrified by the blood of Jesus to offer one word of contradiction. No angel will ever argue against it. God the Father wants to honor it, fulfill it, and glorify Himself by it. Plead the blood of the Son of God. Plead the blood shed on Calvary. Plead the blood of Jesus. In the authority of the name of Jesus, plead the blood of Jesus!

CHAPTER 44

Will You Become Mighty
in Prayer?

YOU BEGAN READING this book with the hunger and hope that you might know more of mighty prevailing prayer in your own experience. You have thrilled to read about the lives of those whom God has used mightily in prayer. As you have read the quotations about mighty prevailing prayer written by some of God's giants of faith and intercession, you have felt both blessed and convicted.

In one sense you have been encouraged and strengthened. You understand much more clearly the scope and power of mighty prevailing prayer. You are more hungry to have God use your prayer life than ever before. Do you dare believe that such mighty prevailings are for you?

Remember that the Holy Spirit is the only real Teacher of prevailing intercession. Mere reading of a book will not transform you unless God helps you to build prayer truth into prayer habit. You will learn to prevail only as you personalize these truths by a new faithfulness, a new deepening hunger, and a new expectant self-discipline in prayer. You learn to pray by praying, but there is one qualifying fact of supreme importance.

Prevailing prayer only prevails through the prevailing Spirit. It is not a work of man, even of the holiest men and women of God. It is the work of the Holy Spirit in you and through your cooperation. Samuel Chadwick confessed, "The biggest thing God ever did for me was to teach me to pray in the Spirit."[1] No one ever becomes a man or woman of prayer except through the Holy Spirit.

How can you prepare His way so the Spirit can intercede in prevailing prayer through your being? Remember, you will always recognize that you are far too weak in prayer to prevail. Rejoice! "The Spirit helps us in our weakness" (Rom. 8:26). Again and again you will need to confess with Paul, "Lord, I don't know how to pray as I ought. I don't know precisely what all the details are for which I should prevail." Rejoice! The Spirit Himself intercedes for you with groans too deep for you ever to be able to express (v. 26).

Since the Holy Spirit is that burdened to help you pray and to prevail through you, God is far more desirous of your prevailing than you ever realized. The Spirit groans for you to become mighty in prevailing prayer. He has infinitely many groanings that are humanly inexpressible—for you to become mighty in prevailing prayer for many, many awesomely great needs in the lives of others.

The Spirit wants to make you mighty to prevail for them. God has no other way. He has ordained to bring His will to pass through your prevailing, joined to the prevailing intercession of both God the Son on heaven's throne of grace and God the Spirit. The Spirit longs to possess you more and more fully that He may pray through you more and more prevailingly.

God understands your heartbroken confession, even as Paul confessed, "I don't know how" (Rom 8:26). At the end of yourself, give yourself again to God in total, total dependence. Can you confess with Oswald J. Smith, "Ah, that burden, that burden for souls—how it has characterized God's anointed ones all down the centuries! . . . A host of . . . mighty wrestlers with God. Theirs, my brethren, is the experience I crave above all other."[2]

God desires you to help mediate the light of the gospel and the saving power of Jesus through your prayer. In redemption there is only one Mediator between God and man, the man Christ Jesus (1 Tim. 2:5). But God needs thousands of cooperating intercessory mediators today. By your prevailing prayer, place one hand on the throne of grace and the other on the need of the world. Moses did. Isaiah, Jeremiah, and Daniel did. Will you? Luther did. Wesley and Whitefield did. Finney, Brainerd, and Hyde did. Will you?

First, get the vision. Ask the Spirit to let you see the world's people and their need with the loving eyes of God. Then you will understand why Nehemiah wept, why Isaiah, Jeremiah, Paul, and a host of others wept. Then you will understand why Jesus wept. Ask the Spirit to let your heart feel earth's pain as the heart of God feels it. Then you will weep. Your heart will weep, and if you prevail long enough, your eyes may also fill with tears.

Next, plead the Spirit's help. Your strongest praying without the Spirit's empowering is impotent. Your feeblest words, empowered by the Spirit, can move Omnipotence. It is not for you to see how much you can do for God. It is for you to see how much more of God you can get into your praying. It is God the Spirit who makes the difference.

Be filled with the Spirit. If you have never received the Spirit's fullness, receive it today. Clear away any controversy, any veil, between your soul and God. Obey God in every step you know to take. Present yourself totally, utterly, eternally to God in absolute surrender, asking the Spirit to fill you. Don't hurry. Be thorough; make sure your surrender is real and total. Then in simple faith appropriate what God has promised: "If you then, though you are evil, know how to give good gifts to your children, how much more will your Father in heaven give the Holy Spirit to those who ask him!" (Luke 11:13).

Now keep filled. Purity can be preserved by the Spirit's help, but power must be renewed. If you wait on God, your strength will be renewed (Isa. 40:31). In Acts the believers were filled and refilled with the Holy Spirit.

As you drive your car, you do not need to get your car repaired every hundred miles or so. But you do need to refill it with the fuel that gives you power. A holy soul often senses spiritual depletion right in the midst of loving service to God and others. We live in a world whose environment depletes us. We war a spiritual warfare that depletes us.

Go alone with God. Ask God. Wait on God. He will refill you again and again. You must stay filled with the Spirit to pray in the Spirit. You must wait on God if you would be refilled. You must feast on His words, chapter after chapter, if you would be refilled. Remember Torrey's words, "The whole secret of prayer is found in those words, 'in the Spirit.'"[3]

In His last teaching before the cross, Jesus revealed to us, His followers, that praying was to take a whole new dimension of power through praying in His name, through His words abiding in us, and through the help of the Paraclete, the Holy Spirit. Are Jesus' words true of your prayer life? They can be. By God's grace, they must be. By your setting your soul's determination, through spiritual discipline and habits of prevailing intercession, they will be.

Prayer power is not something worked up. It is not loudness of voice or physical or emotional self-assertion. It is power of the Spirit within your spirit. Can you paraphrase Paul's words and say, "To this end I pray, struggling with all His energy, which so powerfully works in me" (Col. 1:29)? He will work mightily in you as He prays mightily through you. He will burn the "ought" of prevailing prayer in your innermost soul. He will give you a holy "must" that drives you to your knees.

In this restless, busy age most of us have never learned to give God time in prayer. We would rather work for God than pray. We would rather attend another service than pray. We would rather watch TV than pray. May God forgive us! Bishop J. C. Ryle confessed, "We spend our spiritual strength and forget to renew it. We multiply engagements and curtail prayer.... We work when we ought to pray, because to an active mind work is far easier than prayer.... The servant whom the Holy Spirit is to use must resist the tyranny of overwork. He must resolve to be alone with God even if the hours spent with Him appear to rob his fellowmen of his service."[4]

But, you protest, so often my heart seems cold and prayerless. R. A. Torrey testified, "Many of the most blessed seasons of prayer I have ever known have begun with the feeling of utter deadness and prayerlessness; but in my helplessness and coldness I have cast myself upon God, and looked to Him to send His Holy Spirit to teach me to pray, and He has done it."[5]

Beloved Andrew Murray wrote, "Heaven is still as full of spiritual blessings. . . . God still delights to give the Holy Spirit to them that ask Him. Our life and work are still as dependent on the direct impartation of the Divine power as they were in Pentecostal times. Prayer is still the appointed means for drawing down these heavenly blessings in power upon ourselves and those around us. God still seeks for men and women who will, with all their other work of ministering, specially give themselves to persevering prayer."[6]

Will You Join Me in This Prayer?

WONDERFUL LORD JESUS—my crucified, resurrected, ascended, and enthroned Savior—I worship and adore You. My interceding King, with what everlasting love You give Your holy self to me and to this needy world! Thank You, Jesus, that Your throne is a throne of grace. Thank You that at the right hand of the Father, You are interceding now.

How unworthy I am of all Your amazing grace! You sought me when I was without God and without hope. You died in my place to secure for me Your wonderful salvation. O Son of God, Son of Man, I worship and adore You! How can You love me so? How can you seat me in the heavenlies beside You? How can you make me Your co-intercessor, Your partner in prayer? O Lord, I am so unworthy!

Forgive me for being so slow to learn the secrets of prevailing prayer. Forgive me for so often permitting important duties and even trivial things to rob me of my prayer time with You. Teach me to establish my prayer priorities. Teach me to discipline myself to put prayer in its rightful place. Teach me the ABCs of prevailing prayer, and then through Your grace lead me deeper and deeper in mighty prevailing prayer.

Give me eyes to see others and our world as Your loving eyes see them. Give me a heart that feels the tragedy of sin, the lostness of humankind, the bondage with which Satan enslaves the world. Give me a heart that feels Your love for the church and for all Your own. Give me more of Your love for the lost, more of Your yearning for world harvest, more of Your hunger for the advance of Your kingdom.

O Lord, teach me to pray! Lord, teach me to pray! Fill my

315

heart with Your hunger, my eyes with Your tears, my soul with Your hatred for sin, my will with Your strength to resist the Devil in prayer, my spirit with the mighty power of Your Holy Spirit so that I can prevail with You and for You with holy prevailings and mighty intercession.

I give myself to You anew. Take me! Take all of me! Take me and fill me with Your Spirit that it may be not I but You living in me, not my love but Your love pouring through me, not my power but Your mighty power gripping me and working in and through me. Fill me so that it may be not I praying but the Spirit interceding in might and faith through me.

Help me to pray with prayer's holy and mighty pleas. Help me to bear prayer's burdens when You appoint them to me. Help me to wrestle with the Spirit's mighty prayer wrestlings. O mighty Intercessor on heaven's throne, I am not worthy to be called a prayer warrior. But help me to press prayer battles persistently, vicariously, and victoriously.

Help me to prevail till Satan's plans and strategies are defeated, till Satan's captives are set free and the places Satan has forcibly occupied are captured for You. Help me to back Satan off and force him to retreat from stronghold after stronghold. Help me to press ever forward on my knees. Help me to use the holy authority of Your name, the victory of Your cross, and the power of Your blood.

O Lord Jesus, I am totally unworthy, insufficient, and unable in myself. Yet use me for Your glory. Let me bring joy to Your heart and honor to Your name.

You are able to do immeasurably more than all I could ever ask or imagine. I believe it. I claim it. May Your will be done and Your victory won through my obedience and my prayer. Be the Amen to this my longing and my heart-cry. In Your holy name, my Jesus. Amen.

If God has made this book a blessing to you and you wish to share a testimony or word of encouragement, or if you would like to have the author remember you in a moment of prayer, please feel free to write:

> Dr. Wesley L. Duewel
> OMS International, Inc.
> Box A
> Greenwood, Indiana 46142
> USA

Notes

Chapter 2

[1] Thomas Payne, *The Greatest Force on Earth,* 7th ed. (London: Marshall Brothers, n.d.), 20.

Chapter 3

[1] Andrew Murray, *Ministry of Intercession* (New York: Revell, 1898), 13–14.

[2] R. Arthur Mathews, *Born for Battle* (New York: Overseas Missionary Fellowship and Send the Light Trust, 1978), 74, 72.

[3] E. M. Bounds, *Power Through Prayer* (Grand Rapids: Baker, 1972), 124–25.

[4] E. M. Bounds, *Purpose in Prayer* (New York: Revell, 1920), 83–84.

[5] Murray, *Ministry of Intercession,* 168–69.

[6] R. V. G. Tasker, gen. ed., *The Tyndale New Testament Commentaries,* Vol 17: *The First Epistle General of Peter,* by Alan M. Stibbs (London: Tyndale, 1959), 104.

[7] O. Hallesby, *Prayer* (London: Hodder & Stoughton, 1936), 229, 231; see also Donald G. Bloesch, *The Struggle of Prayer* (San Francisco: Harper, 1980), 87–88.

[8] Hallesby, *Prayer,* 117, 231; Bloesch, *Struggle of Prayer,* 57.

[9] Murray, *Ministry of Intercession,* 13.

Chapter 4

[1] Hallesby, *Prayer,* 48–49.

[2] Leonard Ravenhill, *Revival Praying* (Zachary, La.: Ravenhill, 1962), 12; Murray, *Prayer Life,* 15.

[3] Bloesch, *Struggle of Prayer,* 132.

[4] Murray, *Ministry of Intercession,* 24.

[5] Ravenhill, *Revival Praying,* 54.

[6] An Unknown Christian, *The Kneeling Christian* (Grand Rapids, Zondervan, n.d.), 26.

[7] Murray, *Ministry of Intercession,* 12; idem, *Prayer Life,* 127.

[8] Samuel Chadwick, *The Path of Prayer* (Kansas City: Beacon Hill, 1931), 11–12.

[9] Andrew Murray, *The Prayer Life* (Chicago: Moody, n.d.), 31.

[10]Ravenhill, *Revival Praying,* 11–12.

Chapter 5

[1]F. F. Bruce, *Commentary on the Epistle to the Hebrews*, *New International Commentary on the New Testament*, ed. by Ned B. Stonehouse (15 vols. in print; London: Marshall, Morgan & Scott, 1964), 98.

[2]E. M. Bounds, *The Necessity of Prayer* (New York: Revell, 1920), 66; Payne, *Greatest Force on Earth,* 106–7.

[3]Murray, *Ministry of Intercession,* 135.

[4]Ibid.

Chapter 6

[1]Eva M. Watson, *Glimpses of the Life and Work of George Douglas Watson* (Cincinnati: God's Bible School and Revivalist, 1929), 130.

[2]Charles Haddon Spurgeon, *Twelve Sermons on Prayer* (London: Marshall, Morgan & Scott, n.d.), 60.

[3]Jamieson, Fausset, and Brown, *Commentary Practical and Explanatory on the Whole Bible*, rev. ed. (Grand Rapids, Zondervan, 1961), 1284.

[4]F. J. Huegel, *Reigning with Christ* (Grand Rapids: Zondervan, 1963), 42.

[5]F. J. Huegel, *The Enthroned Christian* (Poole, Dorset, Eng: Overcomer Literature Trust, n.d.), 19.

[6]Murray, *Ministry of Intercession,* 10.

[7]W. E. Vine and John R. Kohlenberger III, *The Expanded Vine's Expository Dictionary of New Testament Words* (Minneapolis: Bethany, 1984), 132; Jamieson, Fausset, and Brown, *Commentary*, 1151.

[8]Huegel, *Enthroned Christian,* 35.

Chapter 9

[1]Mathews, *Born for Battle,* 115.

[2]Mrs. O. J. Fraser, *Fraser and Prayer* (London: Overseas Missionary Fellowship, 1963), 33, 34.

[3]Murray, *Ministry of Intercession,* 104.

[4]Bounds, *Necessity of Prayer,* 47.

[5]Charles G. Finney, *Principles of Prayer,* ed. Louis Gifford Parkhurst, Jr. (Minneapolis: Bethany, 1980), 26.

[6]Murray, *Ministry of Intercession,* 105.

[7]See Duewel, *Let God Guide You Daily,* 79–85, 101–4, 169, 196–97, 202, 209.

[8]Finney, *Principles of Prayer,* 36.

Chapter 10

[1]Charles G. Finney, *Sermons on Gospel Themes* (New York: Revell, 1976), 323.

[2] Murray, *Ministry of Intercession,* 40–41.

[3] J. W. Acker, *Teach Us to Pray* (St. Louis: Concordia, 1961), 31.33.

[4] Bounds, *Necessity of Prayer,* 59.

[5] Bounds, *Purpose in Prayer,* 59.

[6] Chadwick, *Path of Prayer,* 81–82.

[7] Ibid., 68.

[8] R. A. Torrey, *How to Pray* (Chicago: Moody, 1900), 33–34.

[9] Alexander Whyte, *Lord, Teach Us to Pray* (New York: Harper, n.d.), 75.

[10] Finney, *Principles of Prayer,* 71.

[11] Bounds, *Necessity of Prayer,* 59.

[12] Ibid., 56.

Chapter 11

[1] Murray, *Ministry of Intercession,* 53.

[2] D. M. McIntyre, *The Hidden Life of Prayer*, 3d ed. (London: Marshall, Morgan & Scott, n.d.), 86.

[3] Ibid., 87.

[4] P. T. Forsyth, *The Soul of Prayer* (Grand Rapids: Eerdmans, n.d.), 92.

[5] Bounds, *Necessity of Prayer,* 68.

[6] A. B. Simpson, *The Life of Faith* (New York: Christian Alliance Publishing, n.d.), 52.

[7] Bounds, *Necessity of Prayer,* 72.

[8] Ibid., 63.

[9] Bloesch, *Struggle of Prayer,* 79.

Chapter 12

[1] J. Oswald Sanders, *Prayer Power Unlimited* (Minneapolis: Billy Graham Evangelistic Association, 1977), 72.

[2] Bounds, *Necessity of Prayer,* 76.

[3] Torrey, *How to Pray,* 63.

[4] Murray, *Ministry of Intercession,* 10; Payne, *Greatest Force on Earth,* 19.

[5] Sanders, *Prayer Power Unlimited,* 78.

[6] Bloesch, *Struggle of Prayer,* 132.

[7] John Henry Jowett, *The Passion for Souls* (New York: Revell, 1905), 35–36.

[8] Torrey, *How to Pray,* 64.

[9] Bloesch, *Struggle of Prayer,* 80; Kathleen M. Chambers, *Oswald Chambers* (Nashville: Nelson, 1987), 262.

[10] Bounds, *Purpose in Prayer,* 60, 55.

Chapter 13

[1] Unknown Christian, *Kneeling Christian,* 132.

[2] Murray, *Ministry of Intercession,* 166.

[3] James H. McConkey, *Prayer* (Pittsburgh: Silver Publishing Society, 1939), 13.

[4] Unknown Christian, *Kneeling Christian,* 43.

[5] Bloesch, *Struggle of Prayer,* 63.

Chapter 14

[1] Hallesby, *Prayer,* 34; Murray, *Ministry of Intercession,* 42.

[2] Sanders, *Prayer Power Unlimited,* 64.

[3] Ibid., 65.

[4] Fraser, *Fraser and Prayer,* 43.

[5] Ibid.

Chapter 15

[1] McIntyre, *Hidden Life of Prayer,* 91.

[2] Harry E. Jessop, *The Ministry of Prevailing Prayer* (Berne, Ind.: Light and Hope Publications, 1941), 109.

[3] McIntyre, *Hidden Life of Prayer,* 91.

[4] Ibid., 89.

[5] James G. J. McClure, *Intercessory Prayer* (Chicago: Moody, c. 1902), 34.

[6] Mathews, *Born for Battle,* 106.

[7] Huegel, *Enthroned Christian,* 36.

Chapter 16

[1] E. M. Bounds, *The Reality of Prayer* (New York: Revell, 1924), 133.

[2] Murray, *Ministry of Intercession,* 120.

[3] Spurgeon, *Twelve Sermons on Prayer,* 57.

[4] Bounds, *Reality of Prayer,* 129.

[5] Ravenhill, *Revival Praying,* 175.

[6] Payne, *Greatest Force on Earth,* 128.

[7] Ravenhill, *Revival Praying,* 90.

[8] McIntyre, *Hidden Life of Prayer,* 37.

[9] Payne, *Greatest Force on Earth,* 118; Chadwick, *Path of Prayer,* 53.

[10] Murray, *Prayer Life,* 46; idem, *Ministry of Intercession,* 25.

[11] Gordon B. Watt, *Effectual Fervent Prayer* (London: Marshall, Morgan & Scott, 1927), 45.

[12] Spurgeon, *Twelve Sermons on Prayer,* 10.

[13] McConkey, *Prayer,* 10.

Chapter 17

[1] Finney, *Sermons on Gospel Themes,* 56–57.

[2] Torrey, *How to Pray,* 58–59.

[3] Bounds, *Reality of Prayer,* 138.

[4] Ravenhill, *Revival Praying,* 62.

Chapter 18

[1] Payne, *Greatest Force on Earth,* 115–16, 67.
[2] Frank C. Laubach, *Prayer* (Westwood, N.J.: Revell, 1946), 30.
[3] Ravenhill, *Revival Praying,* 124–25.
[4] Rosalind Goforth, *Goforth of China* (Grand Rapids: Zondervan, 1937), 159–60, 230–31.

Chapter 19

[1] Finney, *Principles of Prayer,* 98.
[2] Ibid.
[3] David Bryant, *With Concerts of Prayer* (Ventura, Calif.: Regal, 1945), 104–5.
[4] S. B. Shaw, *Touching Incidents and Remarkable Answers to Prayer* (Chicago: S. B. Shaw, n.d.), 153.
[5] Ibid.
[6] Bryant, *Concerts of Prayer,* 17; Unknown Christian, *Kneeling Christian,* 11.
[7] Arthur T. Pierson, *The Miracles of Missions* (New York: Funk & Wagnalls, 1901), 21–22.
[8] F. J. Huegel, *Successful Praying* (Minneapolis: Bethany, 1959), 85–86.
[9] Bryant, *Concerts of Prayer,* 16.
[10] Ibid., 48.
[11] Sanders, *Prayer Power Unlimited,* 120.

Chapter 20

[1] Charles Haddon Spurgeon, *The Treasury of the Bible,* Vol. 3 (Grand Rapids: Zondervan, 1968), 268.
[2] Unknown Christian, *Kneeling Christian,* 29.
[3] Ibid., 134–38.
[4] Ibid., 100–101.

Chapter 21

[1] John Wesley, *Journal,* Jan. 1, 1739.

Chapter 22

[1] McIntyre, *Hidden Life of Prayer,* 87.
[2] Ibid., 86.
[3] Charles A. Blanchard, *Getting Things From God* (Chicago: Moody, 1915), 128–29.
[4] McIntyre, *Hidden Life of Prayer,* 74–75.
[5] Sanders, *Prayer Power Unlimited,* 139, 120.
[6] Bryant, *Concerts of Prayer,* 132.

[7]George B. Kulp, *Nuggets of Gold* (Cincinnati: God's Revivalist, 1908), 57–58.

[8]Fraser, *Fraser and Prayer,* 47.

[9]McClure, *Intercessory Prayer,* 119–20.

Chapter 23

[1]Torrey, *How to Pray,* 14.

[2]Finney, *Principles of Prayer,* 26.

[3]Michael Baughen, *The Prayer Principle* (London and Oxford: Mowbray, 1981), 90.

[4]Bounds, *Purpose in Prayer,* 62.

[5]Sanders, *Prayer Power Unlimited,* 108.

[6]Bounds, *Power Through Prayer,* 43–44.

[7]Sanders, *Prayer Power Unlimited,* 108.

[8]Bounds, *Power Through Prayer,* 44.

[9]Unknown Christian, *Kneeling Christian,* 21.

[10]Charles Blanchard, *Getting Things from God* (Chicago: Bible Institute Colportage Association), 94–95.

Chapter 24

[1]McIntyre, *Hidden Life of Prayer,* 80.

[2]McConkey, *Prayer,* 82.

[3]Jessop, *Ministry of Prevailing Prayer,* 81.

[4]Chadwick, *Path of Prayer,* 73.

[5]S. D. Gordon, *Quiet Talks on Prayer* (New York: Revell, 1904), 186.

[6]Mathews, *Born for Battle,* 164.

[7]McConkey, *Prayer,* 84.

[8]Blanchard, *Getting Things from God,* 71.

[9]Huegel, *Successful Praying,* 37–38.

Chapter 25

[1]Hallesby, *Prayer,* 207.

[2]McIntyre, *Hidden Life of Prayer,* 91–92.

[3]Huegel, *Successful Praying,* 49–50.

[4]Ibid., 45–48.

Chapter 26

[1]Torrey, *How to Pray,* 27–28.

[2]McClure, *Intercessory Prayer,* 124–25.

[3]Whyte, *Lord, Teach Us to Pray,* 170–71.

[4]A. B. Simpson, *The Life of Prayer* (New York: Christian Alliance Publishing, 1925), 44–49.

[5]Payne, *Greatest Force on Earth,* 97–98.

Chapter 27

[1] John Wesley, "Causes of Inefficacy of Christianity," *Sermons on Several Occasions*, ed. Thomas Jackson, 2 vols. (New York: T. Mason and G. Lane, 1840), 2:440.

[2] Sanders, *Prayer Power Unlimited*, 133–34.

Chapter 28

[1] Torrey, *How to Pray*, 36.

[2] Didache 7:4.

[3] J. G. Morrison, *The Stewardship of Fasting* (Kansas City: Beacon Hill, n.d.), 31

Chapter 31

[1] Bounds, *Necessity of Prayer*, 63.

[2] Chadwick, *Path of Prayer*, 66.

[3] Ibid., 103.

[4] Bounds, *Necessity of Prayer*, 63.

[5] Jonathan Edward, ed., *The Life and Dairy of David Brainerd* (Chicago: Moody, n.d.), 107–8.

[6] McIntyre, *Hidden Life of Prayer*, 22; Bounds, *Power Through Prayer*, 53.

Chapter 32

[1] David Hanes, ed., *My Path of Prayer* (West Sussex, Eng.: Henry E. Walter, 1981), 59.

[2] Bloesch, *Struggle of Prayer*, 113.

[3] Payne, *Greatest Force on Earth*, 140.

[4] Jack W. Hayford, *Prayer Is Invading the Impossible* (Plainfield, N.J.: Logos, 1977), 75.

[5] Charles G. Finney, *Memoirs of Rev. Charles G. Finney* (New York: Revell, 1876), 328–29.

[6] Ibid., 331.

Chapter 33

[1] Bloesch, *Struggle of Prayer*, 51.

[2] Payne, *Greatest Force on Earth*, 15.

[3] McIntyre, *Hidden Life of Prayer*, 94; Ravenhill, *Revival Praying*, 102.

[4] Clara McLeister, *Men and Women of Deep Piety*, ed. E. E. Shelhamer (Cincinnati: God's Bible School and Revivalist, 1920), 383.

[5] Whyte, *Lord, Teach Us to Pray*, 139.

[6] Payne, *Greatest Force on Earth*, 105.

[7] F. F. Bruce, *The Epistle to the Hebrews*, New International Commentary on the New Testament (London: Marshall, Morgan, & Scott, 1964), 98.

[8] Unknown Christian, *Kneeling Christian*, 85.

[9]Finney, *Principles of Prayer,* 39.
[10]Bounds, *Reality of Prayer,* 138.

Chapter 34

[1]Payne, *Greatest Force on Earth,* 122.
[2]Bloesch, *Struggle of Prayer,* 135.
[3]McIntyre, *Hidden Life of Prayer,* 20.

Chapter 35

[1]Mathews, *Born for Battle,* 49.
[2]Ibid., 62.
[3]Ibid., 57.

Chapter 36

[1]Mathews, *Born for Battle,* 27.
[2]Ibid., 27–28.
[3]Huegel, *Enthroned Christian,* 29.
[4]Mathews, *Born for Battle,* 47.
[5]Ibid., 18; Payne, *Greatest Force on Earth,* 118.
[6]Watt, *Effectual Fervent Prayer,* 84.
[7]Ibid., 14.
[8]Gordon, *Quiet Talks on Prayer,* 34.

Chapter 37

[1]Finney, *Principles of Prayer,* 20.
[2]Gordon, *Quiet Talks on Prayer*, 148.
[3]Mathews, *Born for Battle,* 84.
[4]G. Granger Fleming, *The Dynamic of All-Prayer* (London: Oliphants, 1915), 87.
[5]Goforth, *Goforth of China,* 203.
[6]Sanders, *Prayer Power Unlimited,* 143.
[7]Ibid., 67.
[8]Hallesby, *Prayer,* 103–4.

Chapter 39

[1]Unknown Christian, *Kneeling Christian,* 102–4.
[2]McLeister, *Men and Women of Deep Piety,* 318.
[3]Jessie Penn-Lewis, *Prayer and Evangelism* (Dorset, Eng.: Overcomer Literature Trust, 1948?), 56.

Chapter 40

[1]Sanders, *Prayer Power Unlimited,* 50.
[2]Ibid., 49.

[3] Unknown Christian, *Kneeling Christian*, 70.
[4] Simpson, *Life of Prayer*, 70.
[5] Sanders, *Prayer Power Unlimited*, 51.

Chapter 41

[1] Murray, *Prayer Life*, 88.
[2] Hanes, *My Path of Prayer*, 31, 70.
[3] Ibid., 313–14; quotations on pp. 252, 251.
[4] McIntyre, *Hidden Life of Prayer*, 38.
[5] Acker, *Teach Us to Pray*, 29.

Chapter 42

[1] Spurgeon, *Twelve Sermons on Prayer*, 49–50, 43.

Chapter 43

[1] Spurgeon, *Twelve Sermons on Prayer*, 39.
[2] Ibid.
[3] Ibid., 50.
[4] Ibid.

Chapter 44

[1] Chadwick, *Path of Prayer*, 56.
[2] Oswald J. Smith, *The Enduement of Power* (London: Marshall, Morgan & Scott, 1933), 57–58.
[3] Torrey, *How to Pray*, 55.
[4] Payne, *Greatest Force on Earth*, 119–20.
[5] Torrey, *How to Pray*, 56–57.
[6] Murray, *Ministry of Intercession*, 36.

Bibliography

Acker, J. W. *Teach Us to Pray*. St. Louis: Concordia Publishing House, 1961.

Baughen, Michael. *The Prayer Principle*. London and Oxford: Mowbray, 1981.

Blanchard, Charles A. *Getting Things from God*. Chicago: Bible Institute Colportage Association, 1915.

Bloesch, Donald G. *The Struggle of Prayer*. San Francisco: Harper & Row, 1980.

Bounds, E. M. *The Essentials of Prayer*. Grand Rapids: Baker, 1979. Orig., 1925.

_____. *The Necessity of Prayer*. New York: Revell, 1929.

_____. *Power Through Prayer*. Grand Rapids: Baker, 1972.

_____. *Prayer and Praying Men*. Grand Rapids: Baker, 1977. Orig., 1921.

_____. *Purpose in Prayer*. New York: Revell, 1920.

_____. *The Reality of Prayer*. New York: Revell, 1924.

Bruce, F. F. *The Epistle to the Hebrews*. *New London Commentary on the New Testament*. London: Marshall, Morgan & Scott, 1964.

Bryant, David. *With Concerts of Prayer*. Ventura, Calif.: Regal, 1945.

Chadwick, Samuel. *The Path of Prayer*. Kansas City: Beacon Hill, 1931.

Chambers, Kathleen M. *Oswald Chambers*. Nashville: Nelson, Oliver Nelson Division, 1987.

Duewel, Wesley. *Let God Guide You Daily*. Grand Rapids: Zondervan/Francis Asbury Press, 1988.

_____. *Touch the World Through Prayer*. Grand Rapids: Zondervan/Francis Asbury Press, 1986.

Dunning, Norman G. *Samuel Chadwick*. London: Hodder & Stoughton, 1935. Orig., 1933.

Finney, Charles G. *Memoirs of Rev. Charles G. Finney*. New York: Revell, 1876.

_____. *Principles of Prayer*. Compiled and edited by Louis Gifford Parkhurst, Jr. Minneapolis: Bethany, 1980.

_____. *Sermons on Gospel Themes*. New York: Revell, 1976.

Fleming, G. Granger. *The Dynamic of All-Prayer*. London: Oliphants, 1915.

Forsyth, P. T. *The Soul of Prayer*. Grand Rapids: Eerdmans, n.d. Orig., 1916.

Fraser, Mrs. J. O. *Fraser and Prayer*. London: Overseas Missionary Fellowship, 1963.

Goforth, Rosalind. *Climbing!* Grand Rapids: Zondervan, 1940.

_____. *Goforth of China.* Grand Rapids: Zondervan, 1937.

Gordon, A. J. *The Ministry of the Spirit.* Minneapolis: Bethany, 1964. Reprinted by arrangement with Judson Press.

_____. *Quiet Talks on Prayer.* New York: Revell, 1904.

Hallesby, O. *Prayer.* London: Hodder & Stoughton, 1936.

Hanes, David, ed., *My Path of Prayer.* West Sussex, England: Henry E. Walter, 1981.

Harper, Michael. *Spiritual Warfare.* Plainfield, N. J.: Logos, 1970. Reproduced from the Great Britain edition by arrangement with Hodder & Stoughton, London.

Hayford, Jack W. *Prayer Is Invading the Impossible.* Plainfield, N. J.: Logos, 1977.

Huegel, F. J. *The Enthroned Christian.* Poole, Dorset, England: The Overcomer Literature Trust, n.d.

_____. *The Ministry of Intercession.* Minneapolis: Bethany, Dimension Books, 1971.

_____. *Reigning with Christ.* Grand Rapids: Zondervan, 1963.

_____. *Successful Praying.* Minneapolis: Bethany, Dimension Books, 1959.

Jamieson, Robert; Fausset, A. R.; and Brown, David. *Commentary on the Whole Bible.* Grand Rapids: Zondervan, 1961.

Jessop, Harry E. *The Ministry of Prevailing Prayer.* Berne, IN: Light and Hope Publications, 1941.

Jowett, John Henry. *The Passion for Souls.* New York: Revell, 1905.

Kulp, George B. *The Calloused Knees.* Cincinnati: God's Revivalist Office, 1909.

_____. *Nuggets of Gold.* Cincinnati: God's Revivalist Office, 1908.

Laubach, Frank C. *Prayer.* Westwood, N.J.: Revell, 1946.

Lawson, James Gilchrist. *Deeper Experiences of Famous Christians.* Anderson, Ind.: Warner, 1911.

McClure, James G. J. *Intercessory Prayer.* Moody Colportage Library, vol. 130. Chicago: Moody, before 1902.

McConkey, James H. *Prayer.* Pittsburgh: Silver Publishing Society, 1939.

McIntyre, D. M. *The Hidden Life of Prayer.* 3d ed. London: Marshall, Morgan & Scott, n.d.

McLeister, Mrs. Clara. *Men and Women of Deep Piety.* Edited and published by E. E. Shelhamer. Cincinnati: God's Bible School and Revivalist, 1920.

Mathews, R. Arthur. *Born for Battle.* New York: Overseas Missionary Fellowship and Send the Light Trust, 1978.

Moody, D. L. *Prevailing Prayer: What Hinders It?* Chicago: Revell, 1884.

Morgan, G. Campbell. *The Practice of Prayer.* Grand Rapids: Baker, 1971. Reprinted from edition published by Revell, New York, 1960.

Morrison, J. G. *The Stewardship of Fasting.* Kansas City: Beacon Hill, n.d.

BIBLIOGRAPHY

Murch, James Deforest. *Teach Me to Pray*. Secunderabad, A.P., India: Good News Literature Center, Standard Publishing Foundation, 1958.

Murray, Andrew. *The Ministry of Intercession*. New York: Revell, 1898.

_____. *The Prayer Life*. Chicago: Moody, n.d.

Payne, Thomas. *The Greatest Force on Earth*. 7th ed. London: Marshall Brothers, n.d.

Penn-Lewis, Jessie. *Prayer and Evangelism*. Dorset, England: The Overcomer Literature Trust, 1948[?].

Pierson, Arthur T. *The Miracles of Missions*. New York: Funk & Wagnalls, 1901.

Prince, Derek. *Shaping History Through Prayer and Fasting*. Fort Lauderdale, Fla.: Derek Prince Ministries, 1973.

Ravenhill, Leonard. *Revival Praying*. Zachary, La.: Ravenhill Books, 1962.

Sanders, J. Oswald. *Prayer Power Unlimited*. Minneapolis: Billy Graham Evangelistic Association (Special Crusade Edition), 1977, Moody Bible Institute of Chicago.

Shaw, S. B. *Touching Incidents and Remarkable Answers to Prayer*. Chicago: S. B. Shaw, 1897.

Simpson, A. B. *The Life of Faith*. New York: Christian Alliance Publishing, n.d.

_____. *The Life of Prayer*. New York: Christian Alliance Publishing, 1925.

Smith, Oswald J. *The Enduement of Power*. London: Marshall, Morgan & Scott, 1933.

Spurgeon, Charles Haddon. *The Treasury of the Bible*. Vol. 3. Grand Rapids: Zondervan, 1968.

_____. *Twelve Sermons on Prayer*. London: Marshall, Morgan & Scott, n.d.

Stibbs, Alan M. *The First Epistle General of Peter. Tyndale New Testament Commentaries*. London: Tyndale Press, 1959.

Torrey, R. A. *How to Pray*. Chicago: Moody, 1900.

An Unknown Christian. *The Kneeling Christian*. Grand Rapids: Zondervan, n.d.

Van Dooren, L. A. T. *Prayer—The Christian's Vital Breath*. Carnforth, Lancs., England: Latimer Publishing, 1962.

Vine, W. E., and Kohlenberger, John R. III, eds. *The Expanded Vine's Expository Dictionary of New Testament Words*. Minneapolis: Bethany, 1984.

Watson, Eva M. *Glimpses of the Life and Work of George Douglas Watson*. Cincinnati: God's Bible School and Revivalist, 1929.

Watt, Gordon B. *Effectual Fervent Prayer*. London: Marshall, Morgan & Scott, 1927.

Wesley, John. *Sermons on Several Occasions.* Ed. by Thomas Jackson. Vol. 2. New York: Mason & G. Lane, 1840.

Whyte, Alexander. *Lord, Teach Us to Pray.* New York: Harper & Brothers, n.d.

Index